ETHICS AFTER CHRISTENDOM

Ethics after Christendom

TOWARD AN ECCLESIAL CHRISTIAN ETHIC

Vigen Guroian

WILLIAM B. EERDMANS PUBLISHING COMPANY
GRAND RAPIDS, MICHIGAN

© 1994 Wm. B. Eerdmans Publishing Co.
255 Jefferson Ave. S.E., Grand Rapids, Michigan 49503

Printed in the United States of America

00 99 98 97 96 95 94   7 6 5 4 3 2 1

Library of Congress Cataloging-in-Publication Data

Guroian, Vigen.
    Ethics after Christendom: toward an ecclesial Christian ethic /
Vigen Guroian.
        p.   cm.
    Includes bibliographical references and index.
    ISBN 0-8028-0128-5 (pbk.)
        1. Christian ethics — Oriental Orthodox authors. 2. Postmodernism —
Religious aspects — Christianity. 3. Christianity and culture.
I. Title.
BJ1250.5.G85   1994
241 — dc20   94-21943
                                             CIP

Some of the material in this volume has appeared in different form in other publications. The author and publisher gratefully acknowledge permission to use these materials in this book:

"Bible and Ethics: An Ecclesial and Liturgical Interpretation." *Journal of Religious Ethics* 18 (Spring 1990): 129-57.
"Church and Nationhood: A Bonhoefferian Reflection on the 'National Church.'" *Union Theological Seminary Quarterly Review* 46 (1992): 129-57.
"Death and Dying Well in the Orthodox Liturgical Tradition." *Second Opinion* 19 (July 1993): 41-59.
"Family and Christian Virtue in a Post-Christendom World: Reflections on the Ecclesial Vision of John Chrysostom." *St. Vladimir's Seminary Quarterly* 35 (1991): 327-50.
"Is Christian Ethics Any Longer Possible?" In *The Cutting Edge,* edited by Kevin Perotta and John C. Blattner, 33-50. Faith and Renewal Books, 1991.
"Tradition and Ethics: Prospects in a Liberal Society." *Modern Theology* 7 (April 1991): 205-24.
"Toward Ecology as an Ecclesial Event: Orthodox Theology and Ecological Ethics." *Communio* 18 (Spring 1991): 89-110.

To my parents
Grace and Armen Guroian

Contents

Acknowledgments   ix

Introduction   1

I Prospects and Sources for an Ecclesial Christian Ethic

1 Is Christian Ethics Any Longer Possible?   11

2 Tradition and Ethics: Prospects in a Liberal Society   29

3 The Bible in Orthodox Ethics: A Liturgical Reading   53

II The Churches after Christendom

4 The Struggle for the Soul of the Church:
American Reflections   83

5 Church and Armenian Nationhood: A Bonhoefferian
Reflection on the National Church   102

III Applied Ecclesial Ethics: Family, Medicine, and the Creation

6 Family and Christian Virtue: Reflections on
the Ecclesial Vision of John Chrysostom   133

7 Ecological Ethics: An Ecclesial Event   155

8 Death and Dying in the Orthodox Liturgical Tradition:
Toward a Pastoral Ethic of Dying Well   175

Index of Subjects and Names   200

Index of Scripture References   205

Acknowledgments

In my first book, *Incarnate Love: Essays in Orthodox Ethics*, I tried my best not only to mention everyone to whom I owed a debt of gratitude but also to tell how certain persons inspired and encouraged me. Many of those same people have continued to be my friends and correspondents in the years since, during which time this book gradually came together. And new friends have joined them. This time, I'm not going to try to mention everyone, but I do want to mention first and especially three individuals who exerted formative influences on me as I matured as a theologian and who have passed beyond the pale.

Archbishop Tiran Nersoyan (1904-1989) of the Armenian Church, whom I discuss in Chapter 5, was a great encouragement to me for the years I knew him. He was acknowledged to be the most accomplished theological mind of his generation in the Armenian Church. Some of the Armenian liturgical texts that I cite are his translations. And he was gracious enough to read almost everything that I wrote and to comment on it in letters and personal exchanges. I greatly miss his wisdom and counsel.

Paul Ramsey (1924-1989) especially encouraged me to continue to explore the resources of Orthodox liturgy for doing Christian ethics. Although I wrote Chapter 8 several years after Paul's death, it sprang from an idea that he had planted in my mind.

Russell Kirk (1918-1994), author of the classic volume *The Conservative Mind* (1953), who died this year on Eastern Orthodox Good Friday, served on my dissertation committee and for twenty-five years inspired me as a true man of letters and source of vast knowledge. He was instrumental in helping to secure several grants that enabled me to devote summers to writing the essays that appear in this book.

I also want to express my deep gratitude to someone who is still very much alive — Fr. Stanley S. Harakas, the dean of Orthodox ethics in North America. Fr. Stanley has been not only a model of the Orthodox ethicist and a greatly valued colleague with special insights into and knowledge of the Orthodox tradition but also a spiritual counselor to whom I owe a debt deeper and more personal than can be explained here.

Other friends who have encouraged me in all that I have done as a theologian and ethicist include Nathan A. Scott Jr., Gilbert C. Meilaender, Tony Ugolnik, William M. Wilson, Thomas C. Oden, Susan Ashbrook-Harvey, Patrick G. Henry, Edward L. Long Jr., David Little, James F. Childress, and Stanley Hauerwas.

I also wish to thank the individuals and organizations that have helped me with grants and other kinds of support, including the late Edward Mardigan, the Wilbur Foundation, and Archbishop Mesrob Ashjian, Primate of the Armenian Apostolic Church of America. The list of benefactors and friends also includes Ms. Louise M. Simone, who arranged for several trips that I made to Armenia in 1990 and 1991 and helped support my sabbatical in 1988-89.

Among those at Loyola College whom I need to thank in connection with the more practical concerns of preparing and editing the manuscript are Lisa M. Flaherty, secretary to the theology department at Loyola College, and graduating senior Mary Beth McNulty, for invaluable help with the preparation of the index. I also want to thank Jon Pott, editor-in-chief at Eerdmans, and my editor, T. A. Straayer.

Lastly, to my wife, June, my son, Rafi, and my daughter, Victoria, who know what it is like to have a writer for a husband and father, I will simply say once more that I love you.

Introduction

The notion that North American Christendom is at its end has been championed of late by the likes of Stanley Hauerwas and John Howard Yoder. These theologians and others in their camps have equated the end of Christendom with the moral bankruptcy and final dissolution of the historic accommodation of the churches to state and secular order that they call *Constantinianism*. They use this term to refer to the formal arrangements made in the fourth century by the Roman emperors Constantine and Theodosius that brought the church into collaboration with the imperial court and under its protection. In less than a century, Christianity went from being a persecuted sect to enjoying legal toleration, and finally to becoming the official religion of the Empire. Representatives of the Protestant free church tradition, including Hauerwas and Yoder, have consistently argued that the church surrendered its true freedom when it entered into these arrangements. They describe subsequent church history as one tragic story after another of compromising church alliances with the state and the eventual collapse of authentic biblical faith into one form or another of culture religion.

While there is much to be commended in these assessments of Christendom's course, Christendom also had redeeming qualities. Its effects on faith, church, and society were mixed. And there are shades of gray in the concept of Constantinianism. My use of the term in this study is carried on not without an awareness of its drawbacks and limitations. Its use can be misleading, since it may suggest to some that Christendom was formed already by the fourth century, in the reign of Constantine; the critical historical moment actually came in the sixth century, when the Emperor Justinian codified and promulgated an ideological justification for a Christian empire. After this the church

1

certainly became, to a greater or lesser extent, a legitimating instrument of the secular authorities. And it is in this role that Christendom, both East and West, through various forms and transmutations, through schisms and Reformation, has prevailed into the modern era.[1]

Only vestiges of Christendom remain in America.[2] In the midst of the death throes of the cultural establishment of Christianity, American churches are trying to rethink how they might engage the culture and the political order. As American Christians approach the twenty-first century, this is the cultural situation in which we have to enter into reflection on ethics — political ethics, family ethics, and medical ethics.

The thesis that American Christendom is ending is not wholly new. Two decades ago already, church historian Robert T. Handy chronicled the process in a book entitled *A Christian America: Protestant Hopes and Historical Realities* (1971). At roughly the same time, Franklin H. Littell was arguing that "the end of the Constantinian era has brought quite different problems to Europe and America. Europe is certainly 'post-Christendom' and probably 'post-Christian' as well. America is 'post-Christendom,' but the churches yet have a chance to prove the case for Christianity on its merits."[3] When Littell wrote this in 1966, he could still say with some confidence that "the language of secular [America] is created in good part by religious tradition."[4] The synthesis of Protestant piety and Enlightenment liberalism that accounted for the unique character of American Christendom was showing some cracks, but it still appeared salvageable. At mid-century, Reinhold Niebuhr, working out of a Protestant neo-orthodoxy, and John Courtney Murray, working out of a Roman Catholic neo-Thomism, both made effective use of this synthesis in arguing that Judeo-Christian values and natural law principles have a valid role to play in the public square. In the years

1. For a discussion of the differences between the development of Christendom in East and West, see chaps. 4 and 5 of my book *Incarnate Love: Essays in Orthodox Ethics* (Notre Dame, Ind.: University of Notre Dame Press, 1987).

2. The fact that Christmas is celebrated as a national holiday counts as one such vestige, though even in this case the Supreme Court seems to be moving toward an interpretation of the separation doctrine that would prohibit the display in public places of unambiguously religious symbols associated with Christmas.

3. Littell, "The Churches and the Body Politic," *Daedalus* 96 (Winter 1966): 31. Littell's distinction between "post-Christendom" and "post-Christian" is useful. It focuses principally on the degree of disestablishment and secularization that is evident — an important factor for determining how the churches should go about engaging the culture.

4. Littell, "The Churches and the Body Politic," p. 39.

since, however, the synthesis has broken apart — I would say to the point that it is now beyond repair.

Thus it seems to me that for the foreseeable future, the real bone of contention among Christian theologians and ethicists is going to be what constitutes an appropriate ecclesiology and *modus vivendi* for the churches *after Christendom*. In the first three chapters of this book, I deal with this issue in the American context. The title of Chapter 1 — "Is Christian Ethics Any Longer Possible?" — is deliberately provocative and perhaps somewhat disingenuous. Of course Christian ethics is still possible; the real issue is *what kind of* Christian ethics is possible. In Chapter 1 I introduce the problem and take a brief look at trends in America that indicate the need for changes in the churches' strategies for carrying on their historic witness to the gospel of Jesus Christ. My chief contention is that Christian ethics needs to become more ecclesially centered than it has been in recent American history. In Chapters 2 and 3 — "Tradition and Ethics: Prospects in a Liberal Society" and "The Bible in Orthodox Ethics: A Liturgical Reading" — I take up this concern with ecclesiology and explore appropriate ways of being the church after Christendom. I look at sources in tradition, the Bible, and liturgy that contribute to an ecclesially centered Christian ethics — and I discuss what it means to be "ecclesially centered."

There are important differences between Latin and Orthodox Christian views concerning how the church-world relationship is defined and worked out. In Chapter 2 I speak of Christian ethics as *dialogic* and *iconic*, drawing deliberately from the best of the Orthodox tradition. This dialogic and iconic tradition of ethics contrasts with Western *agency* models of the church. In Chapter 3 I argue that the standard explanations of the relationship between the Bible and ethics proposed by Protestant and Roman Catholic ethicists miss an important dimension of the Bible's influence on the church's ethics: they do not consider seriously enough the liturgical contexts in which the Bible is interpreted and applied to Christian living.

In Chapters 1 and 4 I present reasons for rejecting recent recommendations for a new public theology. I believe that Christians can live responsibly in post-Christendom (and post-Christian) societies without resorting to this strategy of engaging the culture. The strategy of a public theology is flawed because it miscalculates the present secular character of the culture and the condition of the churches. I stress two points in particular. First, there are within both the liberal Protestant and the neoconservative camps some who are simply in a state of denial about the advanced condition of secularization and secularism; they do not see that even if the *modus vivendi* of a public theology is in principle a good idea, it is not suited for the present cultural environment. Second, advocates of a renewed public theology fail to take adequate account of the internal disarray of the church bodies. Many churches lack both the conviction and the inner discipline to engage the culture in such a way as to lead to the creation of a new language of public discourse or consensus, and those that might have the conviction and discipline often lack the historic wisdom to attempt this kind of culture formation. But I have a yet deeper theological objection to the new apologetics for a public theology: I maintain that most of the advocates of a public theology tend to have overly functionalistic ecclesiologies that confuse the redemptive mission of the church with the instrumentality of social reform or culture maintenance. Public theologies come in both radical and conservative flavors, but both kinds exhibit flattened ecclesiologies.

After Christendom: An Invitation to Comparative Study

In Chapter 5 — "Church and Armenian Nationhood: A Bonhoefferian Reflection on the National Church" — I extend my analysis to other locations where Christendom once was but is no longer, focusing on the example of the Armenian Church and its struggle to define the church's mission in post-Soviet Armenia. This is a self-described national church that continues to deny in the face of radically new circumstances that the people and culture it once Christianized are no longer uniformly and cohesively Christian. The problem is evident in an encyclical issued jointly in the fall of 1992 by the two supreme patriarchs of the Armenian Church, Catholicos Vazken I of the Holy See of Etchmiadzin in Armenia and Catholicos Karekin II of the Holy See of Cilicia in Lebanon. The patriarchs condemn the aggressive evangelizing activity of Protestant denominations and non-Christian sects in Armenia on the grounds that the country is not "an open and barren field for Christian evangelization," and they uncritically reaffirm "the national character and . . . role of the Armenian Church . . . [as] the spiritual-religious foundation for the buttressing of the unity and strength of the nation."[5] Their position is tellingly anachronistic.

Why do the Armenian church leaders persist in their Constantinian and Ottoman frame of mind? Why do they continue to define

---

5. "H. H. Vazken, H. H. Karekin II Issue Encyclical Denouncing Religious Sects in Armenia," *Armenian Reporter International*, 19 September 1992, pp. 23, 26.

the church as the spiritual organ of the state and special protector of the ethnos? Vazken I and Karekin II want to sound deeply traditional, but in fact they give evidence of a profound and dangerous compromise to modern nationalism. And, regrettably, the Armenian situation is typical of most post-Soviet societies. The Russian, Romanian, Ukrainian, and Serbian churches are all Orthodox national churches, and they among others have been reacting in a fashion similar to that of the Armenian Church. The Soviet system perpetuated (in altered forms, to be sure) the Byzantine arrangement of close ecclesiastical and political collaboration. That is to say that, ironically, the Soviets shielded the churches from the full effects of Christendom's demise.

Dietrich Bonhoeffer's critical description and analysis of the national-church phenomenon as a key component of the whole problem of post-Christendom is applicable to all of these churches. Bonhoeffer understood the crisis of faith and mission that challenges the churches after Christendom. Yet he showed biases common to Western interpreters of the modern church-and-state issue. He accurately identified differences in the paths to post-Christendom trod by Western Europe and North America, but he did not anticipate the third path taken by Eastern Europe and Russia. He outlined the differences between the secularization in the American churches and the European churches in an essay he wrote just after his return from his second visit to the United States in 1939:

> *The secularization of the church on the continent of Europe* arose from the misinterpretation of the reformers' distinction of the two realms; *American secularization* derives precisely from the imperfect distinction of the kingdoms and offices of church and state, from the enthusiastic claim of the church to universal influence on the world. That is a significant distinction. While for the churches of the Reformation the doctrine of the two realms needs a new examination and correction, the American denominations today must learn the necessity of this distinction, if they are to be rescued from complete secularization.[6]

Like Alexis de Tocqueville before him, Bonhoeffer accurately pointed out that the formal separation of church and state in America is deceptive, because there has coexisted with that legal and juridical

---

6. Bonhoeffer, "Protestantism without Reformation," in *No Rusty Swords: Letters and Notes, 1928-1936*, vol. 1 of *The Collected Works of Dietrich Bonhoeffer*, ed. Edwin H. Robertson (New York: Harper & Row, 1965), pp. 108-9.

arrangement a deep cultural fusion of Protestant piety and civic values. The American churches had become as severely compromised to the culture as their European counterparts, even if they had done so by a slightly different mechanism. Bonhoeffer concluded that in this century the church's essential freedom was seriously challenged everywhere — that is to say, in both America and Europe. He came that close to a complete analysis of the meaning of the end of Christendom.

But what about other Old World nations that once referred to themselves as Christian but that have no substantial history of either the Reformation distinction between two realms or the Catholic synthesis and juridical distinction between *sacerdotium* and *imperium?* What special problems arise within the third legacy of *symphonia* in the East, where churches were swept quite suddenly into the maelstrom of modern pluralism and secularism?[7] Surely their situation is unique. Even when governments and churches in the Christian East use the language of "separation of church and state" and "religious freedom," we cannot assume that they have the same connotations that they historically have had in America or Western Europe. The churches and cultures of the Christian East managed to escape the full impact of the Enlightenment and did not develop the church forms, secular consciousness, or language of religious freedom that are characteristic of Western experience. I believe that religious freedom will come to play a role in the future of these churches, though the associated legal and cultural arrangements will produce patterns different from those in the West. In the end, things might well look significantly different in the East, even if the best of circumstances prevail for church and nation.

In Chapter 5 I raise these sorts of issues, providing admonitions and prognostications along the way, sometimes passionately. This chapter is an Armenian theologian's address to his church, though written with the intent of being informative to others. The so-called national church issue that has arisen so dramatically today in the Christian East (viewed here in light of the Armenian case) is a logical focal point. My treatment naturally leads to reflection on the mission of these churches under the new and unfamiliar conditions that they now face. The treatment also opens up fruitful possibilities for comparative study concerning the national church issue. While contemporary trends in America and the Christian East might appear on surface to be radically different

---

7. In the East, the Justinian formulation of a "symphony" of church and civil authority prevailed and was transmitted and transmuted in the Russian czarist Christian empire. See my discussion in *Incarnate Love*, pp. 119-24.

(e.g., secularization in America and Western Europe contrasts with the potential for resacralization in some nations of the post-Soviet world), I maintain that the malaise of the churches in the face of the demise of Christendom East and West calls all churches to a more ecclesially centered Christian ethics.

Liturgy and Ethics: Centering Ethics Ecclesially

If there is one distinguishing characteristic of the Christian ethics proposed in this book and in my previous volume *Incarnate Love: Essays in Orthodox Ethics* (1987), it is that this ethic must incorporate sustained reflection on the liturgical prayer of the church. I contend that liturgy is a primary context and source for Christian ethics — a point that has largely been ignored by mainstream Protestants and Roman Catholics.

In *Incarnate Love,* I point out the dearth of attention to liturgy and lack of appreciation for liturgical praxis as the very doing of ethics. In this book, I attempt to explore further the ways in which liturgy can be a bridge to ethical reflection. I am driven to this study of liturgy by personal and practical concerns. My church needs to retrieve its rich liturgical tradition and then apply this tradition in a lively way to life in contemporary post-Christian and post-Christendom societies. The old medieval commentaries on the rites and liturgy were produced in a monastic and clerical age, and they cannot adequately illuminate the wisdom of the church in this age of the laity. Yes, I am doing ethics, but I also am doing a contemporary form of commentary on the rites of the church. I am consciously exploring ways to bring alive Armenian and Byzantine liturgy and worship. After Christendom, this is the fashion in which liturgical theology needs to be done. The chapters that close out this book are cases in point.

Chapter 6 — "Family and Christian Virtue: Reflections on the Ecclesial Vision of John Chrysostom" — might appear to promise a fairly conventional use of systematic theological texts to construct a theology of marriage and family. But in fact most of the texts from Chrysostom that I cite are taken from sermons that are centered in the Divine Liturgy. Although the liturgical component might elude modern sensibilities, it is real and significant nonetheless. In a perhaps unexpected fashion, in this chapter I also enter the debate prompted by the strong cultural critiques of Alasdair MacIntyre, Stanley Hauerwas, and John Howard Yoder over what constitutes sectarianism and catholicity in a post-Christendom world.

In Chapter 7 — "Ecological Ethics: An Ecclesial Event" — I argue that the profound ecological character of biblical religion has been missed or understated by critics and apologists alike because they ignore the role of blessing in Jewish and Christian faith. Reflection on the content and meaning of the Byzantine and Oriental Orthodox rites of blessing (e.g., baptism, the rites of Epiphany, rites of blessing of fields and crops) underscores this point.[8] The ecological ethic that issues from this activity of blessing is ecclesial. It offers thanksgiving for the blessing of the created order through invocation of the Holy Spirit and praise of the Holy Trinity for the economy (*oikonomia*) of salvation in Christ.

Finally, in Chapter 8 I offer what I believe to be a thesis that is unique in the present literature — namely, that the Orthodox rites of burial and anointing of the sick are crucial sources of moral wisdom on the matters of death and dying. Once again, I seek to speak out of an Eastern context to a culture that on the point at hand is very foreign: in this case, a culture in which traditional biblical and Christian understandings of death and dying are muted or forgotten.

I conceived of this book approximately five years ago, as I was completing *Incarnate Love*. Like that book, this is in some sense also a gathering of essays. Most of this material has been previously published elsewhere, though in all such cases it has evolved further since the initial publication. As diverse as the various topics I address here are, I believe that they do fit together — though perhaps more after the fashion of a mosaic than a symphony. For more than a millennium, Armenian mosaic artistry was prized and sought after by Byzantines and Ottomans alike. I hope that you will find and appreciate the ways in which this volume's essays are tied together by the themes expressed in the book's title and subtitle. I have done my best to place my own Armenian and Orthodox tradition in conversation with Protestant and Roman Catholic traditions and to render the theological riches of my church accessible to all readers. You will have to judge for yourself how well I have succeeded.

---

8. My use of the term *Byzantine* throughout this book refers to churches such as the Russian and Greek, which have a direct origin in Byzantine Christianity and are in communion with one another. These churches are usually referred to as Eastern Orthodox. There is, however, another family of Orthodox churches, the Oriental Orthodox, among which are the Armenian and Coptic churches. These churches are also called non-Chalcedonian churches because they rejected the christological formula issued by the Council of Chalcedon in 451. The rites of these churches often differ significantly from the Byzantine. I use the term *Byzantine*, then, to describe Greek and Slavonic rites as distinct from Armenian rites and prayers.

I. Prospects and Sources for an Ecclesial Christian Ethic

1. *Is Christian Ethics Any Longer Possible?*

> Let this, I say, be our way of overpowering them, and of
> conducting our warfare against them; and let us, before
> all words, astound them by our way of life. For this is the
> main battle, this is the unanswerable argument, the argu-
> ment from actions. For though we give ten thousand pre-
> cepts of philosophy in words, if we do not exhibit a life
> better than theirs, the gain is nothing. For it is not what
> is said that draws their attention, but their enquiry is,
> what we do. . . . Let us win them therefore by our life.
>
> St. John Chrysostom,
> *Homilies on I Corinthians*

Much has been written and said of late about our having entered a
post-Christian era. More often than not the people who make this
assertion fail to explain exactly what they mean by it. If they are asserting that North American culture is bereft of the influences of the church
and the gospel of Jesus Christ, then there is much evidence to suggest
that they are wrong. On the other hand, not all movement under the
banner of Christianity is a genuine sign of life. I have argued elsewhere
that the rise of the religious right in America during the 1970s and 1980s
was not evidence of the persistence or renewal of biblical religion within
the culture but, to the contrary, a symptom of the truly advanced pace
of secularization in our culture.[1] These spasms of political involvement

1. See "The Problem of a Social Ethic," in my book *Incarnate Love: Essays*

11

signified a refusal to acknowledge the fact that the era of American Christendom is over, a refusal to accept the fact that it would be best to lay the notion of Protestant America quietly to rest.

But a vital evangelical faith and practice does persist and does continue to find new life and expression in American Christianity, among Protestant Christians, Catholics, and Orthodox alike. There are hints and suggestions that all the churches still have the capacity to leaven the moral life of society. Even mainline Protestant Christianity, which seems to be in an especially advanced state of spiritual rigor mortis — deeply compromised to secular instrumentalism and immanentism — still manages to contribute in significant ways to the common good within a pluralistic society.

Perhaps it would be most accurate to describe the present relation of the churches to the American culture by saying not that we are living in a post-*Christian* era but rather that we are entering a post-*Christendom* era. This is what I take George Lindbeck to mean when he describes North American Christianity as being "in the awkwardly intermediate state of having once been culturally established but . . . not yet clearly disestablished."[2] Recently, theologians and philosophers such as Lindbeck, Stanley Hauerwas, and Alasdair MacIntyre have been telling Christians that they must abandon a long-held reliance on the culture to affirm biblical faith in crucial social and institutional contexts and to socialize individuals into something approximating a Christian way of life. The churches in America no longer have the internal discipline or conviction necessary to persuade their own, much less others, of the truth in Christianity. When the personal conduct of professing Christians no longer gives evidence of any vital connection with Christian theology, worship, or moral teaching, we cannot expect that sort of influence in the culture at large. Commensurate with a crisis of Christian ethics is an interruption in the transmission of Christian tradition.

This analysis is not so new as is sometimes thought. T. S. Eliot brilliantly put his finger on the phenomenon of a post-Christendom world and its challenge to the church some fifty years ago in his essay "The Idea of a Christian Society." Eliot took the measure of the culture in which he lived and concluded that England (and the rest of the old Christendom) was well on the way to becoming a social order in which

---

in Orthodox Ethics (Notre Dame, Ind.: University of Notre Dame Press, 1987), pp. 117-39.

2. Lindbeck, *The Nature of Doctrine* (Philadelphia: Westminster Press, 1984), p. 134.

the rhythm, structure, and doctrinal content of Christianity no longer influenced pervasively, as it once had, society's self-understanding or articulation of purpose. Western civilization was not without Christian influences and could not yet be said to be pagan, but a social order was emerging in which behavior was no longer "regulated by reference to Christian principle, and [in which] in effect prosperity in this world for the individual or for the group . . . [is] the sole conscious aim."[3]

While not disagreeing entirely with Lindbeck, Hauerwas, Mac-Intyre, or Eliot, Gilbert Meilaender has urged caution of late about overdrawing the current discontinuity between Christianity and the culture as compared with this relationship in the past. He contends that there was considerable economic and cultural pluralism in both East and West as early as the late Middle Ages. He cites historian Francis Oakley's observation that by the eleventh and twelfth centuries, Europe "had become politically too pluralistic, too fragmented, too disorderly, either to sponsor or to admit the successful imposition upon all groups of a single standard of economic behavior."[4] Eliot admonished his readers not to conjure up in their minds "a kind of apocalyptic vision of a golden age of virtue"; after all, "we have to remember that the Kingdom of Christ on earth will never be realised, and also that it is always being realised; we must remember that whatever reform or revolution we carry out, the result will always be a sordid travesty of what human society should be — though the world is never left wholly without glory."[5]

Liberalism, Privatism, and the Lure of Sectarianism

It would be well to keep in mind Meilaender's and Eliot's admonitions when evaluating the present state of the culture or trying to envision a suitable *modus vivendi* for the church after Christendom. While I do not find Eliot's proposal for a new Christian society persuasive, I agree with him that the communal vision of Christianity must not be cultivated exclusively within the body of the faithful. Any temptation to withdraw entirely from the emerging culture must be resisted. This kind of

3. Eliot, "The Idea of a Christian Society," in *Christianity and Culture* (New York: Harcourt, Brace & World, 1949), p. 10.
4. Oakley, quoted by Meilaender in *Faith and Faithfulness* (Notre Dame, Ind.: University of Notre Dame Press, 1991), pp. 8-9.
5. Eliot, "The Idea of a Christian Society," p. 47.

"sectarianism" is impermissible on christological grounds. At the heart of the Christian faith is the conviction that the world's true end is to become the body of Christ. The church is in the world precisely to remember for the world that this is its true end.

The response of mainline American Christianity has been neither sectarian retreat nor reactionary restoration but debilitating accommodation. Eliot identified a source of such compromise in the churches' willingness to accept as a self-description the Enlightenment definition of Christianity as "a mere congeries of private and independent sects."[6] Religion under such conditions is tolerated as a matter of individual conscience. This is the modern heresy that ensures the privatization of Christianity, and in this sense it renders the present state of things unique. But pluralism alone is not the issue: the church has seen that before. There is something more radical and eviscerating at work that is putting in question the very possibility of the Christian life.

We are now getting indications from most unlikely sources of the extent to which a privatized view of religion has permeated the American mind. In April of 1990, for example, the Supreme Court in a majority decision (*Employment Division v. Smith*) written by Justice Scalia denied that members of the Native American Church have a right under the First Amendment to ingest peyote as part of a traditional sacrament. In question was an Oregon state law that prohibits all use of peyote. Conservative columnist George Will praised the decision in an article entitled "The Place of Religion in American Polity," arguing that the decision stood in the best tradition of the "cool realism and secularism of the philosophy that informed the Founders." He went on to say that "a central purpose of America's political arrangements is the subordination of religion to the political order, meaning the primacy of democracy. . . . Hence religion is to be perfectly free as long as it is perfectly private — mere belief — but it must bend to the political law as regards conduct." Will invoked the wisdom of Thomas Jefferson and John Locke, both of whom he interpreted as having viewed religion as something that "can be useful or can be disruptive, but . . . [whose] truth cannot be established by reason." It is on these grounds, he indicated, that Americans declined to establish religion; rather, "by guaranteeing free exercise of religion, they [made] religions private and subordinate."[7]

I suppose one could reasonably argue that forbidding the use of

6. Eliot, "The Idea of a Christian Society," p. 40.
7. Will, "The Place of Religion in American Polity," *Baltimore Sun,* 24 April 1990.

peyote in religious ritual does not vitally jeopardize (as Justices Blackmun, Brennan, and Marshall feared) the court-established principle that "an indissoluble link [exists] between some religious conduct and belief." Will's reasoning, however, has the potential for far more extensive and radical applications. For example, Will ventured to suggest that the court ought to strike down the 1972 decision that exempts the Amish "from complying with Wisconsin law requiring parents to send their children to school until the age of 16."[8]

In "The Idea of a Christian Society," T. S. Eliot warns of a culture driven by a "compulsion to live in such a way that Christian behaviour is only possible in a restricted number of situations." This, he argues, "is a very powerful force against Christianity; for behaviour is as potent to affect belief, as belief to affect behaviour."[9] Will's practical stance, whether one regards it as conservative or classically liberal, is, in my estimate, an accurate reflection of the predominant sentiment in our culture. When I introduced the article to my students at Loyola College, the majority agreed with Will. In discussing the matter, they offered evidence of a deeply ingrained individualism and convictions about the primacy of the self. The authors of the best-selling volume *Habits of the Heart* have referred to this deep-seated belief as "ontological individualism."[10] On a cognitive level, this individualism does not conceptualize beliefs as anything more than personal or private. It gives little evidence of an awareness of the fact that beliefs are not owned apart from communities of memory and tradition. This may amount to a more extreme form of individualism than Will advocates, and yet, for the sake of a social concord that he perceives to be threatened by pluralism, he is ready to restrict religious belief and practice to a private realm.

I believe that we are at a juncture in our cultural history when the churches will have to make some hard choices about how they will define their relationship to society. In this last decade of the twentieth century, we seem almost millennia removed from an American culture that is actually only two or three generations past, in which representatives of the Social Gospel movement such as Walter Rauschenbusch declared confidently that the best values of liberalism and democracy were wholly compatible with those of the kingdom of God and that

---

8. Will, "The Place of Religion in American Polity."
9. Eliot, "The Idea of a Christian Society," p. 24.
10. Robert N. Bellah, Richard Madsen, William M. Sullivan, Ann Swidler, and Steven M. Tipton, *Habits of the Heart: Individualism and Commitment in American Life* (Berkeley and Los Angeles: University of California Press, 1985), p. 334.

the complete Christianization of America was not only a desirable but a realizable goal. The Social Gospel movement did not survive the post–World War II era. Its basic claims about the compatibility of Christianity and culture, significant aspects of its social agenda, and its custodial commitments to American democracy, however, were subsequently embraced by mainline Protestant Christianity, as those churches allied themselves with secular liberalism in a variety of causes. No doubt some good came of this (e.g., in the area of civil rights), but a profound confusion of the standards of the kingdom of God with the underlying convictions of liberalism also ensued.

Eliot said that religious liberalism "may be characterised as a progressive discarding of elements in historical Christianity which appear superfluous or obsolete, confounded with practices and abuses which are legitimate objects of attack."[11] Like secular forms of liberalism, this religious liberalism is "not so much defined by its end, as by its starting point."[12] Religious and secular liberalism share a premise that derives from their common origins in the Enlightenment — namely, that individuals must be emancipated from the tyrannizing grip of outworn traditions. As a result, religious liberalism is destined to lose its force over time, as it yields to the impulse to liberate itself from the shackles of a series of specific historical traditions and communities of memory. This is the path that mainline liberal American Protestantism has taken in the latter half of the twentieth century, gradually de-emphasizing those aspects of its traditions that differentiated it from the surrounding culture and shifting its focus to those principles and virtues that it already held in common with the culture — especially those ostensibly universal truths and human aspirations that could be defined and defended broadly within the culture as justifications for the extension of individual human rights and civil liberties.

Just as postwar Protestant liberalism seemed to be losing steam in the early 1970s, there arose out of other, more "conservative" sectors of American Protestantism an activist Christian Right. The posture of this New Right toward the culture turned out to be something like a mirror opposite of that of the liberal churches. Certainly it rejected the liberal Protestant confidence in the possibility of a constructive synthesis between secular values and Christian values. On the other hand, such representatives of the movement as Jerry Falwell and Pat Robertson confidently asserted that the underlying principles of American

---

11. Eliot, "The Idea of a Christian Society," pp. 12-13.
12. Eliot, "The Idea of a Christian Society," p. 12.

democracy and the rights of individuals (which, they argued, had been betrayed by liberals) are derived from and wholly compatible with biblical norms. Evangelical Christians, precisely because they were good Christians, were the true champions of the republic.

For our purposes here, I need not review the false history invented by Falwell, Robertson, James Kennedy, and others to persuade their ranks that a re-Christianized America ought to be their goal. Suffice it to say that we are beyond the time when a retrieval of such a past order, real or imagined, is either possible or desirable. We have gone on to live in what Eliot called a "Neutral Society,"[13] which is not an alternative to a Christian society but merely a transitional phase on the way to a completely de-Christianized society. Or, using Lindbeck's categories, we might say that a "Neutral Society" is simply an intermediate state between a past in which Christianity was the culturally established faith and a future in which it will be wholly disestablished. The liberal "Neutral Society" is not something to be *decided for* but rather a phase in which society is *deciding whether* it will retain its memory of the role of biblical faith in culture formation and allow for its continued influence, or whether it will embark on a path toward a still-undefined integral secularism (or perhaps even a new paganism or polytheism).

On this matter, I think, heirs of Protestant neo-orthodoxy (e.g, Richard John Neuhaus, before his conversion to Catholicism) and Roman Catholic neo-Thomism (e.g., John A. Coleman) would join theologians and philosophers with whom they share few other views (e.g., communalists Stanley Hauerwas and Alasdair MacIntyre) in warning of the emergence of a society "after virtue" and "after tradition."

The Litmus of the Abortion Issue

No controversy of our time better illustrates where Christianity stands presently within the culture than abortion. It is not surprising that Richard John Neuhaus should have reported that it was the abortion issue that caused him finally to break ranks with liberals: "I . . . discovered how brutally illiberal liberalism can be and how truly bigoted the opponents of bigotry can be."[14] There are resonances of anger and

13. Eliot, "The Idea of a Christian Society," p. 6.
14. Neuhaus, "Advancing the Role of Religion in Public Life," in *Christian Allies in a Secular Age*, ed. Kevin Perrotta and John C. Blattner (Ann Arbor: Servant Books, 1987), p. 54

feelings of betrayal in such words that may suggest what is at the heart of the mistake in a cultural strategy that has, ironically, been shared by liberal and conservative Christians to this point. As a liberal in the 1960s, Neuhaus was committed to the use of "rights" language to bring the Christian conscience to bear on the culture. He was disappointed in his fellow liberals when they did not extend those human rights to the fetus. As a neoconservative, Neuhaus remains committed to a reliance on natural-law and human-rights language to inform a new public philosophy, but he now feels he has established a structure within which he can consistently extend such human rights to the fetus. Yet Stanley Hauerwas has argued forcefully that such reliance on conventional rights language may have been the fatal trap into which religious opponents of abortion unwittingly stumbled, thereby severely jeopardizing their prospects of success:

> Christians . . . assumed that the liberal commitment to the individual carried with it the prohibition of abortion. Yet what they found is that the "individual" whom liberalism has an interest in protecting does not, either conceptually or normatively (though perhaps legally), necessarily include the fetus. . . . [Christians] were prepared to argue about whether certain kinds of abortion might or might not be legally prohibited or permitted, but that . . . [they] would be required to argue whether abortion as an institution is moral, amoral or immoral was simply unthinkable. As Christians we knew generally that we were against abortion, but we were not clear why. We assumed it surely had to do with our prohibition against the taking of life, and we assumed that was surely all that needed to be said.[15]

David L. Schindler has built on this critique, suggesting that when Christians rested their case against abortion on conventional rights language, they failed to realize that they were leaving "intact the deeper logic" of American culture. This logic, says Schindler, "is one of self-centricity which presupposes a primitive (ontological) externality of relation of self and others. Such a logic is the heart of what is called liberalism."[16] The controlling presupposition of the conventional rights

---

15. Hauerwas, *A Community of Character* (Notre Dame, Ind.: University of Notre Dame Press, 1981), pp. 219-20.
16. Schindler, "Introduction: Grace and the Form of Nature and Culture," in *Catholicism and Secularization in America*, ed. David L. Schindler (Notre Dame, Ind.: Communio Books, 1990), p. 18.

position is that autonomous individuals determine by their own decisions how they will be related to others. This autonomous self is the
ultimate irreducible reality. Rights, in turn, are conceived as obligations
that others have toward the self and that the self in turn demands of or
grants to others. "Even when . . . [a] right is extended to all selves, the
direction of obligation — the obliged relation — remains self-centered.
What happens is merely that that self-centricity now becomes universal-
ized."[17] Rights centered in and on the autonomous self relegate relations
of reciprocity and community to the category of epiphenomena at best.
In classical Christian ethics, on the other hand, these communal relations
are held to be as primary as the self and to place obligations on the self
that take precedence over any decisions the self might make about them.
It is no wonder, concludes Schindler, that in a society under the domination of such a language and understanding of rights "those selves who
are least able to act for themselves and thus make demands for themselves" — such as the unborn — are left most vulnerable.[18]

Schindler's analysis is substantiated by the course of recent Supreme Court decisions relating to the abortion issue as well as by the
public responses to these decisions. I consider it ironic that several of
the more recent decisions have been received as efforts by a conservative Court to restrict women's right to have abortions by placing the
power to regulate abortions back in the state legislatures. Perhaps the
most substantial effect of the Court's decision in *Webster v. Reproductive
Health Services* (1989), for instance, was to renew energy within the
pro-choice movement. Once Americans were faced with the *real* pros-
pect of finding serious limits placed on personal autonomy, they backed
off from the principle of the sacredness of life and rights of the fetus.
Liberals detected an opening through which to challenge President
George Bush and the Republicans in the 1990 congressional and guber-
natorial races and in the 1992 presidential contest. While Bush held to
his pro-life position, other Republicans, even within his inner circle,
began to back off. During the Clinton presidency, public support for
the pro-life movement has further diminished, and the movement has
been pushed back on the defensive. Pro-choice advocates have success-
fully capitalized on uncertainties of many Americans whose pro-life
sentiments were quite shallow to begin with.

17. Schindler, "Introduction: Grace and the Form of Nature and Culture,"
p. 18.

18. Schindler, "Introduction: Grace and the Form of Nature and Culture,"
p. 18.

Three years after the *Webster* ruling, in *Planned Parenthood v. Casey* (1992), the Supreme Court refused to strike down *Roe v. Wade*. The justices chose not to challenge the logic of radical personal autonomy that had insinuated itself into law and judicial decisions and prevailed in public opinion. The majority stated that "Roe . . . may be seen not only as an exemplar of Griswold [*Griswold v. Connecticut*, 1965] liberty,[19] but as a rule (whether or not mistaken) of personal autonomy and bodily integrity, with doctrinal affinity to cases recognizing limits on governmental power to mandate medical treatment or to bar its rejection." The *Griswold* case had addressed only the marital *relationship* — "the sacred precincts of the marital bed," as the Court put it (381 U.S. 479 [1965]). But in *Eisenstadt v. Baird* (1972), which held that the state unconstitutionally violated the privacy of the individual by forbidding the distribution of contraceptives to unmarried persons, and in *Roe v. Wade*, the privacy principle was extended to unmarried and single persons. Justice Brennan stated that

> the marital couple is not an independent entity with a mind and heart of its own, but an association of two individuals each with a separate intellectual and emotional makeup. If the right to privacy means anything, it is the right of the individual, married or single, to be free from unwarranted government intrusion into matters so fundamentally affecting a person as the decision whether to bear or beget a child.[20]

Privacy was virtually equated with the autonomous self.

In *Planned Parenthood v. Casey*, the Court upheld a section of the Pennsylvania law that requires teenagers seeking an abortion to secure the consent of parents or guardians, but it struck down a provision requiring a married woman to inform her husband of her intention to have an abortion. The Court stated, "A state may not give to a man the kind of dominion over a wife that parents exercise over their children."[21] Traditional Jewish and Christian faith understands marriage as a conjugal union in which husband and wife *mutually* surrender control of their bodies to one another. They become "one flesh," and the good of procreation is affirmed in the matrimonial blessing. This

---

19. *Griswold v. Connecticut* held that a Connecticut law which banned the use of contraceptives was unconstitutional because it invaded the privacy of the marital bed.

20. *Eisenstadt v. Baird*, 405 U.S. 438 (1972).

21. As quoted in the *New York Times*, 30 June 1992, p. A15.

understanding of marriage is completely irrelevant so far as the Court's new privacy doctrine is concerned.

The Court has gone to great lengths to justify its adherence to this doctrine and its underlying principle of personal autonomy. It has all but conceded that it will not buck the public consensus that rights are lodged solely within and possessed by the autonomous self. In *Planned Parenthood v. Casey*, the judges stated, "The Court must take care to speak and act in ways that allow people to accept its decisions on the terms the Court claims for them, as grounded truly in principle, not as compromises with social and political pressures, having, as such, no bearing on the principled choices that the Court is obliged to make. *Thus, the Court's legitimacy depends on making legally principled decisions under circumstances in which their principled character is sufficiently plausible to be accepted by the nation.*"[22] Which is to say that the Court contended that it had no choice but to stick with the principle of the radical autonomy and privacy of the self because this is what Americans deeply believe.

Is Christian Ethics Any Longer Possible?

The abortion issue is a telling example of how far the American ethos has moved away from biblical and Christian morality. It exposes some profound discontinuities between the culture's deepest beliefs about individualism and the structure of social reality on the one hand and biblical and Christian understandings of personhood, human nature, and community on the other. The Court's "doctrine" and Christian incarnational and trinitarian doctrine do not correlate. In fact, they contradict each other. Is Christian ethics any longer possible in American society? Probably not as it has been conceived and done since the beginnings of Christendom. Christian ethics needs to be rethought, as does the familiar process of correlating Christian truth with social norms. Since Constantine and Theodosius, Christian thinkers have been in the habit of looking for mediating structures within nature and society that correlate with Christian doctrine concerning human nature and divine law. But as Pope Paul VI observed in his apostolic letter *Evangeli nuntiandi*, "The rift between the gospel and culture is undoubtedly the drama of our epoch."[23] This situation would seem to

22. *New York Times*, 30 June 1992, p. A16; italics mine.
23. Paul VI, quoted by Walter Kasper in "Nature, Grace, and Culture: On the Meaning of Secularization," in *Catholicism and Secularization in America*, pp. 44-45.

suggest that a radical review of the church's *modus vivendi* is in order. As Stanley Hauerwas and John Howard Yoder have argued so forcefully, we are at the end of Constantinian Christianity. Our situation has changed, and business as usual will no longer suffice. The question is which new direction we should take.

Those like Hauerwas and Yoder who speak out of the free-church tradition regard Constantinianism and Christendom itself as contrary to the gospel. As I have already indicated, I do not take such a dim view of these historical developments. However, I do agree with the critics that we will not be able to heal our compromised and eviscerated churches unless we abandon the Constantinian outlook once and for all. While I believe that Constantinianism has provided some benefits to the historical church, I also believe that it has saddled the churches of the modern era with a debilitating legacy of compromising or confusing biblical faith with civil religion. The churches have gone so far as to condone political immanentism and nationalism in the name of the kingdom of God. With respect to this history, the free-church tradition contributes an important critique.

At this juncture, I would like to return to the insights of Schindler and Meilaender in order to lay the groundwork for some proposals about what sort of Christian ethics is possible and desirable after Christendom (a discussion that extends into the following two chapters). I find the arguments of Schindler and Meilaender to be more congenial with my own because in their critiques of Constantinianism they manage to offer visions of church and society that are more catholic than those of Hauerwas or Yoder. And I want to focus as they do on the way in which natural law or something like it has functioned within the Constantinian framework, especially in the West, to influence the behavior of rulers and to establish the moral order of the whole of society.

As a Roman Catholic, Schindler does not want to abandon entirely the tradition of natural law as a resource for Christian ethics in a post-Christendom America. Yet we have seen that he is painfully aware of the non-Christian — even anti-Christian — presuppositions in the culture's prevailing notions of human rights and a common human morality. He agrees with Hauerwas's analysis of how Christians miscalculated the effects of making such appeals to a common morality in the abortion debate. But rather than rejecting natural law and human-rights language completely, Schindler argues that we should reserve our skepticism for a liberal form of the natural-law argument that is premised in the autonomy of the self and the self's externality to others. Proponents of this bloodless variety of natural law prize its ostensible neutrality and the fact that it transcends tradition "as a matter of principle."[24]

Schindler maintains that contrary to the sort of ontological individualism and human-rights doctrine associated with this ungrounded and traditionless natural law, catholic Christianity affirms that humanity is created in the image and likeness of a God who in his very essence is a community of being. The true norm of the moral life is the perfectly reciprocal (perichoric) and donative life of the Trinity. Further, Christian faith insists that our human nature in all its diversity is normatively connected to the trinitarian life through love — a love that was revealed fully by the Second Person of the Trinity, who in his humanity lived perfectly the trinitarian life. The agapeic and kenotic love evidenced in Christ's life contrasts sharply with the self-centered logic of modern liberal rights language.

The problem that Schindler wrestles with (and that has not yet been resolved in his thinking) is how Christians might continue to invoke persuasively and without confusion an incarnational and trinitarian-based notion of natural or moral law. This kind of natural law does not presuppose rights of the individual self-centeredly conceived, nor does it give warrant to a common-denominator morality. To the contrary, it reserves a claim for singular, absolute, and final truth in Christian ethics. Schindler does not want to insist that whenever Christians appeal to natural law they have to make explicit their belief that the normativity of our nature resides ultimately in Christ. In one sense, that would controvert the point of such appeals, which seek to establish a common ground based on the fact that "nature and its laws have an integrity of their own." Yet neither should "the Christian . . . , even for a moment, pretend, in his appeal to nature or nature's law, that he is not influenced by grace, by the faith given in and by Christ, or that nature does not have its final end in Christ." To do so would be to make an implicit concession to the falsehood of our culture's individualism, narcissism, and relativism.[25] Schindler argues that while "we cannot force Christian ethics on non-Christians,"[26] neither should Christians concede any use of a natural-law argument in post-Christendom America without appropriate tradition specificity — which is to say, without

---

24. Schindler, "Introduction: Grace and the Form of Nature and Culture," p. 23.

25. Schindler, "Introduction: Grace and the Form of Nature and Culture," p. 23.

26. Schindler, "Introduction: Grace and the Form of Nature and Culture," p. 22.

a serious ontology rooted in christology and trinitarian faith. Our prag-matic and nominalistic culture resists this task of ontology at all turns, and, sadly, Christian theologians and ethicists have not yet adequately taken it up either.

I read Schindler as saying that after Christendom, Christian ap-peals to a natural or higher law must take on a character more radical than conservative. Those who seek to use neutral natural-law argu-ments to establish an apologetic for Christianity will eventually find themselves deeply compromised; those who seek to promote claims that the social order is in fact founded in Christian truth will simply be conducting exercises in anachronism. Unfortunately, the Enlightenment project has been so successful in our culture that few ordinary Chris-tians distinguish between tradition-grounded natural-law arguments and neutral natural-law arguments, with the result that few are able to distinguish a moral life that is Christ-centered and trinitarian from one which is merely "natural." "Any appeal to a natural law argument which does not cost a transformation or conversion in one's being," warns Schindler, "is likely, given the context of contemporary America, to be liberal, which is to say too pale or minimalistic."[27]

Schindler's proposed response to the post-Christendom predica-ment is itself nettled with problems, and yet I feel it is worth the trouble to try to work out these problems because I feel he is basically moving in the right direction. I appreciate his desire to abandon the notion that neutral natural-law discourse is intrinsically compatible with Christian faith and hope, for example. I agree with his plea for a serious Christian ontology rooted in ecclesial practice. On the other hand, he has not yet shown how Christians can at the present cultural moment make effec-tive use of the language of natural law, given the fact that it has histori-cally been bound up with the maintenance of Christendom and has more recently been put to use in the defense of democratic liberalism. In the abstract, the argument for a common morality nourished by Chris-tian belief is not unattractive. It is certainly better than the nihilistic amoralism toward which we seem to be headed. But if we can't engineer a revival of natural-law thinking, perhaps other strategies addressing more immediate needs of the church are called for.

Gilbert Meilaender insists that the fact that "the Christian way

27. Schindler, "Is This the 'Catholic Moment' for the Future?" in *The Twenty-fifth Anniversary of Vatican II — A Look Back and a Look Ahead: Proceedings of the Ninth Bishops' Workshop*, ed. Russel E. Smith (Braintree, Mass.: Pope John Center, 1990), p. 306n.7.

of life — and, indeed, its power and attraction — cannot be made fully intelligible within the restrictions of the public sphere does not mean that no common ground or possibilities for 'translation' exist," even in a fallen world, even in a post-Christendom culture.[28] He grounds his argument in both Christian dogma and historical precedent. Both Scripture and the major ecumenical creeds affirm that in the Incarnation, the Logos is revealed by the Spirit as the One through whom "all things have been created" and in whom "all things hold together" (Col. 1:16, 17). Christians have reason to believe that no thing exists, human or nonhuman, that is not intrinsically related to the Logos. I take it that St. Paul drew courage from this truth in his Areopagus speech, when he proclaimed that the "unknown god" whom Athenians worshiped was in fact the God of Israel and the church. "In him," Paul proclaimed, "we live and move and have our being" (Acts 17:28).

The theology of my own Orthodox tradition has been especially attentive to the sort of christological ontology and epistemology invoked by Meilaender and Schindler. The Greek patristic writers, too, spoke of natural or moral law only on the basis of this christology and trinitarian theology. "Instruction in divine law is not from without," wrote St. Basil of Caesarea, "but simultaneously with the formation of the creature — man, I mean — a kind of rational force was implanted in us like a seed, which, by an inherent tendency, impels us toward love."[29] While a project to reconstruct a public philosophy or common morality is theoretically possible, Meilaender quite rightly notes that establishing a common ground for moral discourse between Christians and non-Christians "is not the same as an elaboration of the Christian way of life."[30] It was not Basil's first concern to find some common morality grounded in human nature or reason between Christians and non-Christians. He was more interested in exploring forms of community and discipline that would enable Christians to live the gospel and show others the way to the kingdom of God. It is my contention that this is the point on which a new *modus vivendi* of the churches in North America and much of Europe must turn in our time as well.

Meilaender suggests that the cultural situation in which the church currently finds itself is in some important sense analogous to

---

28. Meilaender, *Faith and Faithfulness*, p. 22.

29. Basil of Caesarea, *The Long Rules*, in *St. Basil: The Ascetical Works*, trans. M. Monica Wagner, vol. 9 of *The Fathers of the Church* (New York: Fathers of the Church, 1950), p. 233 (q. 2).

30. Meilaender, *Faith and Faithfulness*, p. 22.

the situation the church found itself in during the time of St. Augustine. Like Augustine, we not only have to find some way to carve out a distinctively Christian life in the midst of a decadent civilization but we also have to find some means to maintain contact with all that is still "good in that civilization, to understand that if it is often vicious (in the technical, moral sense), its vice is, at least sometimes, 'splendid.'"[31] I sympathize deeply with Meilaender's sentiment and recommendations. Like Augustine, Christians today must endeavor to find a path between accommodationism on the one hand and sectarianism on the other. But I would also note at least one very important difference between Augustine's time and ours that Meilaender overlooks. Augustine's Christianity was inexplicable apart from existing militant and highly disciplined forms of Christian community. He not only founded such a community in his early years, but, later on as Bishop of Hippo, he fought against one such movement, the Donatists, which exerted a force in North Africa so powerful that it threatened to gain the support of the state and triumph over the catholic church. Contemporary American Christianity exerts nothing like this sort of potent force in the culture; the era of Christendom lies behind us, not before us. So pointing to Augustine may not teach quite the lesson that Meilaender proposes. Neither does it "trump," as Meilaender asserts, Alasdair MacIntyre's suggestion that we await a new St. Benedict. The ethics of St. Benedict and St. Augustine alike makes sense only in the context of their personal histories and involvement with monastic forms of Christian living — and the most important lesson we can learn from these histories is that we need to rediscover the ecclesial context of Christian ethics. Christian ethics is grounded most importantly not in what individual Christian ethicists write but in what all Christians do together in community. The biggest obstacle to Christian ethics today is that Christians are not doing enough together to establish a singularly christic and trinitarian way of life.

In summary, it does appear that there is relatively little common ground left between Christians and non-Christians in post-Christendom America. This is not to say that it has disappeared altogether, however: the work of the creation has not been entirely undone by sin or death, and even at this late date, we can still identify significant threads of our culture's Christian past running through it. And since this legacy remains, we would do well to take advantage of it whenever possible. Yet we must acknowledge that the legacy is scant and it is

31. Meilaender, *Faith and Faithfulness*, p. 32.

diminishing. We must look elsewhere for a ground on which to construct our common moral life. In striving to live moral lives, it has always been imperative — and it is especially imperative in our time — that Christians seek to invigorate those ecclesial forms of teaching, preaching, worship, and *diakonia* that constitute their special inheritance of faith and hope in Jesus Christ.

The Example of St. John Chrysostom

I want to close this chapter with a brief reflection on the pastoral theology of St. John Chrysostom of Antioch.

Chrysostom lived approximately at the same moment in history as St. Augustine in the Latin West. Like Augustine, he early became associated with monastic forms of living and was an unfailing defender of monasticism. Later, as a pastor of the church in Antioch and as bishop of Constantinople, he was known for his scathing criticisms of the culture. He ridiculed its fixation on financial success, material possessions, and amusements. As an alternative, he preached an uncompromising defense of Christian living, both lay and monastic — the distinction between which he minimized by insisting that the Beatitudes are for all Christians.

Chrysostom's theology contrasts with the emerging Constantinian theology of his era. Nor can his efforts to build up energetic and disciplined ecclesial communities be typified as the ethics of withdrawal from the world. As Gerhardt B. Ladner has asserted, "John Chrysostom perished as a martyr for Christian ethical principles in resistance to an unholy alliance of corrupt Church dignitaries with the irresponsible heirs of the Constantinian-Theodosian Empire"; he "tried to reform the 'Polis' within the 'Basileia.' "[32] Chrysostom had a genuine commitment to Christian reform, inspired by the highly disciplined expressions of Christian life existent within — and, yes, as in the case of a vital and thriving monasticism, sometimes also separate from — society. "Chrysostom," wrote Georges Florovsky, "was preaching in the cities [what] monks were fervently practicing in their communities. . . . Chrysostom did not regard monastic life as just an advanced course for the select, but rather as a normal *evangelical* pattern intended for all Christians."[33]

32. Ladner, *The Idea of Reform* (New York: Harper & Row, 1967), p. 129.
33. Florovsky, *The Collected Works of Georges Florovsky*, vol. 2: *Aspects of Church History* (Belmont, Mass.: Nordland, 1975), p. 85.

Chrysostom kept in view the antinomy of church and world through an insistence on an evangelical and catholic ethic of a renewed human being in the image of Christ. His pastoral method is a model for the reinvigoration of Christian living and renewal of confidence in the socially transformative power of the church. Chrysostom's pastoral theology addresses forcefully the cultural pole of Christian ethics, but, perhaps even more significantly for our time, it is capable of redirecting us as well to the ecclesial location of Christian ethics. He reminds us of what is required within the community of believers to make its ethics effective in changing the lives of others. In one of his homilies on 1 Corinthians he wrote,

> A deep night oppresses the whole world. This is what we have to dispel and dissolve. It is night not among heretics, nor among Greeks only, but also in the multitude on our side, in respect of doctrines and of life. For many entirely disbelieve the resurrection; many fortify themselves with their horoscope; many adhere to superstitious observances, and to omens, and auguries, and presages. . . .
>
> [As for the Greeks,] be ye fellow-helpers with me in the battle; by your way of life attracting them to us and changing them. For, as I am always saying, He that teaches high morality ought first to teach it in his own person, and be such as his hearers cannot do without.[34]

---

34. Chrysostom, *The Homilies of S. John Chrysostom,* in vol. 4 of the *Library of Fathers of the Holy Catholic Church* (Oxford: John Henry Parker, 1889), p. 48.

2. Tradition and Ethics: Prospects in a Liberal Society

As I mentioned in Chapter 1, fifty years ago T. S. Eliot addressed what contemporary writers such as Alasdair MacIntyre and Stanley Hauerwas have described as the peculiar threat to Christian tradition posed by contemporary liberal societies. I want to continue that discussion in this chapter and begin to advance proposals for how Christian ethics needs to be conceived after Christendom. In this chapter I will approach these topics through an examination of the relationship between Christian tradition and Christian ethics. In Chapter 3, I will address the question of what the character and location of Christian ethics after Christendom ought to be through a discussion of the Bible and ethics.

In *The Idea of a Christian Society*, Eliot argues that an advanced liberalism is cultivating a spirit of tolerance and a distinction between public secular morality and private religious morality as an alternative to an integral Christian social vision. Liberals have characteristically argued that such a social order does not jeopardize Christian beliefs, practices, or virtuous behavior. To the contrary, they maintain, such a social order provides the necessary space for the various Christian sects to live peaceably with one another. While Eliot grants that there is a partial truth in this conventional description, he insists that something else is at work in advanced liberal societies that undercuts the claim to religious neutrality. "The Liberal notion that religion [is] a matter of private belief and of conduct in private life, and that there is no reason why Christians should not be able to accommodate themselves to any world which treats them good-naturedly, is becoming less and less tenable."[1] The new public morality, he observed, is governed by a

1. Eliot, "The Idea of a Christian Society," in *Christianity and Culture* (New

purely instrumental notion of freedom in which "prosperity in this world for the individual or for the group has become the sole conscious aim" (p. 10). This definition of freedom and the acquisitive, utilitarian morality that liberalism fosters are fundamentally at odds with the Christian vision of life.

Meanwhile, the Christian virtues have been constricted and narrowed in people's lives. The ascendant public morality creates "the compulsion to live in such a way that Christian behaviour is only possible in a restricted number of situations" (p. 24). Christian hope becomes truncated and ultimately is transformed into the secular "notion of *getting on* to which the alternative is a hopeless apathy" (p. 12). Furthermore, liberalism carries within it an impetus toward the dissolution of religious and social tradition. "For it is something which tends to release energy rather than accumulate it, to relax, rather than to fortify. It is a movement not so much defined by its end, as by its starting point; away from, rather than towards, something definite" (p. 12). Liberalism redefines all other traditions as matters of individual or group preference.[2] It subverts the "traditional social habits of people" and dissolves "their natural collective consciousness into individual constituents" (p. 12). Such an environment erodes the influence of Christian morality on the imagination of people until it no longer inspires them with hope and a vision of a highest good. This leads to the creation of "bodies of men and women — of all classes — detached from tradition, alienated from religion and susceptible to mass suggestion" (p. 17).

The problem for Christians, Eliot concludes, is no longer merely that they constitute "a minority in a society of *individuals* holding an alien belief. It is the problem constituted by our implication in a network of institutions from which we cannot dissociate ourselves: institutions the operation of which appears no longer neutral, but non-Christian" (p. 17). The distinction between a private religious morality and a public secular morality becomes increasingly less real in the lives of people. Even among many Christians, private morality simply mirrors the new public ethos. "And as for the Christian who is not conscious of [this] dilemma — and he is in the majority — he is becoming more and more de-Christianized by all sorts of unconscious pressure: paganism holds all the most valuable advertising space" (pp. 17-18). This condition,

---

York: Harcourt Brace & World, 1940), p. 17. Subsequent references to this essay will be made parenthetically in the text.

2. See chap. 17 of Alasadair MacIntyre's *Whose Justice? Which Rationality?* (Notre Dame, Ind.: University of Notre Dame Press, 1988).

judged Eliot, is becoming so typical that "anything like Christian traditions transmitted from generation to generation within the family must disappear, and the small body of Christians will consist entirely of adult recruits" (p. 18).

In hopes of precluding this grim eventuality, Eliot offers a renewed apologetic for the idea of a Christian society. He suggests that the idea of a Christian society ought to be cultivated so that it might be available as an intellectual resource at some inevitable future moment of cultural despair. He believed that in 1940 the idea of a Christian society still had a chance in England, a nation that had retained important institutional features of the old Christendom, including an established church. Yet Eliot's attraction to the idea of a Christian society was not simply the expression of a sentimental yearning for the old Christendom or a hope that the church might one day recapture its role as a major power broker in society. Nor was he interested in promoting a functionalist role for the church and religion as moral supports of the social order. To the contrary, "What is worst of all," he wrote, "is to advocate Christianity, not because it is true, but because it might be beneficial. . . . To justify Christianity because it provides a foundation of morality, instead of showing the necessity of Christian morality from the truth of Christianity, is a very dangerous inversion; and we may reflect, that a good deal of the attention of totalitarian states has been devoted, with a steadiness of purpose not always found in democracies, to providing their national life with a foundation of morality — the wrong kind perhaps, but a good deal more of it" (pp. 46-47).

Eliot stuck to the idea of a Christian society because he believed in the communal nature of Christianity and he believed that a social embodiment of the faith is absolutely necessary for accomplishing the church's mission. He maintained that this social embodiment must not be confined to the church but must extend into the greater society. Such a view is mandated by the Christian belief in the Trinity and the Incarnation.[3] At the same time, he cautioned against any sort of Christian utopianism. A Christian society would itself be subject to decay and ever needful of reform. "I have tried to restrict my ambition of a Christian society," he wrote, "to a social minimum: to picture, not a society of saints, but of ordinary men, of men whose Christianity is communal before being individual" (p. 47).

In the end, I am not persuaded by Eliot's proposal for a Christian

3. Eliot does not say this explicitly in "The Idea of a Christian Society," but the conviction is evident throughout his later writing, as, e.g., in the *Four Quartets*.

society, but I do believe that it raises an issue very much of our time. One of the essay's enduring contributions is its discussion of the problems that liberalism poses for the survival and transmission of Christian tradition. Specifically at issue for us here is the question of whether Christian ethics can persist in a society such as ours. For insofar as Christian tradition is vitiated by the utilitarianism, individualism, and privatism that flourish in the climate of advanced liberalism, a uniquely Christian ethics is likewise endangered. Eliot put his finger on this point when he identified the bifurcation of morality into public and private categories and stressed that such a dualism is inconsistent with traditional Christian virtue and mission. He also recognized the relevance of the truth expressed in the motto *Unus Christianus — nullus Christianus* ("One Christian — no Christian") in this regard: Christian morality is the achievement *of a community* in struggle with and in mission to the world. Such an ethic will not long prosper as mere personal habit or sentiment. The crisis of Christian tradition in a post-Christian society is also a crisis of Christian ethics.

I would like to think that were Eliot alive today, he would take stock of the obstacles presented by latter-day liberal secularism and pluralism and himself conclude that his proposal for a Christian society is no longer plausible, practicable, or desirable. The force of denominationalism alone, particularly in America, constitutes a forbidding barrier to the sort of catholicity he was seeking. The churches in Western liberal societies have yet to propose another strategy of Christian engagement with the world that is faithful to the catholic truth Eliot wanted to protect and the evangelical mission he sought to advance. And the wait for such a strategy may be a long one, for, as Eliot himself said, "between the Church and the World there is no permanent *modus-vivendi* possible" (p. 72).

Liturgy as a Nexus of Tradition and Ethics

The Russian theologian Vladimir Lossky once said of tradition that it is so "rich in meaning" that today it "runs the risk of finally having none." He attributed this to a "secularization which has depreciated so many words of the theological vocabulary — 'spirituality,' 'mystic,' 'communion' — detaching them from their Christian context in order to make of them the current coin of the profane."[4] Lossky includes in

4. Lossky, *In the Image and Likeness of God* (Crestwood, N.Y.: St. Vladimir's Seminary Press, 1974), p. 141.

the "Christian context" a variety of theological and ecclesial loci, including Scripture, doctrine, creeds, patristic sources, and, last but not least, liturgy and prayer. Compelling arguments have been made that the core of tradition resides in the *lex credendi* ("rule of faith"). I will not contest this thesis directly, but I want to advance an alternative way of viewing tradition, especially in its relation to Christian ethics, in order to explore the prospects of both in a liberal society.

Tradition is transmitted and becomes normative for Christian living not only through preaching, doctrine, and theological discourse but also through the prayer and worship of Christians. Liturgy provides a vital link between Christian tradition and ethics, shaping their communal meaning and rendering the truth of the Christian faith persuasive. Exploring this liturgical nexus will give us helpful insights into the crisis of Christian tradition and ethics to which Eliot alerted us fifty years ago and to which so much attention has been paid in recent philosophical and theological literature. Most of the remainder of this chapter is devoted to this topic, though at the close I will return to the subject of what kind of church and society Christians ought to be pursuing.

While Alasdair MacIntyre awaits "another — doubtless very different — St. Benedict" to rescue us from a world in which tradition and virtue are threatened with extinction,[5] I take heart from Jaroslav Pelikan's observation that whatever the decline of tradition, the Christian church may need reform, but it does not need to be reinvented. Pelikan points to the continuity of Christian worship as significant evidence of the persistence of Christian tradition: "Christians have been blessing bread and wine and celebrating the sacrament of the Eucharist nearly every day. If that is a self-evident truth, it is also a massive instance of continuity amid change, and a prime instance of the reality of tradition."[6]

Lossky contends that "tradition in its primary notion is not the revealed content, but the unique mode of receiving," embodying, and enacting it.[7] Tradition thus understood is vitally connected with catechism, sacraments, and liturgy. These practices, in turn, are formative of Christian character and the Christian ethical outlook. In loci of worship and liturgy, Christian ethics obtains the character and function of

5. MacIntyre, *After Virtue*, 2d ed. (Notre Dame, Ind.: University of Notre Dame Press, 1984), p. 263.
6. Pelikan, *The Vindication of Tradition* (New Haven: Yale University Press, 1984), p. 48.
7. Lossky, *In the Image and Likeness of God*, pp. 154-55.   .

bearing and enacting tradition. In Christian liturgy, and in baptism especially, the content of tradition and the manner in which it is handed on are virtually continuous with moral *praxis*. "It is necessary," wrote St. Basil of Caesarea, "to be baptized according to what we have received by tradition (by transmission: *os parelabomen*), and to believe as we have been baptized, and thus to give praise as we believe."[8] St. Basil could have added "and to conduct our lives in a manner consistent with our belief in the One whom we praise."

In Orthodox baptism, the affirmation and transmission of Christian faith assumes an almost undifferentiated identity with the ethics into which the rite inaugurates the candidate. A good example of how this is formulated can be found in the Prayer of Chrismation in the Armenian rite:

> O God, who art great and eternal and knowest all secrets, who art holy and dwellest in the saints and art the Savior of all men, who hast granted the knowledge of thy truth to all them that believe in thee and hast given them the right to be sons of God through the regeneration of water and spirit, who hast also renewed this thy servant (*name*) through the purifying of thy font, sanctify *him* O Lord, in thy truth and in the light of the grace of thy holy Holy Spirit, so that *he* may be a temple and a dwelling of the Godhead and be able to walk in all thy ways of righteousness.[9]

The prayer rehearses the fundamental teaching of the church on the character of God and salvation in Jesus Christ. This deliberate recollection that salvation is achieved "though the regeneration of water and spirit" establishes the basis for Christian hope and the moral imperative that the baptized "walk in all thy ways of righteousness." The prayer is followed immediately by the anointing of the child (or adult) with the holy Myron (oil) on the eyes, ears, nostrils, mouth, hands, heart, back, and feet. With each anointing movement, the priest invokes a virtue or quality of character that the baptized will need in order to live a righteous life. The faith that the church professes through baptism awaits proof and confirmation in the holy lives it hopes to produce through this rite of blessing. The *paradosis*, or handing on, has a distinctly ethical cast.

---

8. Basil of Caesarea, quoted by Yves Congar in *The Meaning of Tradition*, trans. A. N. Woodrow, vol. 3 of the Twentieth Century Encyclopedia of Catholicism, ed. Henri Daniel-Rops (New York: Hawthorn Books, 1964), p. 33.

9. From *The Order of Baptism according to the Rite of the Armenian Apostolic Orthodox Church* (Evanston, Ill.: N.p., 1964), pp. 65, 67.

This connection between tradition and ethics within liturgy and ritual is portrayed vividly by William Faulkner in several of the central stories of *Go Down, Moses*, especially "The Bear." The main character of the "The Bear" is the boy Isaac McCaslin. Along with the preceding story, "The Old People," "The Bear" tells the story of young Isaac's training as a hunter under the tutelage of that peculiar priestly character and master of the hunt, Sam Fathers, an old Indian chief (half Negro, half Chickasaw). The story says something significant about the transmission of tradition through ritual practices, and the language that Faulkner uses to tell the tale has clear religious overtones. In speaking of Isaac's "novitiate to the true wilderness with Sam beside him" and "apprenticeship . . . to manhood,"[10] Faulkner invites us to read the text as a parable of initiation into the Christian life. The ritual practices of the hunt simultaneously teach competence, inspire excellence, and enable the novitiate to recognize and pursue the goods that are the appropriate goals of such practices.

On the literal level, Sam Fathers teaches Isaac about the wilderness and instructs him in the ways of the hunt. Isaac learns what sort of courage and self-discipline are necessary to track and kill the bear. On a deeper level, this knowledge prompts Isaac to explore his human patrimony, mixed up as that is with the destruction of the wilderness and the enslavement and exploitation of one people by another. Through Sam Fathers's instruction in the "liturgy" of the hunt, Isaac appropriates virtues that enable him to renounce and relinquish his inheritance of the McCaslin plantation and the legacy of slavery associated with it.

Faulkner's story is not overtly biblical or Christian. His explorations of the ethical dimensions of tradition and ritual communicate something about human nature and human experience generally. But if the reader is familiar with biblical narrative and Jewish or Christian liturgy, Faulkner's language immediately brings to mind several biblical motifs and Christian rites of initiation and communion. Isaac's goal is to become one of the "true hunters" (p. 164), like Walter Ewell, Major de Spain, old General Compson, and of course Sam Fathers. One of the skills of the true hunter is an ability to distinguish between true hunters and false hunters (it is in the latter category that Isaac places himself in his old age). What distinguishes the true from the false hunter? Faulkner

---

10. Faulkner, *Go Down, Moses* (1940; reprint, New York: Vintage Books, 1973), p. 195. Subsequent references to this volume will be made parenthetically in the text.

suggests that the distinguishing marks are practices and virtues learned in the hunt and the pursuit of the bear. One must learn the tradition and allow it to regulate one's behavior and conduct in the wilderness, beneath "the eye of the ancient immortal Umpire" (p. 181). The true hunters tell stories that the boy, Isaac, appropriates into his own life "about those old times and those dead and vanished men . . . [and] gradually . . . those old times would cease to be old times and would become a part of the boy's present, not only as if they had happened yesterday but as if they were still happening. . . . And more: as if some of them had not happened yet but would occur tomorrow" (p. 171).

On every hunt, rituals are performed — eating the hunter's meat and drinking the hunter's drink — "that brown liquor which not women, not boys and children, but only hunters drank, drinking not of the blood they spilled but some condensation of the wild immortal spirit, drinking it moderately, humbly even, not with the pagan's base and baseless hope of acquiring thereby the virtues of cunning and strength and speed but in salute to them" (p. 192). Isaac would never forget one special hunt when at the age of twelve he killed his first big game with Sam Fathers at his side, when Sam "dipped his hands in the hot smoking blood and wiped them back and forth across the boy's face . . . the old dark man . . . whose bloody hands had merely formally consecrated him to that which, under the man's tutelage, he had already accepted, humbly and joyfully, with abnegation and with pride too" (pp. 164-65). On that occasion an entire legacy had somehow been handed on, and Isaac had become a true hunter, having learned to love "the life he spill[ed]" (p. 181).

There are striking analogies here to Christian baptism and eucharistic communion. As with baptism and the eucharist, the tradition handed on to Isaac is liberating, both in an immediate and in a more removed sense. First, the virtues that hunting and killing in the spirit of love for the life one spills provide to Isaac — courage, patience, humility, and pride (or honor) — are what make it possible for him also to approach and see the bear. At a crucial moment in the story, Isaac relinquishes his gun, his compass, his watch, and "his will" (p. 208). It is then that the bear appears: "It was just there, immobile, fixed in the green and windless noon's hot dappling, not as big as he had dreamed it but as big as he had expected, bigger, dimensionless against the dappled obscurity, looking at him" (p. 209). Second, these very same virtues and the stories of the Old People and the wilderness land enable Isaac to track down the sins of his grandfather and father and uncle and thus relinquish his title to the ill-gotten land. As Isaac says to his cousin McCaslin Edmunds, to whom "possession" of the land will revert, "Sam Fathers set me free" (p. 300).

Freedom is also a sine qua non for Christian ethics — the freedom that is the gift of the Spirit. As St. Paul writes, "the Lord is the Spirit, and where the Spirit of the Lord is, there is freedom" (2 Cor. 3:17). Tradition, Christianly understood, is liberating. "Jesus went to the cross because he would not have any earthly form of the divine (not even, let it be remembered, his own) become a substitute for the ultimate reality of the living God."[11] Isaac's nonpossessive relationship with the wilderness and his relinquishment of his material inheritance have counterparts in the Christian experience of the numinous, in which the ethical is founded and tradition comes alive and is enlivening.

Nevertheless, Faulkner's story is pessimistic about the survival of tradition in the modern world. He wrote *Go Down, Moses* at virtually the same time Eliot wrote "The Idea of a Christian Society," and, like Eliot, he tells the story of the decline of tradition. In the final section of "The Bear," we are told of the last visit Isaac made to the hunting camp "before the lumber company moved in and began to cut the timber." Major de Spain has decided to sell the land and thus to surrender the hunt to corporate enterprises. Even General Compson and Walter Ewell have been smitten by the economic motive. In order to save the hunt, they contrive "a plan to corporate themselves, the old group, into a club and lease the camp and the hunting privileges of the woods — an invention" that Faulkner describes as "worthy of Boon Hogganbeck himself" (p. 315), who in the story represents the democratic and entrepreneurial spirit.

Faulkner's "Delta Autumn" is set more than sixty years later. Isaac still is a hunter. The men with whom he now enters what little remains of the old wilderness of the delta country — "sons and even grandsons" of his companions as a youth (p. 336) — are not true hunters, even if they represent themselves as such. The lesson of "Delta Autumn" is that the tradition has not been passed on. Faulkner is not so much interested in whether Isaac (now old "Uncle Ike") is to blame for the change; he is more interested in focusing on the culture in which the true hunt is no longer possible. The men with whom Ike hunts no longer bring with them into the wilderness the virtues and dispositions and stories that Sam Fathers taught and passed on to Isaac and that even in his youth the town folk did not know or understand. Rather, their character and behavior reflect the economic motives and utilitar-

11. Pelikan, *The Vindication of Tradition*, p. 57.

ianism of the new civilization. Instead of hunter's meat and whiskey, they bring "town meat" with them, "fried slabs of pork, the hot soft shapeless bread, the canned beans and molasses and coffee in iron plates and cups" (p. 344). These are men who believe "that it's only because folks happen to be watching him that a man behaves at all" (p. 346). These are men who are restrained from killing does only by the fact that "if we did . . . in a few years there wouldn't even be any bucks to kill" (p. 347). These are men who never came to own the hunter ethos, never learned to love the life they spill. In the world of which these younger men are so integrally a part, they might be hunters, but by the standards of the stories and virtues of the Old People, they are not. The wilderness is receding, and the true hunt has departed from this new world. The solitary hunter who bears the tradition is no longer grounded in a communal context (or, in Isaac's case, even in the family) in which that tradition might be handed on to others. Faulkner shows us no way out of this tragic circumstance; he simply notes that the "ruined woods . . . dont cry for retribution," because "the people who have destroyed it will accomplish its revenge" (p. 364).

Faulkner brilliantly explores this nexus of liturgy, tradition, and ethics. He also has invented a parable that suggests how Christian liturgy can disintegrate, causing tradition and morality to fade even in the lives of those who retain the church as a part of their lives. One is tempted to question whether Pelikan has it right. In a post-Christendom society, what really is the significance of his assertion that the continuity of Christian worship and prayer proves that tradition is alive? Alexander Schmemann, who devoted much of his energy to explaining and explicating Christian liturgy, repeatedly pointed out that the contemporary crisis of Christian faith is wrapped up with the privatization and disintegration of Christian worship.[12] In a similar vein, I would argue that one of the reasons Christian moral arguments seem so ungrounded these days is that they have become utterly dislocated and dissociated from Christian worship and liturgy. Christians are losing the eschatological experience of the church as the inbreaking of God's kingdom into the world, and so of course this experience is having an increasingly diminished effect on their conduct. They are forgetting that the quest for truth and excellence is part of participating in that kingdom. Of course Pelikan might respond that he is not arguing that the Christian worship that persists is necessarily exemplary; he is simply

12. See, e.g., Schmemann, "Problems of Orthodoxy in America II: The Liturgical Problem," *St Vladimir's Seminary Quarterly* 8 (1964): 164-85.

arguing that whatever its condition, it does persist. I would grant him that, but it would do little to ease my concern on either point. Indeed, I believe we would do well to engage in more serious reflection on the relationship between tradition and ethics in light of the *lex orandi* ("rule of prayer") when the potential for the continued existence of both is in question.

The Liturgical Location of Christian Tradition and Ethics

The greatest challenge of liberalism to all historical traditions, writes Alasdair MacIntyre, is its claim that it brings into existence the ultimate society in which a "tradition-independent moral standpoint"[13] is attainable, while leaving undecided whether that standpoint can be achieved through careful adherence to a Kantian universalizability principle, Jeffersonian intuitionism, a Millsian calculus of utility, or the like. Individuals are granted the freedom to have certain preferences and hold certain opinions (even religious ones), provided they are understood to be ultimately subsidiary to a liberal rationality that overrides the particularisms of contending traditions and individual points of view. There are different opinions as to where this rationality abides: it is variously located in the market economy, management, the new information industry, psychotherapy, the political process, and the legal system.

There is no question that these secular institutions serve as sources of moral wisdom in our culture. Many turn to the market economy, management, or the legal system for criteria to determine what is right or true. But Christians must remind themselves that their identity and morality are grounded elsewhere, in those distinctive practices of the church through which it constitutes itself and remembers, not only in word and thought but in action, the truth it confesses regarding the lordship of Jesus Christ. I am referring specifically here to the rites and liturgies of praise and dedication to the one God whom Christians hold to be the source of life and reason for doing good deeds. While the content of Christian tradition resides in Scripture and doctrine, it is helpful to remember that "Scripture was read first in the context of worship and meditation,"[14] and in a significant sense doctrine can be said to originate in and be confirmed by the *lex orandi*. The

13. MacIntyre, *Whose Justice? Which Rationality?* p. 334.
14. Georges Florovsky, *Bible, Church, Tradition: An Eastern Orthodox View* (Belmont, Mass.: Nordland, 1972), p. 85.

earliest creedal formulas emerged as a product of liturgy (particularly the baptismal rite), and not the other way around.

Jaroslav Pelikan has argued this point persuasively, and he has drawn out some of its implications for the recovery and vindication of Christian tradition. In a discussion of John Henry Newman's work *The Arians of the Fourth Century*, Pelikan writes,

> The specific content of the apostolic tradition had remained secret [even into the fourth century] because so much of it, in the pre-creedal "traditionary system, received from the first age of the Church," had been not dogmatic, but liturgical in its form. It was symptomatic of the loss of tradition in modern times, and of the need for its recovery, that now "we count the words of the Fathers and measure their sentences; and so convert doxologies into creeds . . ." [while] the authentic tradition of orthodoxy was not a matter to be decided by an intellectually formulated "rule of faith" set forth by scholars and theologians, but by the "rule of prayer" of "the thousands of silent believers, who worshipped in spirit and in truth."[15]

Something similar could be said about the condition of contemporary Christian ethics. One clue to the decline of Christian morality is the fact that the "specialists" who propound it seem to have lost all sense of its origins in and relationship to the prayer and worship of Christians. As a result, Christian ethics is often defined as a rational system of rules and principles residing in theological texts available to believer and nonbeliever alike. This way of conceiving Christian ethics (like the theology with which it is associated) has become increasingly strange to "the thousands of silent believers" of which Newman spoke and has lost touch with the full tradition.

The argument from tradition has often referred to the corporate worship of Christians. According to Georges Florovsky, one form of argument from tradition that reached back to the *lex orandi* to effect right belief "was persistently used . . . already by the end of the Second century."[16] Countering fourth-century Arian objections to the co-equality of the Spirit with the Father and the Son, St. Basil appealed to the doxologies of Christian liturgies and the uses of the threefold name in those contexts. And, as Pelikan points out, "When Augustine had been challenged by his opponents to substantiate from tradition his novel

---

15. Pelikan, *The Vindication of Tradition*, pp. 29-30.
16. Florovsky, *Bible, Church, Tradition*, pp. 84-85.

teaching about human nature, the fall, and original sin," he made his appeal "from the tradition of theology and philosophy to the tradition of prayer and devotion, where he located the ancestry of a concept that he was now formulating in the modality of theology and philosophy."[17]

The debate over the use of icons in the East during the eighth and ninth centuries provides an instructive example of this form of argument for and from tradition in liturgy. Both the Iconodules (who supported the use of icons in the churches) and the Iconoclasts (who opposed the use of icons) set out to prove that tradition supported their position. "The main authority of the Iconoclasts," says Florovsky, ". . . was an appeal to antiquity, and this was possibly the strongest point both of their attack and of their self-defense. It was a double appeal to Scripture and Tradition."[18] But this point of strength was also the weakest point of the Iconoclasts' position, for they assumed that the authority of tradition derives from a deposit of proofs in the ancient sources. One of the great defenders of the icons, John of Damascus, asserted to the contrary that the authority of tradition resides in the community of faith itself. Appeals to tradition have to refer to the practices of the church through which Christians in unbroken continuity since apostolic times have articulated their special identity and communal purposes. Did the icons assist them in this task? Were they an enduring element of Christian worship, of prayer and doxological communion? The answer, said John of Damascus, was yes. "The tradition of the church is not only passed on in written documents, but has also been given in unwritten form," he argued. One must also look to the church's worship, which in its specific practices frequently has no explicit scriptural warrant. "What is the origin of the three immersions at baptism, or praying toward the east, or the manner in which we celebrate the eucharist?"[19] And in another context he likewise asks, "Why do we bow down before the cross? Has not unwritten tradition instructed us concerning these things?"[20]

In defense of their position, the Iconoclasts presented a disputed passage from St. Epiphanius condemning the use of icons. The Iconodules countered that the passage was not authentic. Setting the issue of the validity of the passage aside, it is interesting to note the

17. Pelikan, *The Vindication of Tradition*, p. 17.

18. Florovsky, *Christianity and Culture* (Belmont, Mass.: Nordland, 1974), p. 105.

19. John of Damascus, *On the Divine Images*, trans. David Anderson (Crestwood, N.Y.: St. Vladimir's Seminary Press, 1980), p. 31.

20. John of Damascus, *On the Divine Images*, p. 63.

argument that John of Damascus made from the authority of liturgical practice in this context: he asserted that if such a passage were authentic, it would have to have been directed against certain *abuses* of the use of icons, not against the use of icons per se. The proof that Epiphanius did not disapprove of the use of icons generally resided in the fact that they could be "found in his own church, which we see adorned with images to this very day."[21]

There may be no better biblical illustration of the liturgical location of Christian tradition and its relation to the church's ethic than the opening discussion of true and false teaching in the Pauline epistle to the Colossians. The letter was prompted by word that had reached the apostle of the activity of false teachers within the newly formed church. The author of Colossians characterizes these teachers as innovators and refers to the practice of baptism as a source of the true apostolic tradition. Nevertheless, the false teachers also presented themselves as bearers of a tradition, comprising ascetical discipline, legalism, and ritual apparently related to certain Judaic sources, the authority of which was based in "elemental spirits of the universe" (Col. 2:8) and visions connected with angel worship (Col. 2:18). The false teachers were excluding from the church all who failed to conform to such beliefs and practices. Given the rationalistic prejudices of our own contemporary theology, we might think that the appropriate response would involve a forensic or discursive argument with the proponents of the new tradition, exhibiting along the way the main lines of the older tradition. Instead, as Wayne A. Meeks has pointed out,

> the letter as a whole is paraenetic; the readers are recalled to the truths and practices that they already know. The admonitions to "watch out" for the false "philosophers" and not to submit to them are of the same sort as the admonitions about how to behave. The whole is a "reminder of baptism," or rather of the whole process of receiving instruction and entering the Christian community that culminated in baptism.[22]

Alluding directly to baptism and the process of catechetical training accompanying it, the Pauline writer admonishes: "If with Christ you died to the elemental spirits of the universe, why do you live as if you still belonged to the world? Why do you submit to regulations . . . ?

21. John of Damascus, *On the Divine Images*, p. 32.
22. Meeks, *The First Urban Christians* (New Haven: Yale University Press, 1983), pp. 126-27.

These have indeed an appearance of wisdom in promoting self-imposed piety, humility, and severe treatment of the body, but they are of no value in checking self-indulgence" (Col. 2:20-21, 23). The true faith and guarantee of a life lived according to that faith resides in the death and resurrection of Christ recapitulated in baptism (Col. 2:11-12), not in elemental forces of nature or angelic powers. This is the hidden (mystical) reserve of Christian tradition. "So if you have been raised with Christ, seek the things that are above, where Christ is, seated at the right hand of God. Set your minds on things that are above, not on things that are on earth, for you have died, and your life is hidden within Christ. When Christ who is your life appears, then you also will be revealed with him in glory" (Col. 3:1-4).

The apostolic tradition lives and has vitality through the Christian experience of the mysteries of faith in baptism. The author of the Epistle to the Colossians understood Christian ethics to be a necessary outgrowth of this tradition as it takes hold of the lives of persons through the experience of baptism. The death and resurrection in Christ *anamnetically* experienced in baptism has practical consequences, ethical concomitants. As Christ was, as he is known through the Gospel accounts, as he comes to Christians in baptism, as he will appear again in glory — so those who have received baptism must become. "As you therefore have received Christ Jesus the Lord, continue to live your lives in him, rooted and built up in him and established in the faith, just as you were taught, abounding in thanksgiving" (Col. 2:6). This is the main theme of the letter. It is a direct appeal to the tradition as it had been received through an established knowledge and a set of common practices. It is an exhortation, as well, to live by virtues that promote the attainment of that new form of life which the church identifies with the life and teaching of Jesus Christ. "You have stripped off the old self with its practices, and have clothed yourselves with the new self, which is being renewed in knowledge according to the image of its creator" (Col. 3:9b-10). Christians are expected to acquire the virtues of "compassion, kindness, humility, meekness, and patience . . . [and,] above all, . . . love, which binds everything in perfect harmony" (Col. 3:12b, 14). They are expected to become, by dint of participation in the baptismal rite, "the one body" (Col. 3:15) of the risen Christ.

Vladimir Lossky once wrote, "To be in the tradition is to share the experience of the mysteries revealed to the Church."[23] This is a

---

23. Lossky, *The Mystical Theology of the Eastern Church* (Cambridge: James Clarke, 1973), p. 236.

wisdom descriptive of other great religious traditions as well. We have seen how Faulkner captured this wisdom and explored it profoundly in "The Bear." While it is disputed whether the epistle to the Colossians was in fact written by Paul himself, it does share at least one important characteristic with passages of undisputed Pauline authorship such as Romans 6 and 1 Corinthians 11: the appeal to tradition and attendant obligations to right conduct are grounded in a reference to the readers' shared experiences of Christ in worship. As Robert Bellah and his collaborators have argued in *Habits of the Heart,* this sort of argument from tradition founded in communal practices in defense of moral standards and commitments that transcend individual preference or choice runs contrary to the pervasive individualism in our culture. In our liberal culture, Christians are pressed to eschew the sort of wisdom about mystery and faith described by Lossky. Those who are committed to the good or the betterment of society frequently focus almost exclusively on the cognitive and conceptual attributes of Christian ethics — certain universalizable rules and principles — which, they argue, are rationally apprehensible by autonomous individuals, religious and nonreligious alike. But this strategy involves an implicit concession to the presuppositions of advanced liberalism, and it eventuates in an abandonment of the eschatological urgency and hope of the Christian tradition and a severe diminution of the capacity and calling of Christian ethics to provide a social vision and inspire people to work for a community of goods — ends that were addressed so effectively by the author of the epistle to the Colossians.

Eucharist, Eschatology, and Tradition

In the endeavor to describe how tradition norms Christian ethics, I am attracted to John Howard Yoder's suggestion that instead of the strong organic metaphor of "a tree (or family tree)," which stresses uninterrupted continuity, "the process of traditioning ethics might better be compared to a vine: a story of constant interruption of organic growth in favor of pruning and a new chance for the roots." Even while proposing this metaphor, however, Yoder warns against trying to use it to support a scriptural fundamentalism or a naive primitivism that seeks to "capture some pristine purity" in the historical origins of the church.[24]

24. Yoder, *The Priestly Kingdom* (Notre Dame, Ind.: University of Notre Dame Press, 1984), p. 69. At this point, I want to emphasize that while I find Yoder's vine

What we . . . find at the heart of our tradition is not some proposi-
tion, scriptural or promulgated otherwise, which we hold to be
authoritative and to be exempted from the relativity of hermeneutical debate by virtue of its inspiredness. What we find at the origin
is already a process of reaching back again to the origins, to the
earliest memories of the event itself, confident that that testimony,
however intimately integrated with the belief of the witnesses, is
not a wax nose, and will serve to illuminate and sometimes adju-
dicate our present path.[25]

Neither does Yoder want to be perceived as advocating a simply
linear view of history. The process of interpretation and evaluation in
Christian tradition not only incorporates historicity but supersedes or
transcends it. Turning to yet another metaphor, he explains,

We are not talking about "the authority of tradition" as if tradition
were a settled reality and we were then to figure out how it works.
We are asking how, within the maelstrom of traditioning processes,
we can keep our bearings and distinguish between the way the

---

metaphor to be helpful in understanding how tradition works in Christian ethics,
I view it as only one among several available metaphors, and I do not believe that
it should be the controlling metaphor in our understanding of tradition generally,
as Yoder certainly seems to suggest. It seems to me that in matters of church dogma,
for instance, the tree probably serves as a more appropriate metaphor than the vine.
Once a church doctrine or dogma has been firmly established through the church's
internal argument and formal consensus has been reached, such teaching is virtually
immutable. Doctrinal definitions establish the boundaries of error and right belief
and are not subject to the sorts of immediate empirical verification that matters of
morality are subject to. Still, while the dogmas of the church will not change, there
is nothing in principle that says the *formulation* of that dogma cannot change.

To illuminate the pneumatic quality of tradition and the continuity of tradition, Yoder himself uses the metaphor of a stream or river (milieu). This metaphor
has the additional advantage of serving as a heuristic corrective to rigid and overly
conservative interpretations of tradition as immutable. Once Christians enter the
stream (of tradition), they have to determine the prevailing current and stay with
it even as they make adjustments to historical contingencies and new insights. On
this point I defer to Vladimir Lossky: "In fact, if Tradition is a faculty of judging in
the Light of the Holy Spirit, it obliges those who wish to know the Truth in the
Tradition to make incessant efforts: one does not remain in the tradition by a certain
historical inertia, by keeping as a "tradition received from the Fathers" all that which,
by force of habit, flatters a certain devout sensibility. On the contrary, it is by
substituting this sort of tradition for the Tradition of the Holy Spirit living in the
Church that one runs the most risk of finding oneself finally outside the Body of
Christ" (*In the Image and Likeness of God*, pp. 155-56).

25. Yoder, *The Priestly Kingdom*, p. 70.

stream should be going and side channels which eddy but lead nowhere. Can we do this by some criterion beyond ourselves? The peculiarity of the term "tradition" is that it points to that criterion beyond itself, to which it claims to be a witness. We are therefore doing no violence to the claim of tradition when we test it by its fidelity to that origin. A witness is not being dishonored when we test his fidelity as an interpreter of the events to which he testifies.[26]

Some might charge that Yoder is stating the obvious when he proposes that the Jesus rendered by the Gospel narratives and worshiped in the Spirit by the church is the ultimate criterion of Christian tradition. But Yoder has shown in his books *The Politics of Jesus* and *The Priestly Kingdom* how the "obvious" has eluded major strands of Protestant and Catholic ethics, which for one reason or another have gone a long way toward denying the relevance of Jesus and his teaching to social ethics.

More needs to be said, however, about how Jesus Christ is recognized and accepted by the church as the ultimate criterion of truth in all arguments from tradition. The memory of the church is not merely historical. The argument from tradition is not just an appeal to the past, to a Jesus who once lived in ancient Palestine. Jesus Christ the ultimate criterion of truth for Christian tradition and ethics cannot be found simply by tracing one's way back to some original historical figure or *kerygma*. Arguing from tradition is a process of remembering and interpreting who Jesus Christ is and what he did while on this earth in order to discern the most appropriate path to the eschatological kingdom that was revealed in his person. If Christ is the ultimate criterion of truth for Christians, writes John D. Zizioulas, it is because the church has continually experienced him as "the heart of history, . . . the ground of creation, and . . . the end of history."[27] The memory of the church is both *anamnetic* and *epicletic*, and it is eucharistically centered. Eucharistic worship puts history to the service of doxology and calls on the Holy Spirit to place in communion with Christ those who remember him and consume his body and blood. Ultimately, Christian tradition and ethics are bound up with sacrament and eschatology. "That action is right which fits the shape of the Kingdom to come," says Yoder. "Moral validation is derived from the imminent Kingdom which Jesus announces, not from the righteous state of affairs our action promises to

---

26. Yoder, *The Priestly Kingdom*, pp. 77-78.
27. Zizioulas, *Being as Communion* (Crestwood, N.Y.: St. Vladimir's Seminary Press, 1985), p. 98.

bring about."[28] In other words, Christian ethics is fundamentally eschatological rather than consequentialist. Yoder has not developed this description in a sufficiently eucharistic direction, however; he lacks a eucharistic ecclesiology.

On any number of occasions, Alexander Schmemann returned to the observation that the weakness of recent Christian theology is its lost sense of the sacramental and eschatological dimensions of Christian tradition.[29] Christian tradition is not merely a selective form of historiography, historical reasoning, or historical memory; it is a eucharistic and eschatological science, a eucharistic and eschatological way of knowing. In the final analysis, the continuity of tradition is not located in theological texts, creeds, liturgical forms, or ecclesiastical offices. The continuity that contemporary writers such as Pelikan, Zizioulas, and Schmemann have identified is a product of the eucharistic *anamnesis* of the gathered worshiping community. The collective remembrance of this community, in the power of the Holy Spirit, makes Christ and his sacrifice present and also affords a passage into and a proleptic experience of God's eschatological kingdom. This Christian eschatology, argued Schmemann, is "the very source and foundation of the Christian doctrine of the world and of the Church's action in the world," of the church's social vision.[30] This means that out of its own experience as the distinct human community that worships Jesus Christ as Lord and Savior, the church reaches an initial understanding of the world on terms established by the kingdom of God rather than by the world. And to that world, stated Schmemann, the church offers

> an emphatic acceptance, a *yes*, but also an equally emphatic rejection, a *no*. "God so loved the world that he gave His only Son. . . . God sent the Son into the world, not to condemn the world, but that the world might be saved through Him" (John 3:16-17) and then — "Do not love the world or the things in the world. If anyone loves the world, love for the Father is not in him" (John 2:15).[31]

This Christian truth, this ultimate criterion of Christian discernment, which originates in the enduring eucharistic experience of Christ and

28. Yoder, "To Serve Our God and to Rule the World," in *The Annual of the Society of Christian Ethics, 1988* (Washington: Georgetown University Press, 1988), p. 10.

29. See, e.g., Schmemann, *Church, World, Mission* (Crestwood, N.Y.: St. Vladimir's Seminary Press, 1979), especially chaps. 7 and 9.

30. Schmemann, *Church, World, Mission*, p. 153.

31. Schmemann, *Church, World, Mission*, p. 148.

his kingdom that the Holy Spirit provides, is the source and the *raison d'être* of Christian tradition and Christian ethics.

Become Learners in the Kingdom of Heaven

> When, therefore, a teacher of law has become a learner in the kingdom of Heaven, he is like a householder who can produce from his store both the new and the old. (Matt. 13:52, NEB)

Christians become learners in the kingdom of heaven in a variety of ways, liturgy not being the least of these. Christian tradition entails not merely instruction concerning matters of the community's important past but also activity that brings out of this remembered past new things for the future. Christian ethics involves both recollection of and instruction concerning conduct that pleases God. It is, moreover, a discerning exercise that takes into account present reality and future possibilities in order to reevaluate and revise old ways of exercising the liberty and responsibilities of citizenship in the kingdom of God.

How is it possible for Christian tradition to continue to yield new things in a society of the sort described by Eliot? And how might Christian ethics effectively extend its reach beyond the community of faith and out into the larger culture short of declaring it to be the fertile field for a new Christendom? In this closing section, I want to venture three observations or suggestions in response to these questions.

1. I submit that the church needs to work much harder at exercising in new situations the Pauline style of parenesis that we have seen at work in the epistle to the Colossians and that St. Paul used with perhaps even greater effect in 1 Corinthians. By means of this form of ethical instruction and exhortation, Paul focused those whom he addressed on important moral issues, moving the received tradition along to new perspectives. Such parenesis is dialogic. Its initial movement is intraecclesial. It insists on "letting all the legitimate voices (within the community) be heard, and [encouraging] all the vociferous speakers to become listeners, too, and then to act within that polyphonic world."[32] Wayne Meeks has argued that St. Paul thus sought to expand the knowledge of the communities he addressed and broaden their

---

32. Wayne A. Meeks, "The Polyphonic Ethics of the Apostle Paul," in *The Annual of the Society of Christian Ethics, 1988* (Washington: Georgetown University Press, 1988), p. 19.

wisdom, and that he included the "voices" of Scripture, apostolic teaching, and liturgical practice within the conversation. The lesson here is that the church's authority is dialogic rather than autocratic. The community in *all* its parts is responsible for achieving the moral competency necessary to settle internal arguments discerningly and to address the world at large with wisdom. For the Pauline communities this often meant defining for the first time Christian attitudes on institutions and conventions that involved both church and society. In this connection, the tradition was mined to reach a new resolve on such issues as sexuality (1 Cor 6:9-20), marriage (Eph. 5:21-33; 1 Cor. 7), the relation of Christians to the Roman judicial system (1 Cor. 6:1-7), and the Christian's obligations to the Roman state (Rom. 13).

Were tradition functioning similarly in the church today, its witness might not only bear greater spiritual fruit but could have a powerful moral effect. While Christians ought not to expect the advent of a new Christian society, their presence in this society as a dialogic community of memory and tradition nonetheless makes possible practical embodiments of the Christian faith even within secular institutions.

2. John Howard Yoder has argued that renewed attention ought to be given to "the vision of a Christian cultic commonwealth as the model for the civil commonwealth."[33] Those who take exception to the idea that the church offers a social ethic through its status as a disciplined believing community in witness to the gospel are more often than not wedded to liberal ideas of agency. They believe that in order to be "effective," the church must devote itself to lobbying for its own special interests in the larger marketplace of ideas. Such critics dismiss the church-as-model vision on the grounds that it is static and sectarian. This is a misjudgment, however. Yoder's more recent emphasis on the dialogic structure of peoplehood controverts glib assertions that his proposals are sectarian. He recasts and deepens our understanding of agency, moving it beyond liberal notions of the autonomous self (or collective entity) that acts over and against other autonomous agents. Yoder redefines agency in relational and communal terms. The ultimate biblical point of reference for this is St. Paul's assertion in 1 Corinthians 14 that the body is made up of many members with diverse gifts and that God speaks within and through the dialogic life of that body.

Orthodox theology and ecclesiology embrace a similar dialogic paradigm, joining it with a theology of icon and image. Accordingly, the icon is not, as is so often wrongly suggested, a static aesthetic entity;

---

33. Yoder, *The Priestly Kingdom*, p. 166.

rather, it is credited in theology with having a remarkable capacity to *attract* people into the reality of which it is an image. Liberal agency models almost never speak of attraction but rather of argument, persuasion, and power in their efforts to describe the nature of the church and its mission. This agency theory emphasizes reason and will, whereas the theology of the icon emphasizes imagination, perception, and interpretation. The power of the icon, says Anthony Ugolnik, resides in its capacity to "prepare the believer to look outward, even into the secular world, to find the image of the Creator. This claim on the imagination will allow the very act of interpretation, the structures of meaning that the Christian assigns to the world and experience, to transfigure the culture of his or her people."[34] The icon is a material embodiment of the truth that the church has agreed upon. It draws people into a deeper and fuller relationship with Christ and the saints within worship. It is a material representation of the human and divine dialogue that constitutes the church and in which the church invites others to participate. When Orthodox speak of the church as the ultimate icon or representation of the kingdom in the world, they have in mind these dialogic and kenotic qualities of the icon. Orthodox ethics is, in a fundamental sense, iconic ethics.

3. With such an understanding of the church, the problem of communicating Christian tradition and ethics in a pluralistic society may indeed boil down to "finding ways," as Yoder puts it, "to translate and to work at reciprocal adjudication of the varieties both of perception and of evaluation, where one provincial vision clashes and overlaps with another." When he says "overlap," he means "that two provincial visions are dealing with the same subject matter of bringing people into common enterprise." When he says "conflict," he is referring to the fact "that people may have different commitments behind these common enterprises."[35] The process of adjudicating and securing firm mutual resolve among persons and communities holding differing visions and perceptions may ironically be hindered by the prevailing liberal notion that reason can offer some common and neutral language that will thoroughly liberate us from parochial, tradition-bound beliefs. Yoder, like Alasdair MacIntyre, criticizes this liberal conviction and endeavor as imperialistic. My own belief is that all cultures endeavor to produce and maintain a common moral language to bind the social fabric to-

---

34. Ugolnik, *The Illuminating Icon* (Grand Rapids: William B. Eerdmans, 1989), p. 61.
35. Yoder, *The Priestly Kingdom*, p. 44.

gether. These common moralities are inevitably imperialistic vis-à-vis other moral traditions. Wherever the church is situated, it will be engaged in a struggle not merely to convert individuals but to transform the dominant linguistic structures and ethical norms of the society.

I agree with Yoder and MacIntyre, however, that what makes the liberal variety of this common morality especially troublesome is its confident claims to neutrality and tribe-transcendent rationality. Speaking as an Orthodox, I do not want to reject the natural law that Yoder and MacIntyre revile as the bugbear behind this imperialism. But neither, as I argue in Chapter 1, do I feel that Orthodox or other Christians in post-Christendom societies need to turn to natural law as the primary stratagem for resolving arguments between traditions. Greek fathers such as St. Basil and St. John Chrysostom held to a belief in natural law, but, unlike Western theologians and proponents of the Enlightenment, they never went so far as to make natural law the linchpin of apologetics for Christian faith and a Christian society. This dubious legacy has been passed on in increasingly secular forms to provide an ideological defense for liberal democracy and pluralism, but, as we have seen, it has had the additional effect of exiling all competing traditions that propound any special claims about what constitutes universal truth — and hence especially religious traditions — to the private sphere.

Yoder is right to suggest that the best way for Christians to meet the challenge of this imperialism is not to become less specifically Christian but to become better practiced in their own language of faith and the dialogues they pursue. Even the liberal cultural hegemony is not fixed. All common moralities and civil religions are fluid. The goal should not be to replace the language of the liberal cult with that of the Christian cult; rather, it should be to work strenuously at drawing people outside the church into a dialogue that engages their imagination so that they will experience the capacity of Christian truth to illumine the nature of the problems they face and the moral decisions they must make. The church must strive to transform perception and understanding of what is morally at stake in the lives people lead.

Conclusion

I do not know whether the proposed *modus vivendi* for the church would have satisfied T. S. Eliot. I do think the course indicated respects and affirms Eliot's legitimate concern that the Christian witness to the liberal society should not be premised primarily in an apologetic of social utility or in claims of a convenient correlation of Christianity with things held to be of value in the culture but rather that it should be premised in the confident proclamation of the church's redemptive truth. Eliot also was of the persuasion that because the Christian faith is incarnational and trinitarian, it must resist mightily the propensity of liberalism to redefine it as purely a matter of individual preference and personal habit. Unless Christian tradition and Christian ethics reside in the church, they will have no integrity. The church seeks not merely the salvation of individuals but the reclamation of the fallen social, political, and economic life of humankind.

3. The Bible in Orthodox Ethics: A Liturgical Reading

Stanley Hauerwas has suggested that one reason the use of the Bible in Christian ethics has not been wholly persuasive is that Christian ethicists and moral theologians have failed to interpret Scripture in its liturgical settings. "There is certainly nothing intrinsically wrong," writes Hauerwas, "with individuals reading and studying scripture, but such reading must be guided by the use of the scripture through the liturgies of the church. . . . As Aidan Kavanagh has observed, 'the liturgy is scripture's home rather than its stepchild, and the Hebrew and Christian bibles were the church's first liturgical books.'"[1] Who would deny that within the large corpus of systematic and applied ethics hardly a glance is given to the liturgical contexts of Scripture in the church? In this chapter I want to take up Hauerwas's challenge to Christian ethicists and take a serious look at the liturgical settings of Scripture. A recovery of the church's biblical hermeneutics displayed in liturgy is essential for reclaiming an ecclesial Christian ethic.

A Methodological Gambit

Before beginning the constructive argument, I want to engage in a brief methodological gambit with the intent of offering some impressions of the contemporary discussion on the relationship of the Bible to Christian ethics and getting at what is at stake theologically in such talk.

1. Hauerwas, *A Community of Character* (Notre Dame, Ind.: University of Notre Dame Press, 1980), p. 240n.9. Hauerwas's citation of Kavanaugh is taken from *The Shape of Baptism: The Rite of Christian Initiation* (New York: Pueblo, 1978), p. xiii.

Some twenty-five years ago, Paul Lehmann published his valuable and often-cited systematic study *Ethics in a Christian Context.* In the opening of that book, Lehmann refers to the hermeneutical problem of understanding the relationship between the Bible and Christian ethics. He argues that modern biblical scholarship would seem to indicate that biblical ethics needs to be clearly distinguished from Christian ethics. He says that contemporary Christian ethicists have not paid sufficient attention to the hermeneutical issue or the methodological problems it raises. In Troeltschian fashion, Lehmann argues that a gulf was created between New Testament ethics and all subsequent Christian ethics by the delay of the parousia in the church's early experience. New Testament ethics was based on a presumption of the imminent return of Christ, whereas Christian ethics is the outcome of the church's subsequent efforts to define and work out what it means to be faithful followers of Christ with responsibilities in the world during the extended interim between the Lord's first coming and the fulfillment of his kingdom.[2]

In raising this distinction, Lehmann did not set out to deny the authority of the Bible in the ongoing life of the church. Nor did he deny that biblical ethics and Christian ethics can be — and usually are — closely related. Rather, he sought to address forthrightly modern questions about how the Bible can continue to be normative for Christian living. He determined that a successful solution would be possible only if Christian ethicists were serious about ecclesiology. For it is in the eucharistic gathering, he maintained, that the gap between the New Testament church and all subsequent Christian existence is bridged, in which the tension between New Testament ethics and Christian ethics is worked out.

I agree with Lehmann that the eucharistic gathering is the primary location in which Christians learn how to put the Bible to lively effect in their own lives and in the world. And, as I have indicated already, my goal is to explore how this happens and is important for Christian ethics. But I reject Lehmann's claim that Christian ethics differs from New Testament ethics as a consequence of the delay of the parousia. Christian ethics (which includes the ethics of the New Testament) is grounded in the fact that the Word has become flesh and dwelt among us (John 1:14), leaving those who seek to become his disciples with the responsibility of imitating and following him with discernment in all times and circumstances until his return.

2. See Lehmann, *Ethics in a Christian Context* (1963; rpt., Westport, Ct.: Greenwood Press, 1979), pp. 28-29.

Lehmann is not alone in thinking that the hermeneutical problem is somehow the key to doing Christian ethics responsibly. Earlier in this century, Reinhold Niebuhr raised the issue in his *Interpretation of Christian Ethics* (1935), and later James Gustafson in his well-known essay "The Place of Scripture in Christian Ethics" worried about closing the gap between the knowledge of the meaning of the texts gained through biblical studies and the uses that Christian ethicists make of them.[3] This concern has led still others to increasingly formalistic accounts of the uses of Scripture in Christian ethics. The search for the meaning of the texts in and of themselves has often led to a neglect of the kind of ecclesiological reflection that Lehmann called for. One notable exception is Thomas W. Ogletree, who, in *The Use of the Bible in Christian Ethics* (1983), insists that the ecclesial context of Scripture is a key to understanding how the Bible continues to be normative for Christian ethics.

Attention to ecclesiology has been even more pronounced in recent books and articles by John Howard Yoder, Stanley Hauerwas, and James William McClendon Jr.[4] Unlike Lehmann, however, these authors do not take up the discussion of ecclesiology because they believe eucharistic community is crucial for bridging a gap between biblical ethics and contemporary Christian ethics. They emphasize not one but several ecclesiological contexts of Christian ethics, including liturgy, preaching, and *diakonia.* Study of the actual practices of the believing community is essential, these writers insist, for a fruitful exploration of the uses of the Bible in Christian ethics. They shift attention away from prevalent notions that there is a tension between New Testament ethics and so-called Christian ethics, and they minimize the importance for Christian ethics of correlative concerns about definitions of genre, conceptual tools (such as covenant, prophecy, or law), and the development and original meanings of texts. These theologians value

3. Gustafson, "The Place of Scripture in Christian Ethics: A Methodological Study," *Interpretation* 2 (October 1979): 430-55. See also Gustafson's *Christian Ethics and the Community* (Philadelphia: Pilgrim Press, 1971) and *Theology and Christian Ethics* (Philadelphia: Pilgrim Press, 1974).

4. See, e.g., Yoder, *The Politics of Jesus* (Grand Rapids: William B. Eerdmans, 1972) and *The Priestly Kingdom* (Notre Dame, Ind.: University of Notre Dame Press, 1984); Hauerwas, *A Community of Character,* especially chaps. 2 and 3; McClendon, *Systematic Theology,* vol. 1: *Ethics* (Nashville: Abingdon Press, 1986); Bruce C. Birch, *Let Justice Roll Down* (Louisville: Westminster/John Knox Press, 1991); Bruce C. Birch and Larry L. Rasmussen, *Bible and Ethics in the Christian Life,* rev. ed. (Minneapolis: Augsburg, 1989); and Stephen E. Fowl and L. Gregory Jones, *Readings in Communion* (Grand Rapids: William B. Eerdmans, 1991).

the scholarly study of the Bible, but they strongly suspect that the sorts of questions that biblical scholars bring to the texts will seldom help to improve our understanding of how the church employs the Bible ethically as a guide for moral formation and Christian witness.

Yoder, Hauerwas, and McClendon reflect understandings of Scripture from the Anabaptist tradition. Paul Lehmann seems to see some connection between their position and that of Orthodox theologians. Early in *Ethics in a Christian Context*, he acknowledges that his way of doing ethics (in the light of the hermeneutical problem) is fundamentally different from that of either the Orthodox Church or "the so-called 'sects.'" Initially he points to a sharp distinction between the Anabaptist and Orthodox approaches, stating that "the tension between New Testament ethics and Christian ethics is *more* acutely felt" in the so-called sectarian branch of Protestant Christianity than it is in the mainline Protestant churches, whereas among the Orthodox this tension is *less* acutely felt. But despite this difference, says Lehmann, neither of the traditions encounters the hermeneutical problem. He asserts that the Anabaptists make a more serious attempt than the mainline Protestant churches "to encourage the individual Christian as a member of a holy community toward as close an approximation to the ethical behavior of Jesus Christ as the conditions of a sinful world allow."[5] And he asserts that "the intimate connection between liturgy and life which marks the piety of Orthodoxy is designed to foster the direct implementation of the ethic of the Gospels in and through the ethics of the church."[6] Thus, if I understand him correctly, Lehmann maintains that although the Orthodox Church and the Protestant "sects" represent opposite poles of interpretation with respect to relationships among New Testament ethics, Christian ethics, and the *ecclesia*, they nevertheless evidence a kindred spirit in the extent to which neither finds it necessary to turn to the modern hermeneutical problem as a preface to or starting point for Christian ethics.

Lehmann seems content simply to let the situation stand in this way, as if the sizable Orthodox and Anabaptist exceptions to his approach were not significant. But it will not suffice to dismiss these exceptions with the argument that the Orthodox and Anabaptist traditions have somehow or other remained precritical in their reading and use of the Bible. Perhaps he is assuming that *every* use of the Scriptures that does not presuppose an inherent tension or break between biblical

5. Lehmann, *Ethics in a Christian Context*, p. 42n.3.
6. Lehmann, *Ethics in a Christian Context*, p. 42n.3.

ethics and Christian ethics is precritical. But on what grounds can he make that assumption? There are other weaknesses in his analysis as well. For example, although Lehmann's description of the relation between Scripture, worship, and ethics within Orthodoxy is fairly accurate, Yoder's work would seem to indicate that the Christ-against-culture or the Bible-against-church model does not adequately capture the character of Anabaptist Protestantism as a living community of faith. The fact is that neither the Orthodox nor the Anabaptists have defined themselves in worship, evangelism, or communal organization in the terms prescribed by the hermeneutical problem that Lehmann and so many other contemporary Christian theologians believe is essential to understanding or doing Christian ethics. To the contrary, both traditions, albeit for different reasons, strongly insist that the Bible belongs to a particular community and that the use of the Bible in Christian ethical thought must reflect the ecclesial context of Scripture. Lehmann cannot simply dismiss the weight of these positions out of hand.

A Communal Hermeneutic

At one point in his posthumously published work *The Eucharist*, Alexander Schmemann comments, "I daresay that the gradual 'decomposition' of scripture, its dissolution in more and more specialized and negative criticism, is a result of its alienation from the eucharist — and practically from the Church herself — as an experience of a spiritual reality."[7] Significantly, Schmemann makes this comment in the midst of a discussion of the Little Entrance of the Byzantine Liturgy. He insists that the liturgy is Scripture's home. But what do Schmemann and Orthodox theology mean by this? Likewise, what does Schmemann mean by the " 'decomposition' of scripture"? I will deal with these two questions together in an effort to clarify the notion of the communal hermeneutic of the Orthodox Church.

Wayne A. Meeks helps to answer these questions in an intriguing article entitled "A Hermeneutics of Social Embodiment." Meeks suggests an alternative to what he depicts as two equally deficient and misleading ways of reading the Bible that have arisen from within New Testament studies. "One is a rigorously historical quest, in which all the early Christian documents alike, canonical and extracanonical, are

---

7. Schmemann, *The Eucharist* (Crestwood, N.Y.: St. Vladimir's Seminary Press 1988), p. 66.

treated as sources for reconstructing the diverse and curious varieties of the early Christian movement. The other way . . . cares not at all where the texts came from or what they originally meant; by purely literary analysis it wishes to help text and reader to confront one another continually anew."[8] Meeks's alternative is to seek "to uncover the web of meaningful signs, actions, and relationships within which that text did [or does] its work."[9] Put another way, biblical texts obtain their significant Christian meaning through the authoritative roles they assume within the church. Such meaning is grasped by observing and, even better still, by participating in those liturgical, preaching, and evangelical activities through which the church defines its social identity and pursues its communal goals. "Perhaps it is not too much to say that the hermeneutical circle is not completed until the text finds a fitting social embodiment," says Meeks.[10] This is very near to what Schmemann means when he laments the ill effects of the "rupture" between word and sacrament.[11]

"The scriptures and the Church," wrote Schmemann, have been reduced "to the category of two formal *authorities,* two 'sources of faith' — as they are called in the scholastic treatises, for which the only question is which authority is the higher: which 'interprets' which." In a move that established the norm in the West, the Reformers declared "holy scripture to be the supreme authority for teaching the faith." But how are we to determine the meaning of Scripture once it has been disembodied and removed from the liturgical context in which its meaning has formerly been explored and enacted by the community of believers? Sooner or later we will have to turn to "biblical science" for a determination of meaning, and when this happens, "the meaning of scripture is dissolved in a multiplicity of private" albeit "scientifically" governed theories or opinions. The reigning model of biblical interpretation becomes the autonomous interpreting self confronting the text with all the tools of the science. The individual located within the craft of biblical exegesis stands as an authority over Scripture. Schmemann saw that the Orthodox proclivity is to react against this modern individualistic trend by insisting that the church is the definitive authority on Scripture. But this argument for the supremacy of

---

8. Meeks, "A Hermeneutics of Social Embodiment," *Harvard Theological Review* 79 (1986): 176.

9. Meeks, "A Hermeneutics of Social Embodiment," pp. 183-84.

10. Meeks, "A Hermeneutics of Social Embodiment," p. 184.

11. Schmemann, *The Eucharist,* pp. 67-69.

ecclesial authority, he explained, has itself forgotten how Scripture becomes eucharistically incorporated. This embodiment is accomplished when the community of believers interprets the meaning of Scripture in prayer and in doxological and serviceable response to the preaching and eucharistic presentation of the word in the Liturgy. "It is precisely through the sacrament that the word is interpreted," says Schmemann, "for the interpretation of the word is always witness to the fact the Word has become our life. . . . The sacrament is his witness, and therefore in it lies the source, the beginning and the foundation of the exposition and comprehension of the word."[12]

In fact, argued Schmemann, the issue is not one of authority, still less of two competing authorities, Scripture and church (or Scripture and tradition); rather, it is about truth and how that truth comes to life, how it is hypostatized (or enfleshed) in the communion of believers. From the eucharistic perspective, the Bible cannot be an authority over the community, because in the eucharistic assembly of God's Word the Word becomes flesh, the very flesh of those who have gathered around the gift offering, and in this way the community itself becomes the evangelical truth. Moreover, from this eucharistic perspective, the church is not an authority either, at least not in the sense of *auctoritas*.[13]

Contrary to the assumptions of Western textualism and individualism, the truth that the church becomes is not confined to the text but includes the response to the text and the enactment of that response by the community that receives it and uses it as Scripture. Tradition is in some real sense Scripture performed and embodied ecclesially. It is the communal action of receiving and proclaiming the gospel. Eucharistically speaking, therefore, neither the content of Scripture nor the content of tradition is confined to a text. From the standpoint of this eucharistic and communal hermeneutic, the prevalent Western model — namely, that two authorities, Scripture and tradition, are subject to interpretation by the autonomous intellect — is very questionable. The communal hermeneutic also obviates the need for what John E. Tiel has described as the "romantic paradigm" of the theologian, in which the church is presumed to depend on original and creative individual theologians who reconstruct the communal life of the church.[14]

12. Schmemann, *The Eucharist,* pp. 66, 67, 68.
13. See John D. Zizioulas, *Being in Communion* (Crestwood, N.Y.: St. Vladimir's Seminary Press, 1985), pp. 114-15.
14. See Tiel, "Theological Responsibility: Beyond the Classical Paradigm," *Theological Studies* 47 (December 1986): 580-82.

Nicholas Lash says much the same in his book *Theology on the Way to Emmaus*. Lash is particularly helpful in dealing with some of the thorny issues associated with such a description of the ecclesial employment and interpretation of the Bible. While he maintains that the "fundamental form of the Christian interpretation of scripture is the life, activity and organization of the believing community," he insists that this emphasis does not remove the need for "experts" or their special skills. While it rejects individualism and the tyranny of private reason, it embraces fully the notion that those "who engage in the activity of reading a text bear personal responsibility for their reading."[15] The experts *do* have a role to play; it is simply the case that their role is subordinate to the actual "enactment" of Scripture by the believing community. Among other things, the experts have an important role to play in keeping the community of believers honest about the "script," true not only to the spirit of its authors but to the tradition of interpretation.

The Social Embodiment of Scripture: An Example from the Byzantine Liturgy

Let us return for a moment to Wayne Meeks's observation that "perhaps . . . the hermeneutical circle is not complete until the text finds a social embodiment." Meeks proposes that "a hermeneutical strategy entails a social strategy. . . . Texts do not carry their meaning within themselves, but 'mean' insofar as they function intelligibly" — for example, insofar as they organize groups and establish their communal purposes — within specific contexts and histories. Meeks proposes a "strategy" that obliges the individual exegete to participate, "at least in the imagination" or empathetically, "with the kind of communal life which 'fits' the text."[16] But I do not see why, on the basis of Meeks's analysis, this should not also apply to the interpretation of Scripture that occurs within the ecclesial community.

The question of how the beatitudes (Matt. 5:1-12//Luke 6:17, 20-23) belong to Christian ethics — especially Christian *social* ethics — has long been a point of controversy in the church. Meeks's recommendations about a hermeneutic of social embodiment exposes the limita-

15. Lash, *Theology on the Way of Emmaus* (London: SCM Press, 1986), pp. 42-43.

16. Meeks, "A Hermeneutics of Social Embodiment," pp. 183-84.

tions of the debate over this issue. Several of the positions that have been proposed concerning the ethical meaning and application of the beatitudes reflect the struggle of biblical criticism and biblical theology to come to terms with Jesus' sayings on the basis of literary form, historical criticism, biblical eschatology, or such concepts as law and gospel. Many of these approaches function to minimize the extremeness of the beatitudes and other parts of the Sermon on the Mount. Some have ascribed these sayings to an Oriental tendency to use hyperbole for pedagogical purposes. Others have explained Jesus' radical teachings as an "interim" ethic fitted for the short time that he and the early church expected to pass before the kingdom came (or, alternatively, as a futuristic ethic for the eschatological kingdom itself). And still others have argued that the sayings reflect Jesus' effort to stress the interiority of the moral and religious claims that the Law implied but did not fully reveal. These interpretations all have some value in having opened up helpful perspectives on Scripture, and the best of them have struggled fruitfully with the recognition that there exists in the beatitudes a tension between, or perhaps a synthesis of, an ethic of rules and commands on the one hand and an ethic that is dispositional and eschatological on the other. Yet the hermeneutical strategies that these interpretations propose almost inevitably fail to consider that the beatitudes might *in fact* already have obtained viable meaning and embodiment in the believing community through its liturgical life and practice.

Charles E. Curran's interpretation of the beatitudes is illustrative of this pervasive short-sightedness:

> The radical and seemingly impossible ethical teaching of Jesus is more than mere rhetoric. Jesus indicates the goal and direction that should characterize the life and actions of his followers. "Give to everyone who asks" is an impossible ethical imperative, but such a demand indicates the constant thrust that characterizes the life of the Christian. . . . Eschatological considerations introduce an inevitable tension into Christian ethics. The tension results from the fact that the reign of God in Christ is now present, and is going forward toward its fullness.[17]

Thus, according to Curran, the beatitudes make an actual and present claim on Christians because Jesus in his own life, death, and resurrec-

17. Curran, *Themes in Fundamental Moral Theology* (Notre Dame, Ind.: University of Notre Dame Press, 1977), pp. 15-16.

tion inaugurated the reign of God. Furthermore, they indicate the quality of that future mode of existence in God's kingdom that Christians hope for and to which Christians must conscientiously strive to orient their lives.

Curran does not provide his reader with any benchmarks of actual Christian practice in which this biblical eschatology is embodied, however. Instead, he shifts the focus from the ecclesial settings of the beatitudes as they relate to the church in sacrament and pilgrimage to certain moral issues affecting the secular order, such as war, women's equality, colonialism, and human rights. It is to these issues, he argues, that the radical teachings of Jesus are applicable. Presumably he is asking us to look for the embodiment of these teachings in such human struggles. Curran's original goal of holding biblical eschatology in tension with Christian ethics begins to sound like a religious version of a familiar ethical idealism with which Americans especially are quite comfortable. Precisely because Curran fails to identify the ecclesial and liturgical locations of Christian eschatology and the symbol of the kingdom of God, he risks leaving his readers with the impression that the evangelical counsels that he has described as radical demands are actually assimilable in culturally familiar moral ideals of benevolence and justice. Ironically, it is not far from this point to the kinds of cultural accommodation that Curran pointedly warns against and that he charges the Roman Catholic Church with having lapsed into.

Curran could have pursued another strategy to explain the significance of the beatitudes for the church. For example, he could have taken up the liturgical interpretation of the beatitudes on the Feast of All Saints. The origins of the present feast lay in several commemorations of martyrs from the days of the early church. One fifth-century Syrian celebration fell on Easter Friday. A similar Byzantine celebration fell on the octave day of Pentecost. In Rome a feast for All Martyrs and All Saints came just after Easter on the thirteenth of May. In all cases, the meaning of the commemoration was unambiguously paschal and messianic: they were occasions on which the fullness of Christ's victory over sin and death might be proleptically experienced. In the ninth century, the Latin Church moved the feast from May to the 1st of November, where it remains today. There, as the last major feast before Advent, it still invites a messianic interpretation: the feast is a proleptic and eschatological experience of the future kingdom inaugurated by the birth of the Christ child. The Roman Catholic lectionary juxtaposes Matthew 5:1-12 with 1 John 3:1-3 and Revelation 7:2-4, 9-14, thus interpreting the beatitudes as constitutive of the character, disposition, and relationships of those who will be among the multitudes standing before the Lamb at his throne and in a resounding doxological hymn receive from Christ his new creation. This liturgical performance of Scripture lends an immediate concrete sense of personal and communal meaning to the beatitudes. They are illuminated as eschatological, yet also as morally transformative and definitive for Christian character and living.

In the Slavonic version of the Byzantine Liturgy of St. John Chrysostom, the beatitudes are put to yet another important use that illustrates the full range of their ethical application by the church. In the Byzantine Liturgy, Matthew 5:1-12 is the text of the third antiphon of the Lesser Entrance. Historically, this beginning of the present liturgy belonged to the processional performed on appointed feast days. In Constantinople, for example, the procession led from Hagia Sophia to a stational church that bore the name of the feast or of that saint with whom a feast was associated. Alexander Schmemann explains: "The singing of the *antiphons* took place during this procession and was completed at the doors of the church with the reading of the 'prayer of entrance,' and only then did the clergy and the people of God actually enter the church for the performance of the eucharist." Thus it is clear, says Schmemann, that the Lesser Entrance not only "comprises the *beginning* of the eucharistic ceremony, but also the *entering,* dynamic character of the ceremony, the eucharist as *movement*" into the kingdom of God.[18]

The words of the first antiphon are from Psalm 103, describing the character of God. "Bless the Lord, O my soul: . . . Who forgiveth all thy sin, and healeth all thine infirmities. . . . The Lord is full of compassion and mercy, long-suffering and of great goodness." The accompanying prayer stresses the utter transcendence of this God, the fact that his love and mercy are of infinite measure and beyond all human comprehension. "O Lord our God whose might is ineffable, whose glory is inconceivable, whose mercy is infinite, and whose love toward mankind is unutterable. . . ."[19] The second antiphon is taken from Psalm 146 and depicts God as the agent of creation and redemption

18. Schmemann, *The Eucharist,* pp. 51, 52-53. The history and function of the antiphons give them a character that varies from one feast to another. My analysis here is restricted to the antiphons for ordinary Sundays.

19. From the *Service Book of the Holy Orthodox-Catholic Apostolic Church,* ed. and trans. Isabel Florence Hapgood (Englewood, N.J.: Antiochian Archdiocese, 1975), p. 81.

who loves especially his chosen people, who in turn call on him as Lord and King. "Blessed is he that hath the God of Jacob for his help, and whose hope is in the Lord his God; who made the sea, and all that therein is, who keepeth his promise forever. Who helpeth them to right that suffer wrong; who feedeth the hungry . . . : as for the way of the ungodly, he turneth it upside down. The Lord thy God, O Sion, shall be King forevermore." The prayer for this antiphon names the church as God's vessel of holiness in the world. "O Lord save thy people, and bless thine heritage. Preserve the fulness of thy Church: sanctify those who love the beauty of thy house."[20]

In this liturgical setting, the beatitudes assume an utterly christological meaning, emphasizing holiness as a virtue for believers. The new humanity that God brings into existence through Christ is called to be holy. It is not that the kingdom of God is contingent upon the holiness of any creature; it is rather that those who would enter God's kingdom must be conformed to the likeness of the One who is holy in order to be fit for it. The first two antiphons function figurally and typologically, anticipating Christ and his new creation. The beatitudes are sure signs that the kingdom is present among us, because he who spoke them also fulfilled them in his life. Their utterance liturgically is intended to achieve the fulfillment of the kingdom that has been realized in Christ.[21] Christ is the revelation of the kingdom in person. The rubrics for the antiphons instruct the deacon to stand before the icon of Christ as they are sung, holding his stole with three fingers of the right hand. This christological interpretation is deepened by the anthem that follows the second antiphon: "O Only begotten Son and Word of God! Thou who art immortal yet didst deign for our salvation to become incarnate . . . Save us."[22]

The entrance is completed and the beatitudes are sung as the deacon passes through the iconostasis onto the altar.[23] At the conclusion of the Lesser Entrance, the christological, social, and eschatological meanings of the beatitudes are joined. The beatitudes themselves are

---

20. *Service Book of the Holy Orthodox-Catholic Apostolic Church*, p. 82.

21. See Dumitru Staniloae, *Theology and the Church* (Crestwood, N.Y.: St. Vladimir's Seminary Press, 1980), p. 168.

22. *Service Book of the Holy Orthodox-Catholic Apostolic Church*, pp. 82-83.

23. In the current procession, the altar plays the role that the entire sanctuary played in the original Byzantine processions. Schmemann explains that this substitution of the altar for the entire sanctuary "weakened the perception and experience of the 'assembly as the Church' itself as the entrance and ascent of the Church, the people of God, to the heavenly sanctuary" (*The Eucharist*, p. 59).

prefaced by the words "In thy Kingdom remember us, O Lord, when thou comest into thy Kingdom. Blessed are the poor in spirit for theirs is the kingdom of heaven. . . ."[24] This is followed by the great doxological hymn of the Trisagion: "O holy God, who restest in the Saints, who art hymned by the Seraphim . . . accept from the mouths of us sinners, the Thrice-Holy song, and visit us with thy beneficence. . . . Sanctify both our souls and bodies, and grant that we may serve you in uprightness all the days of our life."[25] Those who would enter the kingdom must bear the character of the One who is its Lord and who spoke and fulfilled the beatitudes in his life. This character is the product of both human striving and divine grace. At issue is obedience to Christ's command to "be perfect, therefore, as your heavenly Father is perfect" (Matt. 5:48) and the free gift of God's grace to those who believe in his Son.

Liturgically, the beatitudes are experienced as both moral imperative and eschatological promise. We need never run the risk of idealizing, spiritualizing, or otherwise disembodying them if we recall that they come to us as Christ's commentary on his own life, a life that led not only to the cross but to the resurrection.[26] The beatitudes are compelling for Christians not because they are precepts that are somehow or other metaphysically true but because Christ lived them. They are evangelical because he who taught and practiced them did so for our sakes. Those who in gratitude for this become his disciples must be for others what Christ is for them. We know that it is possible to live the beatitudes because the church exists.

The liturgical uses of the beatitudes point up the inadequacies of much of the debate over whether or how they belong to Christian ethics. The questions ordinarily raised in such discussions ignore the ecclesial and liturgical contexts in which the beatitudes obtain ethical force and eschatological significance for the worshiping community. In this sense, the ecclesial and liturgical employment of the beatitudes already answers questions of whether they are primarily elements of a personal ethic or whether they embrace a social vision. The Orthodox Church has interpreted the beatitudes as the very constitution of the kingdom of God. At the start of a sermon on Matthew 5:1-2, St. John Chrysostom asks, "What kind of foundations of His new polity doth

---

24. *Service Book of the Holy Orthodox-Catholic Apostolic Church*, p. 83.
25. *Service Book of the Holy Orthodox-Catholic Apostolic Church*, p. 85.
26. See Staniloae, *Theology and the Church*, p. 167. The idea here is that the words interpret Christ's conduct, and his conduct interprets the words.

He [Christ] lay for us?"[27] His answer is that this new polity is based on the beatitudes. Yet this constitution is not a founding charter or a set of theoretical statutes that can be abstracted from its original location in the church. It is, rather, the abiding presence of the One in whom the beatitudes have been revealed as the will of God. The goal of church polity, therefore, is to understand and do God's will in the world.

Biblical Typology and Christian Ethics

The preceding example of the use of the beatitudes within Orthodox liturgy leans heavily toward a figural or typological biblical exegesis. This kind of exegesis retains a strong sense of historicity and is attentive to the narrative locations of biblical passages as comparisons are drawn between biblical events or characters along a scale of time. It is often said that by contrast allegory abstracts texts from historical or narrative contexts and makes them speak for certain eternal truths or concepts. By pointing up the typological use of the beatitudes in the Byzantine rite, I have identified what is also judged to be the presiding form of biblical exegesis in Orthodox liturgy and tradition. Yet in doing so, I do not want to deny the legitimate use of the allegorical method in the Orthodox tradition.[28] Thus, although I refer to contemporary advocates of the typological method such as Hans Frei and George A. Lindbeck in my attempt to draw out the significance of typology for an ecclesially centered Christian ethics, I want to point out here that I do not concur in their belief that allegory is an unhelpful deviation from that norm, nor do I endorse narrative theologies that

27. Chrysostom, *Homilies on the Gospel of Saint Matthew,* vol. 10 of the Library of Nicene and Post-Nicene Fathers, 1st series, ed. Philip Schaff (New York: Christian Literature, 1889), p. 91. Chrysostom hedged not a bit on the applicability of the beatitudes to all Christians. Addressing married people in a homily on the epistle to the Hebrews, he wrote, "And if these beatitudes were spoken to solitaries only, and the secular person cannot fulfill them, yet He [Christ] permitted marriage, then he has destroyed all men. For if it be not possible, with marriage, to perform the duties of solitaries, all things have perished and are destroyed, and the functions of virtue are shut up in a strait" (*Homilies on the Epistle to the Hebrews* in vol. 14 of the Library of Nicene and Post-Nicene Fathers, 1st series, ed. Philip Schaff [New York: Christian Literature, 1890], p. 402).

28. Much of Orthodox and ascetical and mystical theology is heavily allegorical. St. Gregory of Nyssa was a master of this form. A prime example is his *Life of Moses.* A good modern translation can be found in the Classics of Western Spirituality series — *The Life of Moses,* trans. Abraham J. Malherbe and Everett Ferguson (New York: Paulist Press, 1978).

pay little attention to the liturgical contexts of the church's biblical exegesis.[29]

In any event, a retrieval of the typological method is in order. Anton Ugolnik's admonition to Orthodox who would engage in that task is pertinent. He understands all too well the Orthodox propensity to be merely reactive when challenged with the modern Western quandary over hermeneutics. Ironically, such Orthodox negativity works against a truly effective engagement of the biblical texts within contemporary Orthodoxy. "Let us assume, for a moment," writes Ugolnik, "that in response to the western hermeneutic we seize upon the figural interpretation of scripture, draw it from the liturgy and justify it as 'premodern.' In that very justification we cancel an assumption about time about which the figural mode is based."[30] The "return" to a figural use of the Bible, he argues, must be proactive. It must help contemporary Christians to conform their lives to the Christ in whom all such figural interpretation is founded.

This is the sense in which Georges Florovsky issued a challenge to the Orthodox and other Christians to regain their biblical minds.[31] It is also the message of George A. Lindbeck when he explains that in New Testament times "typology was used to incorporate the Hebrew Scriptures into a canon that focused on Christ, and then, by extension, to embrace extrabiblical reality." Typology in its seriousness about the literal meaning of events or personages continues to provide "a powerful means for imaginatively incorporating all being into a Christ-centered world." Lindbeck cautions, however, that typology should not be used to help "believers find their stories in the Bible." Rather, Christians should be encouraged to use typology to "make the story of the Bible their story. The cross is not to be viewed as a figurative representation of suffering nor the messianic kingdom as a symbol for hope in the future; rather, suffering should be cruciform, and hopes for the future messianic."[32]

29. This question of the relation of allegory and typology and the claim I make that within Orthodox theology the two do abide together defensibly as part of Christian piety and practice is undoubtedly related to the whole matter of Platonism in Orthodox theology. The liturgies to which I refer include Platonic as well as allegorical elements. But I also maintain that the cited texts support my claim that the presiding method is typological.

30. Ugolnik, "An Orthodox Hermeneutic in the West," *St. Vladimir's Theological Review* 27 (January, 1983): 111.

31. See Florovsky, *The Collected Works of Georges Florovsky*, vol. 1: *Bible, Church and Tradition: An Eastern Orthodox View* (Belmont Mass.: Nordland, 1972), pp. 9-16.

32. Lindbeck, *The Nature of Doctrine* (Philadelphia: Westminster Press, 1984), pp. 117-18.

Some years back, biblical scholar James Barr questioned whether or to what extent this typological exegesis is useful for contemporary Christians. He was skeptical of the efforts of biblical scholars to rehabilitate typology, and he was especially critical of the renewed emphasis on typology by some in the *Heilsgeschichte* school of New and Old Testament studies (e.g., G. W. H. Lampe, Gerhard von Rad, and Martin Noth). According to Barr, the best argument these scholars had to offer in favor of typology was that it served to counterbalance the spiritualizing propensities of allegory. The *Heilsgeschichte* school identified a salvation history of divine events as the core of the Bible. But Barr argued that this typological approach was not consistent with the way that the authors of the New Testament and the early church read Scripture: "The character of the [New Testament] scene is not adequately described if we say that it is one in which a new saving event, or a representation of the older saving events, or a new turn of the *Heilsgeschichte*, is looked for; it is, rather, much more precisely one in which a Christ is expected, and in which the [typological] use of the Old Testament passages is heavily biased in this direction."[33] But Barr found that this messianic and christological orientation was not sufficiently appreciated by the *Heilsgeschichte* school.

This debate among biblical scholars is not my primary concern here, however. Suffice it to say that in more recent years, Barr has expressed an interest in Hans Frei's assertion in *The Eclipse of Biblical Narrative* that figural or typological exegesis goes hand in glove with the biblical authors' interests in weaving together a realistic narrative that, though history-like, is not wedded to the strict view of literality and temporal sequence of modern historiography to which the salvation history concept owes its inspiration and method of exegesis.[34] I suspect that Frei has shown Barr a way out of his earlier pessimism about finding an effective means of implementing typology to edify contemporary Christians.

In the history of Christianity there has been no better practitioner of the figural or typological use of Scripture than St. John Chrysostom. It is instructive to look at Chrysostom's technique. The sermons he delivered as a priest in Antioch and later as Bishop of Constantinople draw relentlessly from biblical stories, juxtaposing in figural fashion

33. Barr, *Old and New in Interpretation* (New York: Harper & Row, 1966), p. 133.

34. See Frei, *The Eclipse of Biblical Narrative* (New Haven: Yale University Press, 1974), especially pp. 27-28, 173-75.

Old and New Testament stories and characters with Christ as the lodestar. Chrysostom had a purpose — to transform the minds and the hearts of his listeners, people that he knew to be (and often publicly accused of being) more pagan than Christian. Chrysostom was definitely not trying to translate the biblical stories into the idiom of the culture in order to solve the so-called social or moral questions of the day, nor did he translate these stories into symbols or cyphers through which the meaning of ostensibly universal human experiences might be grasped. Rather, he invoked these stories and events in order to get his listeners to regard and conduct themselves as participants in the Christianly normative world of the Bible.

One powerful example of Chrysostom's use of typology appears in his fourth sermon on Jesus' parable of Lazarus and the rich man (Luke 16:19-31). The story itself makes use of the promise and fulfillment motif that is at the center of New Testament typology. When the rich man asks Abraham for permission to return from the dead to warn his five brothers about what will be awaiting them if they do not change their ways, he is told, "If they do not listen to Moses and the prophets, neither will they be convinced even if someone rises from the dead." For those who refuse to be attentive to the lives and words of Moses and the prophets, whom Luke presents throughout his Gospel as types of the Christ, even the miraculous resurrection of the dead will not provide sufficient warning of judgment and the great reversal that Christ brings about. On the other hand, the implication is that those who do pay heed to these Old Testament types and the Law will recognize Christ and obey his teaching.

Chrysostom draws attention to the special character of Abraham in this parable. "Abraham was hospitable. The rich man sees Lazarus with Abraham, in order that Lazarus also may convict him of inhospitality. For that patriarch hunted out those who were going past and brought them into his own house; but this rich man overlooked the one who was lying inside the gate."[35] The rich man, a Jew who calls Abraham "father" (v. 24), is supposed to have lived his life in the manner of Abraham. Chrysostom's unwritten "texts" in this connection are the baptismal rite and the eucharist, from which his congregation could recollect that they too were "offspring" of Abraham, meaning that God expected them to strive conscientiously to imitate Christ, in

---

35. John Chrysostom, *On Wealth and Poverty*, trans. Catherine P. Roth (Crestwood, N.Y.: St. Vladimir's Seminary Press, 1984), pp. 50-51. Later, Chrysostom also mentions Job as one whose "door was open to every comer" (Job 31:32).

whom God's promise to Abraham was fulfilled. "The poor man has one plea, his want and his standing in need; do not require anything else from him; but even if he is the most wicked of all men and is at a loss for his necessary sustenance, let us free him from hunger. Christ also commanded us to do this, when he said, 'Be like your father in heaven, for he makes his sun rise on the evil and on the good, and sends rain on the just and the unjust' [Matt. 5:45]."[36]

The eucharistic context of this sermon cannot be overemphasized, however. In his first sermon on Lazarus and the rich man, Chrysostom deliberately alludes to the eucharistic table. He invokes the image of eating at the dinner table, mentioning how the rich man gorged himself while ignoring the starving man at his gate. And he admonishes,

> As for you, my beloved, if you sit at table, remember that from the table you must go to prayer. Fill your belly so moderately that you may not become too heavy to bend your knees and call upon your God. Do you not see how the donkeys leave the manger ready to walk and carry loads and fulfill their proper service? But when you leave the table you are useless and unserviceable for any kind of work. . . . The time after dinner is the time of thanksgiving, and he who gives thanks should not be drunk but sober and wide awake.[37]

As Michael G. Cartwright has helpfully pointed out,

> The imagery of the Lukan parable, Paul's first letter to the Corinthians [chap. 10], the riotous gathering outside all created a rich associative setting within which Chrysostom addressed the Christians of Antioch. Festive tables outside the door, the tables at home, the table of the Lord before them, the table of the rich man's feast — the table to which Lazarus looked up with eyes of hunger and longing; all these "tables" become the multivoiced matrix within which the Gospel is proclaimed, heard, and responded to — in short, *enacted* in the context of community. Moreover . . . the sermon is itself set in the context of the pro-anaphora which prepared the faithful for the Eucharistic banquet.[38]

36. Chrysostom, *On Wealth and Poverty*, p. 52
37. Chrysostom, *On Wealth and Poverty*, p. 27.
38. Cartwright, "Practices, Politics and Performances: Toward a Communal Hermeneutic for Christian Ethics" (Ph.D. diss., Duke University), pp. 10-11. I owe Cartwright a special debt of gratitude for the help I received from his dissertation as well as from personal conversations and correspondence that helped to define the thematic content of this chapter.

It is against this background that Chrysostom forcefully insists in his second sermon that Christian prayer and good works should be directed first of all to the poor, to the likes of Lazarus. "For this reason Christ said, as He welcomed those who had acted [hospitably toward strangers and outcasts], 'As you did it to one of the least of these, you did it to me' [Matt. 25:40]."[39] Abraham was hospitable, as was Christ after him, and Christ demanded the same of all who would identify their lives with him. This instruction prepared Chrysostom's congregation for his final radical prescription: "I beg you remember this without fail, that not to share our wealth with the poor is theft from the poor and deprivation of their means of life; we do not possess our own wealth but theirs." Those who would be nourished with Christ's body and blood must likewise be "nourishing Christ in poverty here and laying up great profit hereafter."[40]

I recognize that Chrysostom's use of the Bible here is not the purest example of typology, which properly involves setting out type and antetype in explicit fashion. It is not that such "pure" examples are difficult to find in Chrysostom's vast corpus of New Testament homilies; indeed, his writings are replete with them. But I am interested in a broader definition of figural or typological exegesis than such examples would lead us to. Chrysostom knew the Bible well, and it is fair to say that he presumed that his congregation also would recall (if from no other source than his own preaching) what the Pauline epistles, in particular, say about Abraham as a type of the man of faith whose hope was in Christ. This recollection would have been reinforced by the eucharistic context of the preached word and a liturgical theology so deeply indebted to this typological claim as to leave no one uncertain that the one holy and eternal sacrifice of which Christ is both offering and offerer is the antetype (or fulfillment) of all the Old Testament sacrifices.[41]

Hans Frei describes figural exegesis as "at once a literary and a

---

39. Chrysostom, *On Wealth and Poverty*, p. 51
40. Chrysostom, *On Wealth and Poverty*, p. 55.
41. In the Anamnesis of the Byzantine liturgy of St. Basil, the celebrant prays, "Look upon us, O God, and behold this our service, and accept it as thou didst accept the gifts of Abel, the sacrifices of Noah, the burnt-offerings of Abraham, the priestly offices of Moses and Aaron, the peace-offerings of Samuel. Even as thou didst accept at the hands of the holy Apostles this true ministry, so also do thou in thy beneficence, O Lord, accept these gifts; that having been accounted worthy blamelessly to minister at thy holy Altar, we may receive the recompense of wise and faithful stewards, in the terrible day of thy just requiting" (*Service Book of the Holy Orthodox-Catholic Apostolic Church*, p. 99).

historical procedure, an interpretation of stories and their meanings by weaving them together into a common narrative to a single history and its patterns of meanings." He goes on to explain that this procedure means to depict a (biblical) world that lays claim to being "the one and only real world." It becomes the duty of the Christian "to fit himself into that world . . . [and] to see his disposition, his actions and passions, the shape of his own life as well as that of his era's events as figures of that storied world."[42] John Chrysostom was an artful teller of the biblical stories. He painted his listeners into the world of the Bible. When in his sermon he describes the failure to share one's wealth with the poor as "theft from the poor and a deprivation of their means," he is not claiming possession of a rationally apprehensible, universalizable principle but rather is adding one more detail to the picture of the biblical world into which he invites his listeners. This is what makes the prescription so powerful and so difficult to reject for the listener who desires to belong to that world.

An Application: The Matter of Surrogacy

We have seen how John Chrysostom was an exemplary practitioner of a communal and typological hermeneutic. I have wondered on occasion how Chrysostom might have addressed the issue of surrogate motherhood and in what circumstances he would have found the opportunity to do so. As I read his homilies on marriage and family life,[43] I am repeatedly impressed by how his moral instruction is consciously founded in the stories of the biblical marriages (e.g., Abraham and Sarah, Isaac and Rebekah) and familial relationships (e.g., Joseph and his brothers, Hannah and Samuel). The Orthodox rites of marriage richly allude to the biblical marriages that illustrate divine and human fidelity. And so I imagine that if Chrysostom were living today, he would locate a discussion of surrogate motherhood in a homily on marriage, with no apologies to his more pagan or secularly oriented parishioners. Surrogacy is an issue that needs a Christian response not primarily because the future of contract law is at stake or even the happiness of couples but because it denies the church's understanding

---

42. Frei, *The Eclipse of Biblical Narrative*, pp. 2-3.
43. See especially *St. John Chrysostom on Marriage and Family*, trans. Catherine P. Roth and David Anderson (Crestwood, N.Y.: St. Vladimir's Seminary Press, 1986).

of marriage as a "one flesh" unity with a vocation to expand and extend the kingdom of God into the lives of children and strangers.

Over the past decade we have heard much about surrogacy. The debate was prompted especially by the highly publicized "Baby M" case of the mid-1980s. In this case, the father's custody of a child born through a surrogate arrangement was contested by the woman with whom he legally contracted to conceive and give birth. The plea for custody of the child by Mary Beth Whitehead, the biological mother of Baby M, was denied by the New Jersey Supreme Court. William Stern and his wife were granted custody of Baby M, and Mrs. Whitehead received only visitation rights.

Within the body of literature on surrogacy published thus far, Christian ethicists have said surprisingly little of a theological nature. On the whole they have simply rehearsed the arguments of legal scholars, psychologists, and sociologists. Their position seems to be that the issue of surrogacy is mostly a matter of weighing certain legally guaranteed personal rights, calculating consequent economic practices or psychological effects and the like, and setting policy. I would not dismiss the importance of such considerations, but I think it is telling how little of this discussion *starts* from normative claims about the nature and the purposes of Christian marriage. One would think that from the Christian standpoint this is where the surrogacy issue is to be engaged. But perhaps this presumes a biblical mind that contemporary Christian catechism and seminary or graduate school training is no longer inculcating.

The Orthodox marriage rites place every new Christian marriage within the history of the biblical marriages in which God has shown his steadfast love and through which has pursued his promise of redemption. Moral instruction about the meaning and purposes of marital life is gleaned from these stories. The great patriarchal and matriarchal marriages are recalled. Each new Christian marriage is set within the history of these biblical marriages, beginning with Abraham and Sarah and the divine covenant and culminating with the marriages of Zechariah and Elizabeth and Joseph and Mary, through whose offspring, John and Jesus, the promised kingdom of God breaks dramatically into human history. In this way marriage, the union of the two in one flesh, is defined as a primary form of participation in God's redemptive purpose — indeed, as an ecclesial event. A Christian marriage well lived, measured by the standards (and mistakes) of the holy marriages that have preceded it, is a proleptic sign of God's eschatological kingdom.

The story of Abraham and Sarah, which is always recalled in the Orthodox rites, is particularly informative in this regard because it specifically involves a case of surrogacy. God promises Abraham an heir, but as Abraham and Sarah age they begin to despair of having a child on their own and select Hagar to serve as a surrogate mother. The Orthodox marital rites present their adoption of this strategy as yet another failure of faith in the context of their marriage (along with Abraham's attempts to pass Sarah off as his sister in order to save his life and his household — Gen. 12:10-20; 20:1-18), actions that jeopardized rather than assisted the fulfillment of God's covenant promise. It is significant, however, that the biblical authors tell the story in such a way as to indicate that Abraham and Sarah made their mistakes with the intent of pursuing the larger soteriological purposes that they saw governing their lives. Abraham did not lie about his relationship with Sarah merely to preserve his own life, for example. Nor did he and Sarah turn to the surrogacy alternative merely because they personally desired children. The Orthodox Church honors the patriarchs and matriarchs as holy figures not because they lived faultless lives but because they learned their lessons well and struck the path to salvation. The same is expected of those who marry in Christ, the One whose relationship to the church the Old Testament marriages foreshadowed.

The presence of Hagar and Ishmael threatened the peace of Abraham's household and, thus, all that God had sought to accomplish through it. The slave girl was emboldened to ridicule her mistress, who was unable to bear a child; and later, after Isaac's birth, Sarah grew jealous of Ishmael's presence and joint claim to the covenant. Ultimately, Hagar and Ishmael were expelled permanently from the household. There is good practical wisdom and psychology in these stories that Christians and Jews today ought not to overlook in their reasoning about surrogacy. But precisely because the Abraham and Sarah and Hagar stories are read and enacted liturgically in typological fashion as key elements of the biblical narrative of redemption culminating in the Incarnation, the Orthodox Church will derive from them an ethic that exceeds the measure of even this practical wisdom. In such a context, the Abraham and Sarah narratives, along with the other stories of patriarchal-matriarchal marriages, tell us that spousal union, motherhood, fatherhood, and children participate in purposes beyond the legal obligations — and beyond the wishes and pleasures — of those who aspire to be parents, to conceive, give birth to, or raise children. The Byzantine rite makes this abundantly clear in the prayer of crowning:

O God most pure, the Creator of every living thing, who didst transform the rib of our forefather Adam into a wife, because of thy love towards mankind, and didst bless them, and say unto them: Increase, and multiply, and have dominion over the earth; and didst make the twain one flesh: and what God hath joined together, that let no man put asunder: Thou who didst bless thy servant Abraham, and opening the womb didst make him to be father of many nations; who didst give Isaac unto Rebecca, and didst bless her in child-bearing; who didst join Jacob unto Rachel, and from that union didst generate the twelve Patriarchs; . . . who didst accept Zecharias and Elizabeth, and didst make their offspring to be the Forerunner; who, from the Root of Jesse according to the flesh, didst bud forth the ever-Virgin One, and wast incarnate of her; and wast born of her for the redemption of the human race; who, through thine unutterable gift and manifold goodness didst come to Cana of Galilee, and didst bless the marriage there, that thou mightest make manifest that it is thy will that there should be lawful marriage and the begetting of children: Do thou the same all-holy Master, accept the prayer of thy servants. As thou wert present there, so likewise be thou present here, with thine invisible protection. . . . Bless this marriage and vouchsafe unto these thy servants, . . . a peaceful life, length of days, chastity, mutual love in the bond of peace, long-lived seed, gratitude from their posterity, a crown of glory which fadeth not away.[44]

Thus, Orthodox are encouraged to formulate decisions concerning surrogacy not just on the basis of considerations about its immediate effects on spousal relationships or its psychological impact on the parents and children involved but with a view to how the practice influences their understanding of marriage and child rearing and how it affects the mission of the Orthodox Church. They are called to make a decision about the moral permissibility or impermissibility of surrogacy in light of the faith, hope, and charity that the Byzantine prayer identifies as the virtues of the patriarchs and matriarchs and that belonged to the One whose blessings are beseeched for every married couple that believes in him. They will have to judge how surrogacy measures up to the standard that the church sets for marriage — that it be a one-flesh union bound up with the eschatological promise of God's kingdom.

---

44. *Service Book of the Holy Orthodox-Catholic Apostolic Church*, p. 295.

The Eucharistic Locus of an Ecclesial Hermeneutic:
The Pauline Model

A central ecclesial image of the New Testament writers is that of the "body," a gathered community that is obedient to the governance and rulership of the One whom it identifies as the founder of that community and the One in whom that community's identity is secured. I have argued, with help from Schmemann, Meeks, and Lash, that it is this body that carries the normative hermeneutic for Christian living and that the primary locus for that communal hermeneutic is the liturgy of the church. Through the example of the surrogacy issue, I have endeavored to show how that communal hermeneutic can be brought to bear on ethical practice. Now I want to conclude with an examination of how the typological and communal themes join to form a hermeneutical basis for an ecclesial Christian ethic.

St. Paul offers a model for this hermeneutic in 1 Corinthians 10–11 by typologically identifying the church with Israel. Speaking to certain controversies raging within the Corinthian community over church discipline and ethics, the apostle anchors his counsel with references to baptism and the eucharistic meal, reminding the Corinthians that through these practices they gain and sustain their identity as a peculiar community.

> You should understand my brothers, that our ancestors were all under the pillar of cloud, and all of them passed through the Red Sea; and so they all received baptism into the fellowship of Moses in cloud and sea. They all ate the same supernatural food, and all drank the same supernatural drink; I mean, they all drank from the supernatural rock that accompanied their travels — and that rock was Christ. And yet, most of them were not accepted by God, for the desert was strewn with their corpses.
>
> These events happened as symbols [*typoi*] to warn us not to set our desires on evil things, as they did. (1 Cor 10:1-6, NEB)

Thus, according to St. Paul, the eucharist and baptism are the primal activities of remembrance through which the *ecclesia* discerns and defines its historical and spiritual relation to Israel, recognizes itself as the fulfillment of God's promise to redeem Israel, and prepares itself to become a people worthy of inheriting the kingdom of which the church itself is the eschatological and sacramental sign. On the basis of this *remembrance*, St. Paul draws authority and warrant for his admonitions and counsel to the Corinthian Christians. For Paul the issue was not primarily whether the Corinthians were breaking certain theological, customary, or secular rules when they ate meat consecrated to an idol (1 Cor. 8:1-13), when women neglected to wear veils in worship (11:3-17), or when they broke up into factions at the common *agape* meal, the wealthier refusing to share what they brought with the others (11:17-33). Obedience to an external authority or ethical code is not the fundamental issue for the church when it gathers as a eucharistic community or seeks to extend its life to the rest of society. Rather, the full measure of Christian character and conduct is to be derived from a typological understanding of the saving events that extend back to ancient Israel and forward to the Incarnation. These events are what secure Christian identity. Properly interpreted, they serve as guides and teaching tools for following and imitating Christ faithfully (1 Cor 11:1). When, at the beginning of chapter 10, St. Paul links the identities of the church and Israel through baptism and its type (the crossing of the Red Sea) and the eucharistic meal and its type (the manna from heaven and the water from the rock) and then brings this typological way of narrating the Christian story into a critical conversation about current realities, he is, in fact, showing the Corinthian Christians how Christian ethics is done.

Later in chapter 10 (vv. 14-18) and again in chapter 11 (vv. 23-26), St. Paul directs the Corinthian Christians to the primary location of this remembrance and discernment. "So then, dear friends, shun idolatry. I speak to you as men of sense. Form your own judgement on what I say. When we bless 'the cup of blessing', is it not a means of sharing in the blood of Christ? When we break the bread, is it not a means of sharing in the body of Christ? Because there is one loaf, we, many as we are, are one body; for it is one loaf of which we all partake" (1 Cor. 10:14-17, NEB). The apostle's word on the subject is not sufficient: the Christians of Corinth must "form their own judgement." Through eucharistic worship and identification with Christ, they must discern whether it is proper either to participate in pagan worship or eat meat that has been dedicated to pagan deities. A general moral good is not what is at stake here; they must set their sights on the saving truth that is made available to all those who participate with belief in the eucharistic banquet. In the shared meal, the Word becomes flesh, the very body of those who have gathered in remembrance and praise of him who is their Messiah and Redeemer. Either the community itself becomes the evangelical truth or it does not. Participation in pagan worship is strictly prohibited because it is a denial of that truth and the refusal to become it. "Look at the Jewish people. Are not those who partake in the sacrificial meal sharers in the altar? What do I imply by this? that an idol is anything but an idol? or food offered to it anything more than food? No; but the sacrifices the heathen offer are offered (in the words of Scripture) 'to demons and to that which is not God'; and I will not have you become partners with demons. You cannot drink the cup of the Lord and the cup of demons. You cannot partake of the Lord's table and the table of demons" (10:18-21, NEB). This soteriological truth is not at issue in the purchase and consumption of meat consecrated in pagan sacrifices. Hence, a Christian must make the decision about whether to eat it on the basis of a concern about whether doing so would offend or harm other members of the Christian fellowship or whether it would create harmful divisions within the one body of believers (10:23-33; cf. 8:4-13). As Meeks has shown in his book *The First Urban Christians*, by using Scripture and the tradition as he does here and elsewhere in 1 Corinthians, St. Paul undertakes two important self-interpretive activities for the church: he clarifies the nature of the Christian polity and the social boundaries that separate Christian from non-Christian, and he defines the terms on which that polity can with integrity engage and bear witness to the larger society. I believe St. Paul is also teaching us that a liturgical reading of Scripture is sometimes also a more appropriately scriptural reading.

I should say in closing that in describing the eucharist as the primary locus of Christian ethics, I do not want to detract from the doxological significance of worship. I agree with Paul Lehmann, however, that "as the politics of God give to the eucharistic liturgy its occasion and significance, so the ethical reality of the *koinonia* gives to the celebration of the Eucharist its integrity."[45] The ethical character of the *koinonia* is rooted in the messianic promise. Christian ethics springs to life through the hope inspired by faith that this promise of redemption is fulfilled in and through the church. Christian doxology gives substance to this hope. It affirms that the God who has made the promise has also tabernacled among us (John 1:1-5, 14) and that he is now and ever has been the Lord and Judge of all creation. I do not know how else to understand the great eucharistic prayers of Orthodoxy that narrate the biblical story of creation, fall, and redemption in Jesus Christ. It is also powerfully dramatized at the close of the Divine Liturgy of the Armenian Church in its lection from the first chapter of the Gospel of John and recitation of Psalm 34. Here doxology combines with ethical instruction about the character of God as the

---

45. Lehmann, *Ethics in a Christian Context*, p. 103.

Lord and Judge of creation: "Keep thy tongue from evil; and thy lips that they speak no guile. Eschew evil and do good, seek peace and ensue it."[46] Geoffrey Wainwright sums it up when he states that the liturgy "is the locus in which the story of the constitutive events [of Christian existence] is retold in order to elicit an appropriate response in worship and ethics to the God who remains faithful to the purposes which his earlier acts declare."[47]

Conclusion

While I have sought in this chapter to address the role of the Bible in Christian ethics, I would not have that inquiry limited by academic arguments concerning the meanings and proper uses of texts or concerning the nature and legitimate concerns of Christian ethics. For in the last analysis, neither biblical scholars nor ethicists decide these questions: the churches decide them. In so many cases, when theologians and ethicists have allowed such questions to determine what they do, it has blinded them to the ecclesial context and liturgical performance of the Bible. I think a disquieting though largely unexamined awareness of this situation accounts for the strong attraction of narrative theology in recent years. The blinding formalism and constrictive conceptualism to which I am referring have had deleterious consequences for the use of the Bible in Christian ethics. Many have sought to mine the Bible for narrow and abstract pronouncements on specific issues or for statements that will substantiate the credibility of some concept such as justice or peace. Christian ethics is ever in jeopardy of becoming, or being mistaken for, someone else's ethics when it drifts too far from singularly Christian practice.

As we have seen by looking at Chrysostom and St. Paul, there is another way to understand the relation of the Bible to Christian ethics. The Bible should not be reduced to a resource for moral decision making or an authority from which to address prized theological or cultural concepts. Rather, it must be allowed to define what is normative for how Christians behave, to serve as the image of what they as a community are to be. I have tried to show that the Orthodox tradition possesses a rich treasury of liturgies and rites in which the biblical world

46. *Divine Liturgy of the Armenian Apostolic Orthodox Church* (New York: Delphic Press, 1950), p. 105.

47. Wainwright, *Doxology* (New York: Oxford University Press, 1980), p. 153.

with its images is powerfully narrated, enacted, and embodied communally. Such are the occasions — whether in ordinary worship, the great feasts of the church, or the sacraments and blessings of baptism, marriage, ordination, and burial — in which Christian identity and destiny are defined and secured.

It remains to be seen whether these ecclesial and liturgical renderings of the biblical world will be applied in an ethical way. Nothing less is at stake than a renewal of the scriptural mind, transcending all the formalisms, foundationalisms, narrativist theologies, and fundamentalisms to which the Orthodox Church, like its sister churches, has been mightily attracted here in its new American home.

II. The Churches after Christendom

4. *The Struggle for the Soul of the Church: American Reflections*

It is not possible to do Christian theology or ethics today unless one pays serious attention to the fact that as America closes out the twentieth century the churches are facing the emergence of a new cultural situation. Disagreements persist over just how "Christian" America was in the past and over the value of this status if it ever did apply. But most contemporary observers are at least agreed that the old cultural configurations, which were explicable only against the background of historic Western Christendom, are increasingly less at the heart of what defines American culture.

There is virtually complete agreement that by the middle of the twentieth century, one could no longer accurately speak of America as a Protestant Christian nation; certainly the concerted aspirations of the American Protestant churches toward that end had ceased. In the 1950s and 1960s, Will Herberg's thesis seemed to fit: America had become a "triple melting pot" (actually, Herberg preferred "transmuting pot" to "melting pot") of Protestant, Catholic, and Jewish religious communities. In this mix, the Protestants still had the predominant public religious presence, and the Anglo-Saxon type remained an ideal by which the Americanness of ethnic and religious identities was judged.[1] But the Protestant hegemony of ecclesiastical and cultural authority and ideology had broken up under the forces of immigration, urbanization, pluralism, and secularism. Denominationalism, that uniquely American form of church polity, continued. Indeed, it was showing signs of encompassing Roman Catholic and Jewish identity and religious con-

1. See Herberg, *Protestant, Catholic, Jew: An Essay in American Religious Sociology* (Garden City, N.Y.: Doubleday-Anchor, 1960), p. 21.

sciousness as well. But the denominational arrangement was now subsumed under the effects of the triple melting pot. "The religious unity of American life implies an institutional and ideological pluralism," wrote Herberg. "The American system is one of stable coexistence of three equi-legitimate religious communities grounded in the common culture-religion of America."[2] Herberg called this common culture-religion "the American Way of Life." He was among the first to identify the essential features of American civil religion, much discussed during the 1960s and 1970s.

Herberg's description and analysis indicates the persistence of key elements of "Christian America." But it also uncovers the forces that were bringing a wholly new cultural order into existence. American religion had become so "thoroughly secularist," he wrote, "that the familiar distinction between religion and secularism appears to be losing much of its meaning. . . . Both the 'religionists' and the 'secularists' cherish the same basic values and organize their lives on the same fundamental assumptions."[3] A generic religion that promised to help ensure success, happiness, and prosperity was embraced by "religious" and "nonreligious" Americans alike.

This equilibrium of pluralism and unity, religiosity and secularity that Herberg described had come about through the peculiar dynamics of the American Way. The constitutional and legal separation of church and state and the prohibition against religious establishment, joined with practical need of the nation's many churches to find some way to coexist with one another, provided the incentive and the structure for mutual tolerance. The old Protestant ideological hegemony of religion and nationhood remained sufficiently strong in a transmuted form to provide an overarching cultural unity under which a plurality of churches and historic faiths worked out a peace and pursued common and conflicting causes. Secularism and religion coexisted relatively peaceably — ironically, because secularism itself was "being generated out of the same conditions that are, in part at least, making for the contemporary religious revival." Motivated by desires to preserve ethnic and religious identity within the assimilative process and also by a hunger for success and personal fulfillment, increased numbers of Americans sought out the churches. "It is not secularism as such that is characteristic of the present situation," concluded Herberg, ". . . but

2. Herberg, *Protestant, Catholic, Jew*, p. 259.
3. Herberg, *Protestant, Catholic, Jew*, pp. 270-71.

secularism within the religious framework, the secularism of a religious people."[4]

In recent years, several sociologists of American religion have added a new chapter to Herberg's book. In *The Struggle for America's Soul*, Robert Wuthnow asks, "How did Herberg's tripartite system, in which the basic religious and *religio-political* divisions occurred between Protestants and Catholics and between Christians and Jews, come to be replaced by what some have called a 'two-party system' " of liberals and conservatives?[5] In *Culture Wars*, James Davison Hunter argues that "in the wake of the fading Judeo-Christian consensus has come a rudimentary realignment of pluralistic diversity. . . . The major rift is no longer born out of theological or doctrinal disagreements — as between Protestants and Catholics or Christians and Jews. Rather the rift emerges out of a more fundamental disagreement over the sources of moral truth."[6] Both Hunter and Wuthnow describe a two-way split between the "orthodox" and the "progressivists," a split that cuts across the denominations and major historic faiths. The struggle to define America, they say, now centers on such intensely debated issues as sexuality, abortion, education, family, the arts, and the moral role of government and law.

I will not pursue any further the line of analysis taken by these authors in their efforts to make sense of this conflict of moral visions. Wuthnow and Hunter are concerned with where the culture is going, who the major players in it presently are, and who they will be in the future. My interest lies elsewhere. I want to ask whether the cultural conditions described by these authors signal the final demise of religious America, for example. And I want to ask what the church's mode of engagement with the culture should be, given its new minority status.

After Herberg's Tripartite Religious America, What?

The paled but not spent manifestations of historic biblical faith in America that Wuthnow and Hunter describe correspond to trends that Herberg detected in the 1950s. The culture's orientation, however, has now

4. Herberg, *Protestant, Catholic, Jew*, p. 271.
5. Wuthnow, *The Struggle for America's Soul: Evangelicals, Liberals, and Conservatives* (Grand Rapids: William B. Eerdmans, 1988), pp. 31-32.
6. Hunter, *Culture Wars: The Struggle to Define America* (New York: Basic Books, 1991), p. 77.

moved decisively toward secularism. Herberg could rightly say of America at mid-century that "secularism as such is [not] characteristic of the present religious situation" but that it was advancing within a religious framework. Wuthnow and Hunter tell us that the situation today is more ambiguous. Secularism has gained autonomy ideologically and institutionally within a variety of voluntary organizations and social movements. The state itself has become distinctly secular. Hunter argues that the latter is true in two ways: "The formal relations between religion and government" have shifted, with the government assuming "more and more jurisdiction over areas of social life previously controlled by churches and synagogues" (e.g., welfare services, family life, education), and "a secular orientation is manifested in the way the . . . state is organized" under "bureaucratic principles. Thus the very *ethos* of the modern state is unsupportive of a broad cultural system rooted in, legitimated by, and promoting (through public policy) a commitment to transcendent ideals."[7] Hunter reverses Herberg's formula when elaborating the grounds for the present struggle to define America. "The practical effects of the birth of Christianity and the Reformation have, at least in the U.S. context, become both politically and culturally defunct," he says. "Another world event has become paramount . . . the secular Enlightenment of the eighteenth century and its philosophical aftermath. This [secularism] is what inspires the divisions of public culture in the United States today."[8]

Herberg had warned that the pluralism, individualism, historicism, and relativism running through the culture might reduce the historic religious communities to creatures of the very secularism which at that time grew symbiotically with biblical faith. He addressed the deleterious consequences to biblical faith and ecclesial polity that a surrender to these forces would foster. The Americanization of the churches had already brought about a distinct loss of the sense of "uniqueness and universality: each of the three 'faiths,' insofar as the mass of its adherents are concerned, tends to regard itself as merely an alternative and variant form of being religious in the American way. . . . The authentic character of Jewish-Christian faith is falsified, the faith itself is reduced to the status of an American culture-religion."[9]

Since the publication of *Protestant, Catholic, Jew,* much has transpired in America that confirms Herberg's warnings about the thinning

---

7. Hunter, *Culture Wars,* pp. 301-2.
8. Hunter, *Culture Wars,* p. 132.
9. Herberg, *Protestant, Catholic, Jew,* p. 262.

and deracination of the historic faiths. Hunter does well to point out that the "most recent expansion of pluralism signifies the collapse of the long-standing Judeo-Christian (mostly Protestant) consensus in American public life." Who can deny either that "symbols of moral discourse, informed . . . by biblical imagery and metaphor" have receded from public discourse?[10] The privatization of religion in America has advanced greatly since Thomas Luckmann diagnosed the trend in *The Invisible Religion* (1967). And when Hunter says that the divisions and tensions between "religious" Americans no longer express confessional and doctrinal differences, that the sole source of controversy centers on symbolic moral-cultural issues, I take this as persuasive evidence of the radically secularized condition of historic biblical faith. The churches are powerfully tempted to become involved in the culture wars. Perhaps the temptation is humanly unavoidable. But it entails a great risk of the further reduction of biblical faith to an instrumentalistic morality. Involvement in the culture wars inherently contributes to a strictly functionalistic understanding of biblical faith as good for morality. It leads to a conception of the church as a "party" or interest group for the preservation of society. Even so-called "orthodox" or "evangelical" Christians who give in to the temptation thereby lose hold of the meaning of the gospel as salvation for individual human beings. The church's measure of "success" and mission, even its very being, are assessed on the basis of whether the society endorses abortion, looks favorably or not on homosexuality, sets looser or stricter limits on pornography, and the like.

Real Pluralism: Is a Public Theology What We Need?

The legacy of the Constantinian era and the reign of what has justifiably been called Christendom came to an end at different moments throughout the Old World "after the churches had exhausted their credit, after they had lost both proletariat and intellectuals, after they [often] gave birth to violent anti-Christian ideologies."[11] When the separation of church and state came, it was often forced on the churches as a result of the triumph of anticlerical and secular ideologies. Not infrequently, the old religious sacralism was replaced with some new

10. Hunter, *Culture Wars*, pp. 76-77.
11. Franklin H. Littell, "The Churches and the Body Politics," *Daedalus* 96 (Winter 1967): 31.

form of secular "sacralism." The legally or culturally disestablished church came to be seen by church apologists as a moral and spiritual institution and reserve of freedom that balanced the state's claims to sovereignty over human society.

But America proved the exception to this rule. "In America," says Franklin H. Littell, "the Constantinian pattern and style were proclaimed at an end by Christians [and non-Christians] who had a new vision of the nature of high religion and just government."[12] This entailed "neither establishment nor secularism."[13] That is why the Troeltschian typology of church and sect does not quite capture the American reality. Here churches and sects became denominations — a hybrid of church and sect types. No single denomination managed to lay claim to society or state for long. The relationship between church and state was defined early on by separation and nonestablishment. Religious pluralism was a given, not an afterthought. This is not to suggest that the American story in this regard is simple or that there were no exceptions to this basic thesis. Still, the overall pattern is unique and remarkable.

In this light, the idea of an American Christendom, or of Christian America, can be seen as something of a myth; but so too is the notion of a radical separation of church and state. In fact, the state has sought to maintain a formal neutrality concerning religion while presiding over a de facto integration of Protestant piety, belief, and polity with the democratic ethos. In the mid-nineteenth century, Alexis de Toqueville captured the relationship of religion and state accurately:

> While the law allows the American people to do what they please, religion prevents them from conceiving, and forbids them to commit what is rash and unjust.
>
> Religion in America takes no direct part in the government of society, but it must be regarded as the first of their political institutions; for if it does not impart a taste for freedom, it facilitates the use of it. I do not know whether all Americans have a sincere faith in their religion . . . but I am certain that they hold it to be indispensable to the maintenance of republican institutions.[14]

This civil religion held up at least until the time of the publication of Herberg's *Protestant, Catholic, Jew.* It could be argued that the fact that it

---

12. Littell, "The Churches and the Body Politics," p. 31.
13. Littell, "The Churches and the Body Politics," p. 29.
14. Tocqueville, *Democracy in America*, vol. 1, ed. Phillips Bradley (New York: Vintage Books, 1945), p. 316.

was talked about so much by academics and theologians during the 1960s and 1970s constitutes the surest sign that its demise had commenced.

Noting the demise of this civil religion may be another way of marking the beginning of a new relationship between the churches and the culture. The weakening of denominational commitments and the decline of ecumenical institutions and processes based in denominational Christianity are further indications of profound changes in the American order. Tocqueville's religious America and Herberg's secularly religious America have faded from the scene. The legal and customary arrangements for the separation of church and state and nonestablishment may have been articles of religious and civil peace, as John Courtney Murray put it in 1960, but that is not necessarily a good thing. As long as the vast majority of Americans experienced religion and culture as interwoven, and the leaders of American democracy identified with religious America, this peace was easy for the churches to accept and perceived as "good" for religion. In today's context, however, the so-called New Class and cultural elites are not alone in abandoning the old forms of religious identification and the moral legacy of American Protestantism. Hunter makes the special point in *Culture Wars* that "the most unnoticed but momentous way in which religious and cultural pluralism expanded in the postwar period can be found in that part of the population claiming no particular religious faith."[15]

In his 1993 study *Christianity in the Twenty-first Century*, Wuthnow questions whether Herberg didn't even overstate the extent to which religion served as a source of identity for Americans in the 1950s. Certainly "a generation or two later," Wuthnow concludes, "identity comes from multiple sources . . . [and] the share that comes from religion may be even less."[16] Wuthnow and Hunter agree, in any case, that vast numbers of Americans today live in real cognitive dissonance respecting their claims to being religious and the conduct of their lives. These Americans retain a vague notion of religious identity but their lives are distinctly secular, with the experience of God in worship and prayer not figuring very prominently in all that they do. Increasingly these nominally Christian or Jewish Americans embrace the heady hedonism and narcissism of popular culture and do not see that this contradicts biblical faith. Middle-class suburbia is teeming with such persons.

15. Hunter, *Culture Wars*, p. 754.
16. Wuthnow, *Christianity in the Twenty-first Century* (New York: Oxford University Press, 1993), p. 188.

In view of this, it is surprising that some American religionists continue in a state of denial. I can find no other description than denial for the insistence by theologians and social critics such as Richard John Neuhaus and George Weigel that America remains a religious nation even while they lament the existence of "the naked public square."[17] These critics concede that the symbols and language of historic biblical faith are being expelled from the public arena by the courts and that they weigh ever less on the political process. But if this is really so, why persist in arguing that America is no less religious in the 1990s than it was thirty or forty years ago?

In the midst of the new secularity, the multiplication and differentiation of beliefs and loyalties in America accelerates. Gerrit G. de Kruijf commented several years ago in a paper delivered at an annual meeting of the Society of Christian Ethics that "the American churches are approaching, though from a different side, the same issue that the churches in Europe have faced since the French Revolution. . . . The basic question in the American context . . . [is] whether the churches are prepared to accept pluralistic democracy even when society has become really pluralistic [and really secularistic]."[18] Under these conditions of "real pluralism and secularism," the churches certainly need to redefine their *modus vivendi* vis-à-vis the culture. They need not rule out the possibility that a new public philosophy will emerge to hold the center together, but the churches cannot assume that this public philosophy will embrace biblical faith or even be neutral about it. Recent Supreme Court decisions such as *Lee v. Weisman* (1992), which bans prayers from student exercises and graduation ceremonies, do not so much reflect a new conservative philosophy of the justices — long feared by both religious and secular liberals — as they signal shrewd and pragmatic concessions to the new secular autonomy and non-religious character of a critical mass of Americans.

Thus, I am skeptical of the calls issued by some theologians,

---

17. For Neuhaus's assertions, see *The Naked Public Square: Religion and Democracy in America* (Grand Rapids: William B. Eerdmans, 1984) and "From Providence to Privacy: Religion and the Redefinition of America," in *Unsecular America*, ed. Richard John Neuhaus (Grand Rapids: William B. Eerdmans, 1986), pp. 52-66. For Weigel's assertions, see especially chap. 1 of *Catholicism and the Renewal of American Democracy* (New York: Paulist Press, 1989), "Is America Bourgeois?" *Crisis* 4 (October 1986): 5-10, and "Is America Bourgeois? A Response to David Schindler," *Communio* 15 (Spring 1988): 77-91. Schindler's response immediately follows: "Once Again: George Weigel, Catholicism and American Culture," pp. 92-120.

18. De Kruijf, "The Christian in the Crowded Public Square," in *Annual of the Society of Christian Ethics* (1991): 24.

especially within the academy, for a new public theology as the appropriate answer to a perceived decline of public morality. The proponents of a public theology typically argue that Americans have lost both a moral consensus and a public language through which we might reach agreement about the common good. They maintain that a public theology would provide a language of mediation between religious and moral truth on the one hand and public debate on the other.[19] Yet the task of formulating a new democratic ideology to bridge the gap between religious truth with public policy is probably impossible given the actual pluralism and secularity of America. In Herberg's secularly religious America, Reinhold Niebuhr and John Courtney Murray could still hold out hope for such a public theology, because the cultural synthesis of biblical faith and Enlightenment liberalism held together. Since that time, however, corrosive post-Enlightenment processes have damaged the synthesis more than many contemporary religionists are willing to admit. On one side, the biblical origins of Christian faith in the transcendence and providence of God and the concept that human being are created in the image of God are not remembered by many Americans. On the other side, much of what gave us confidence in the Enlightenment's claims about the moral foundations of liberal society

---

19. The calls for a public theology are issued in a handful of representative ways, including the following:

> In my judgment, we shall have a civilization in which religion is a force and it shall shape public polity and policy. The question is whether we will be able to develop a public theology to guide, refine, critique, and vindicate, as fitting, the dynamic, spiritual, ethical . . . center, which gives every society its internal guidance system. (Max L. Stackhouse, "Piety, Polity, and Policy," in *Religious Beliefs, Human Rights, and the Moral Foundation of Western Democracy*, 1986 Paine Lectures in Religion, ed. Carl H. Esbeck [Columbia, Mo.: University of Missouri Press, n.d.], p. 26)

> I return to the point that we need something like an ideology. Perhaps I might say we need a "common faith" or a "democratic faith." My own preference is for "public philosophy." . . . Public philosophy is the mediating language between religious truth and public decision. (Neuhaus, "From Providence to Privacy," p. 64)

> But does the Hauerwas project [of narrative theology] give us the tools needed to construct a religiously-informed public philosophy for the renewal of the American experiment? This seems doubtful. . . . If our goal is *public* moral argument, by which we mean an argument open to all Americans irrespective of confessional allegiance, then the passage from the naked public square to the civil public square will be charted through the revivification of natural law, or its functional equivalent. (Weigel, *Catholicism and Renewal*, pp. 196, 200)

and the correctness of democratic government has been put to question. Historicism and relativism have had their way with both traditional religion and Enlightenment liberalism.

In this new situation, the search for public theology is fraught with danger. Protestant and Roman Catholic liberals drift toward a Rousseauistic conception of a civil theology that translates the Christian hope for salvation into humanistic reform and looks only to the state for guarantees of personal liberty and social security. Neoconservative theologians talk about the founding fathers' vision of a virtuous republic. They wax nostalgic over a past utopia, and in their efforts to retrieve it, they deny that cultural conditions have changed. Liberals and neoconservatives alike fail to distinguish satisfactorily between a renewal of confessional faith within the churches and the construction of a new civic faith. Neither liberals nor neoconservatives have squarely faced the demise of the unique American cultural synthesis of Protestant faith and Enlightenment liberalism. The pluralistic yet cohesive Christian/Enlightenment culture described by Tocqueville, which flavored legal disestablishment and separation of church and state with a definite religious bias, is coming to an end. If there is any substance in the claim that we are at the end of American modernity, it involves these phenomena.

In an essay entitled "The Tower of Babel," Michael Oakeshott characterized modernity this way:

> [Ours is] a world dizzy with moral ideals [in which] we know less about how to behave in public and in private than ever before. Like the fool, our eyes have been on the ends of the earth. Having lost the thread of Ariadne, we have put our confidence in a plan of the labyrinth, and we have given our attention to interpreters of the plan. Lacking habits of moral behavior, we have fallen back upon moral opinions as substitute. . . . We exaggerate the significance of our moral ideals to fill the hollowness of our moral life. . . . No doubt our present moral distraction . . . springs partly from doubts we have in respect to the ideals themselves; all the effort of analysis and criticism has not yet succeeded in establishing a single one of them unquestionably. But this is not the root of the matter. A moral ideology . . . [may even] be established and maintained because this appears the only means of winning the necessary moral stability for the society. But in fact it is no remedy; it merely covers up the corruption of consciousness, the moral distraction inherent in morality as the self-conscious pursuit of moral ideals.[20]

20. Oakeshott, *Rationalism in Politics* (New York: Basic Books, 1962), p. 74.

I fear that much of what constitutes the search for a public theology or public philosophy is an exercise in drawing up plans for the labyrinth when, truly, the "thread of Ariadne" has been lost. Whatever our judgments about the wisdom of Christianity's former alliances with culture and the church's collaboration with states and empires in the effort to organize Christendom, it is at least clear that such strategies are not appropriate at the present cultural moment. The best a desire for a public theology can hope to produce is a desolate halfway house between Christendom and secularism. At worst, ironically, it contributes ideological frenzy and viciousness to the ensuing culture wars.

Prospects for a Public Church

A dozen years ago, Martin E. Marty published *The Public Church*. As the title suggests, the book is concerned with the privatization of religion in America under the impact of pluralization and secularization. The publication of the volume initiated a decade of debate about what constitutes an appropriate strategy for the churches in a new, more secular and less cohesive public order. With reference to Supreme Court decisions of the sixties and seventies, Marty measured the extent to which "the civil religion was becoming so diffuse that it was ungraspable."[21] And the collapse of the American consensus on fundamental values within the legal realm reflected a growing fragmentation and pluralization in the culture at large.

Marty looked back to John Courtney Murray's classic statement on the American consensus *We Hold These Truths* (1960) as an anchor and marker for possible courses of ecclesial and public life. He made the case for a new reading of Murray that stressed not so much his theory of consensus and effort to develop a public theology as his vision of disparate but potentially collaborative religious communities.[22] That is to say, Marty emphasized Murray's pluralist impulse; he argued in effect that Murray had anticipated the present cultural moment of centrifugal pluralism. The dangers of such pluralization were privatism and tribalism at one extreme and the "administrative despotism" of which Tocqueville warned at the other extreme. Marty proposed that the most effective way to counteract sectarianism and administrative despotism would be to gather the churches together in a "communion

---

21. Marty, *The Public Church* (New York: Crossroad, 1981), p. 159.
22. See Marty, *The Public Church*, pp. 160-61.

of communions," or a "public church."[23] Participating churches and denominations would get the opportunity to join with others in a common worldly Christian calling without having to sacrifice their unique traditions. Moreover, the public church did "not await discovery": it already existed in the network of voluntary and benevolent associations and ecumenical bodies that the Protestant churches had created during the nineteenth and early twentieth centuries. During that period, the constituency of the "communion of communions" had expanded to include not only the old mainline churches but "the newer evangelicalism and Catholicism" as well.[24]

Over the past decade, others have endorsed this vision of a public church. Dennis P. McCann, for example, has argued that the public church is a "more modest and more promising" strategy than outright calls for a restoration of moral consensus through a public theology. In continuity with Murray and Marty, McCann focuses his advocacy on the concept of civility. "The 'public church' is less a strategy for coalition-building," he says, "and more a collective learning process for cultivating the churches' common 'faith in civility.' "[25] He goes on to say,

> Pluralism may exist without "civility," but a pluralistic society cannot, if it lacks the sense of social interdependence which this virtue fosters among diverse communities who, both because of and in spite of their differences, remain pledged to one another for the sake of the common good.
>
> The "public church," then, is merely the process that institutionalizes the practice of civility within the Christian "communion of communions" in order to promote "the harmonious exercise of the [nation's] social life."[26]

Whether civility as a virtue of the public life has a future is an open question. There is nothing that guarantees its survival. With the breakdown of the synthesis of Christian piety and Enlightenment republicanism that historically engendered civility in the American citizenry, tribalism or administrative despotism are real possibilities. I am sympathetic with McCann's contention (1) that the public church is less ideo-

---

23. Marty, *The Public Church*, p. 161.
24. Marty, *The Public Church*, p. 3.
25. McCann, *New Experiment in Democracy: The Challenge for American Catholicism* (Kansas City: Sheed & Ward, 1987), p. 176.
26. McCann, *New Experiment in Democracy*, p. 176.

logically charged than certain versions of public theology issuing from the right and the left and (2) that it is "more faithful to Tocqueville's pioneering insight into the relationship between religion and democracy in America."[27] Nevertheless, I remain skeptical about the public church proposal because of the ways in which shifts along the fault lines indicated by Wuthnow and Hunter have reconfigured religion in America and the roles that it is possible for churches to play in the culture. If Hunter is correct, we are witnessing the end of the symbiotic relationship of biblical faith and society that Tocqueville described.

Herberg accurately identified the public church more than thirty years ago, although he did not use the term then: "America has emerged as a 'three-religion country,' in which the Protestant, the Catholic, and the Jew each finds his place. Insofar as America knows of a church in the Troeltschian sense — a form of religious belonging that goes along with being a member of a national community — it is this tripartite unity of Protestant-Catholic-Jew."[28] Neither Marty nor McCann would argue that this configuration holds as it did when Herberg observed it. Both are acutely aware of the radical pluralism of religion in contemporary America. Denominational affiliations are far less important today than they were when Herberg wrote *Protestant, Catholic, Jew,* for example. As Hunter has pointed out, "Whether one is Protestant, Catholic, or Jew does not mean very much when attempting to explain variations in peoples' attitudes or values. . . . Evidence strongly suggests that the significant divisions on public issues are no longer defined by the distinct traditions of creed, religious observance, or ecclesiastical politics."[29] Herberg had monitored this trend during the 1950s, and he saw that the narrowing of the once-substantial theological and ecclesiastical gaps between Protestants, Catholics, and Jews left room for a common alliance in a communion of communions that fostered the American Way and the American national consensus.

Hunter teaches us a new lesson. He asserts that the impetus toward common alliance and consensus that Herberg described no longer obtains. Instead, the ideological divisions between "progressives" and "orthodox" cuts through the major communions and denominations. This is bad news for the advocates of a renewed public church, because it means that the churches and denominations themselves have become divided houses. On specific issues — abortion, say

27. McCann, *New Experiment in Democracy,* pp. 176-77.
28. Herberg, *Protestant, Catholic, Jew,* p. 258.
29. Hunter, *Culture Wars,* p. 105.

— conservative Catholics, Protestants, and Jews will join forces in opposition to more liberal Catholics, Protestants, and Jews. Marty's and McCann's broad vision of the public church as a "communion of communions," a proximate reality in Herberg's America, looks increasingly remote and unrealistic in the age of the culture wars.

Hunter has shown that the major historic faiths and their denominations have internalized the culture wars. They mirror the conflicted moral vision in American life within themselves and precipitate conflict elsewhere. Indeed, precisely because religious communities cultivate moral sensibilities and convictions, the conflict is often more intense and divisive within their ranks than it is within the public at large. McCann's more modest definition of the public church as "a collective learning process for cultivating the churches' common 'faith in civility'" deals only partially with what Hunter uncovers. It is difficult to see how even a learning process could be common to religious houses as resolutely divided against themselves as those in America today.

But why even argue that cultivating a "faith in civility" is what makes a church public or that it should be the first priority for the churches in America? I am inclined to think that the churches have no more idea than the culture at large about what civility amounts to — beyond some form or other of "liberal" tolerance. Civil society has come to mean a "neutral" society, in which conviction and deeply held beliefs (especially religious beliefs) that make claim to public profession are held in suspicion and viewed as candidates for "deconstruction." Tolerance requires that belief and conviction be removed from public discourse in deference to "personal preferences" and "lifestyles." "Preferences" and "lifestyles" are more acceptable because they are more easily negotiable in a variety of business, familial, artistic, educative, and therapeutic environments.

Marty argues correctly that the contribution that civility makes to the common good is less an offering of the churches than of the Enlightenment spirit, which is itself in eclipse.[30] Frankly, I think that if there were to be a restoration of faith in true civility that respected and left space for belief and conviction, it would be just as likely (if not more likely) to issue from secular sources as from within the religious communities. Certainly, there is no reason to presume that religious people possess the moral insight and means to accomplish such ends whereas nonreligious people do not.

30. Marty, *The Public Church*, p. 132.

Back to Ecclesial Ethics

Everything that I have said thus far leads back to the position that when the churches set themselves to the task of serving the neighbors and strangers among them in public and private worlds, they do more for the general good than when they draw up programs for fostering public theology and a faith in civility. Moral education in virtue, character, and social living has always been at the heart of Christian ethics. But such education must respect not only the limited freedom of the human person but also the unlimited freedom and love of God. I commend Gilbert Meilaender's admonition and prescription:

> Communities that seek simply to remain "open" and that do not inculcate virtuous habits of behavior will utterly fail at the task of moral education. Communities that do not permit the virtues they inculcate to be transcended by the good will ultimately cut themselves off from the very source that inspired their efforts to shape character. In short, the development of true virtue requires both grace and a community dedicated to shaping character; yet those two requirements stand in considerable tension with each other. Perhaps communities that seriously attempt to inculcate virtue while also gathering regularly to confess their failures and await a moment of felicity are the best we can manage.[31]

However much modern "liberal" people are tempted to define virtue as something strictly private, the church as proleptic sign and eschatological vehicle of the kingdom of God knows and experiences virtue's deep and profound public dimensions. And when the church forgets, as it so often has, that its ethic transcends the values and virtues of any particular culture, it jeopardizes not only the salvation of neighbors and strangers but the felicitous outcome of a greater common good. "Wisdom about virtue," Meilaender reminds us, "involves a note of the 'felicitous.' The churches and other communities of virtue do not 'possess a moral superiority' so much as they witness to the gift-like character of the good. In this way they keep themselves open, and help other institutions to be open, to the God who has called them into existence."[32]

---

31. Meilaender, "Virtue in Contemporary Thought," in *Virtue — Public and Private,* ed. Richard John Neuhaus (Grand Rapids: William B. Eerdmans, 1986), p. 29.
32. Meilaender's position is summed up by Richard John Neuhaus in "Exploring Virtue: A Report on a Conversation," in *Virtue — Public and Private,* p. 73.

In *Protestant, Catholic, Jew* Herberg wrote that "the American church has tended to be activist in a way that almost borders on what Pius XII . . . described as the 'heresy of action'" — the notion that "the world can be saved by . . . external activity."[33] If there has ever been a time that the American churches need to take this admonition to heart, it is today. The social-agency model of the church pioneered by mainline Protestantism has been at the source of the dissipation of ecclesial life. H. Richard Niebuhr understood this dynamic and the arriving histori- cal moment when he wrote in 1935 of the final collapse of the Protestant quest for Christianizing America:

> A converted church in a corrupt civilization withdraws to its upper rooms, into monasteries and conventicles; it issues forth from these in the aggressive evangelism of apostles, monks . . . and missionar- ies; . . . it enters into inevitable alliance with the converted emperors and governors, . . . merchants and entrepreneurs, and begins to live at peace in the culture they produce under the stimulus of their faith; when faith loses its force, . . . discipline is relaxed, repentance grows formal, . . . idolatry [and] . . . corruption [follow]. Only a new withdrawal followed by a new aggression can save the church and restore to it salt with which to savor society.[34]

Niebuhr's short narrative of the course of faith and culture would likely draw accusations of sectarianism from some contem- porary critics of comparable analyses and prescriptions made recently by the likes of Stanley Hauerwas and John Howard Yoder, but I believe my argument in Chapter 2 undercuts this criticism. I maintain that the ethics of the church after Christendom must embrace a particular set of behaviors or strategies that cannot rightly be labeled sectarian. I described the first of these strategies as a renewed exercise of the Pau- line style of parenesis — an ethical instruction that is dialogic and ini- tially intraecclesial but that quickly moves toward defining the bound- aries of the ecclesial community and the secular world. This necessarily calls forth moral prescriptions about institutions and conventions that involve both church and society, such as relations between the sexes, marriage and family, law, and obligations to the state. I have argued that this dialogic paradigm should be joined with an iconic understand- ing of the church — that is to say, the church conceived not as a mere

---

33. Herberg, *Protestant, Catholic, Jew*, p. 149.
34. Niebuhr, quoted by Robert T. Handy in *A Christian America* (New York: Oxford University Press, 1971), pp. 211-12.

static model of the good or virtuous community but as a dynamic and attractive enactment, "picturement," and embodiment in belief and act of the human good. Inasmuch as ecclesial life has become dissipated and hence "unattractive," movement toward the dialogic paradigm may have to be "inward" at the outset — but it cannot remain just that and be truly dialogic and iconic.

In his very insightful book *The Company of Strangers*, Parker Palmer points to the power of liturgy in building up the public life — a view that I clearly endorse. In this context, it seems reasonable to return to that claim in order to illustrate how the dialogic and iconic ethic of the church comes about. Palmer laments how worship today "is public only in the sense that anyone may enter the sanctuary on Sunday morning and join with us." He proposes that "the church could help to build a public by worshiping in public places. . . . Public space is available to us. Do we have the imagination to use that space to pronounce the promise of unity and healing of wounds?"[35] He anticipates the objection that such practices in a pluralistic society might offend others. He rightly attributes this objection to "the disastrous conclusion which Americans have drawn from pluralism — that diversity requires religion to retreat into private, to withdraw from the public realm."[36] He argues that precisely the opposite can be true: going out in public with liturgy can be a way of engaging in dialogue with others about the human good and affirming the worth of other traditions and religious communities. Liturgy is a near-perfect example of how the church moves simultaneously inward to strengthen ecclesial life and outward in dialogic and iconic fashion to draw others into its life and communicate its vision of the human good to the society at large. For example, I have argued frequently in Armenian church settings that our rites of the blessing of the fields or the blessing of the water should be performed at toxic waste sites and other environmentally endangered locations — at polluted rivers and lakes — or at our local and national parks. Likewise, the ancient practice of the baptismal processions out of doors should be restored. The joyful, truly public celebration of baptizing persons and welcoming them into the church will have special healing power in a society in which loneliness and alienation afflict so many people.

Of course, the *modus vivendi* of the church in the post-Christendom North American world should not be limited to a renewal

---

35. Palmer, *The Company of Strangers* (New York: Crossroad, 1990), p. 136.
36. Palmer, *The Company of Strangers*, pp. 137-38.

of public liturgical acts. I have not yet addressed the topic of education in this book, but I believe this, too, is an aspect of human culture in which the dialogic life of the church can be powerfully expressed. When American Christians have come to terms with the fact that they really do live in a post-Christendom world, perhaps they will find the freedom to devote their energies to the renewal and founding of Christian schools and colleges in which the trinitarian faith is unapologetically learned and confessed. Perhaps in the face of the pronounced decadence of much of secular education, Christians and Jews will increasingly find the courage and confidence to affirm and explore how serious, cosmopolitan intellectual training is possible within a confessional environment.[37]

Conclusion

In preceding chapters I have referred to St. Augustine and St. John Chrysostom as exemplars of a Christian ethics for our time. Both stood at the historic juncture between the early Christian church and medieval Christendom. While both were conversant with classical culture and engaged society through their ecclesial vocations, neither gave much thought to committing the church to a consuming role as transmitter and translator of moral values for the whole of society. Instead, Augustine and Chrysostom championed a *particular* way of life that they felt was best exemplified by monasticism built on the model of the apostolic church. Thus their understanding of reform and social transformation was at once more dialogic and iconic (ecclesially centered) and less instrumental and ideological (society centered) than the understanding of many of today's advocates of either a public theology or a public church.

Today, a more agnostic attitude toward the culture is called for, along with a recommitment to faithful pilgrimage and redemptive mission. The churches must "let go" culturally. This is not to say that Christians should withdraw from public life. To the contrary, it is part of their calling to bring their Christian convictions into play in society. Nor do I have difficulty with Christians speaking selectively for or

---

37. For a probing analysis of the historic role the churches played in American education as well as the reasons for the expulsion of religion from contemporary education and the ways in which the liberal mainline churches ironically contributed to it, see George M. Marsden, *The Soul of the American University* (New York: Oxford University Press, 1994).

against specific public policies in the language of the culture. I have found this to be necessary and fruitful when addressing the issue of genocide, for example. But Christians must keep clear in their own minds the difference between the culture's language and their primary language, between Christian ethics and the secular ethics around them. Christians may properly make selective use of the culture's idiom, such as the rhetoric of human rights and the sanctity of life, as they enter into debate in the public square, but in doing so they should be aware of the secular connotations of this rhetoric (e.g., the way in which such principles as self-autonomy underlie the secular understanding of human rights and freedom), and they must repudiate these presuppositions of secular liberal ethics. There will be moments in public and political debate when Christians feel that they must affirm the christic and trinitarian basis of their own understanding of human freedom and flourishing. These kerygmatic moments are bound to make Christians look countercultural and provoke the criticism of secular antagonists.

My principal point here is that in the present situation, the churches are being called not to new projects of culture formation but to habits of virtuous living. The churches need to think of themselves less as agents and lobbyists for social change and more as exemplars and catalysts of human flourishing. The culture wars tell us that we are entering a time that is not only about redefining America but also about rejoining the struggle to determine what it means to be church in America. Wuthnow speaks of the struggle for America's soul, but we are also engaged in a struggle for the soul of the church.

5. Church and Armenian Nationhood: A Bonhoefferian Reflection on the National Church

As we close out the twentieth century, the cultural contexts in which the churches pursue their mission are in most places and in most respects quite different from what held at the beginning of the century. A hundred years ago, the American Protestant churches were buoyant with the hope and expectation that the complete Christianization of the nation was within reach. Instead, as we have seen, Christendom has passed from the scene. However the American churches may feel about this new situation, its reality is inescapable, and they will have to learn new ways to relate to the culture and witness to God and Jesus Christ.

Few theologians of this century understood better than Dietrich Bonhoeffer what it means for the Christian churches to face a post-Christendom world. Bonhoeffer said that we live in a "world-come-of-age." His criticism of the churches in this new context seems ever more prescient. Bonhoeffer saw that large numbers of people living in the nations that had made up Christendom no longer experienced God in the old religious sense. Throughout his life he assessed with devastating trenchancy the new situation of the European churches, especially those of a national and establishmentarian character. He concluded that they were becoming fossils in a changed world, failing to bring the gospel to modern people.

But Bonhoeffer also believed that the passing of Christendom presented the churches with a special opportunity. It was giving them a chance to lay hold of their birthright, the true freedom that had been compromised through the long history of Christendom (both Roman Catholic and Protestant). The collaboration of the German national church with Nazism came as no real surprise to Bonhoeffer, but it did constitute devastating proof of where the conservative and accommo-

102

dationist proclivities of this historic type of church could lead. In the face of this, Bonhoeffer stressed that the church cannot attain true freedom by sacralizing the temporal order, nor can it extract this freedom as a privilege from the state. Moreover, the true freedom of the church does not consist of exemption from state interference, as Anglo-American Christianity thought. "The freedom of the church is not where it has possibilities," he wrote, "but only where the Gospel really and in its own power makes room for itself on earth, even and precisely when no such possibilities are offered to it."[1]

Six months before his death, as he was losing hope for release from a Nazi prison, Bonhoeffer wrote a sermon for the occasion of the baptism of his infant nephew and namesake Dietrich Wilhelm Rudiger Bethge. In it he spoke as if he were anticipating the possibility of what really happened after the war. He hoped and expected that the German "church, which has been fighting in these years only for its self-preservation, as though that were an end in itself," would change greatly by the time his nephew were grown up. He warned, however, that much still needed to be done. "Any attempt to help the church prematurely to a new expansion of its organization will merely delay its conversion and purification."[2] It has been said that Dietrich Bonhoeffer's death was the greatest tragedy to befall the German church, for it meant he could not be there to guide it when, immediately following the war, his worst fears came to pass and the Western allies and conservative forces within Germany used the national church structure once again to service the German state. Church leaders rushed "to secure again their privileges in the shell of the same old state church."[3]

Similarly, today the churches of formerly Soviet lands enter the world scene with a propensity and drive to reclaim lost privilege and power, and new national governments find advantage in such concordats also. Church leaders show little understanding of the challenges that the post-Christendom environment poses for the historic faith and ecclesial polity. Tragedies for Christian existence threaten as these churches grope their way toward freedom. Soviet imperialism re-

1. Bonhoeffer, "Protestantism without Reformation," in *No Rusty Swords: Letters, Lectures and Notes, 1928-1936*, vol. 1 of *The Collected Works of Dietrich Bonhoeffer*, ed. Edwin H. Robertson (New York: Harper & Row, 1965), p. 104.

2. Bonhoeffer, *Letters and Papers from Prison* (New York: Macmillan, 1972), p. 300.

3. Thomas I. Day, "Conviviality and Common Sense: The Meaning of Christian Community for Dietrich Bonhoeffer," in *A Bonhoeffer Legacy: Essays in Understanding*, ed. A. J. Klassen (Grand Rapids: William B. Eerdmans, 1981), p. 229.

strained tendencies to preserve pointedly nationalistic ecclesial identities at the same time it shielded them from religious and secular pluralism. The net result was that for as much as seventy-five years, many of these churches, frozen in medieval establishmentarian attitudes, stood as the sole symbol of national pride and identity in their country. As events unfold, Bonhoeffer's analysis and criticism of national churches promises to shed crucial light on the church-state situation in Eastern Europe, Russia, and the Caucasus.

The circumstances in these parts of the world belong to the larger picture of the end of Christendom. Although America figures in the larger post-Christendom ecclesial context, the American situation is virtually sui generis. The national churches and states of Eastern Europe and the former Soviet Union have little if any firsthand experience of the religious pluralism and denominationalism that have so characterized America. The historical evolution of American Christianity lends at the very least a certain plausibility or even an axiomatic flavor to the early constitutional arrangements for separation of church and state and the later distinction in the American mind between denominational religious affiliation and national identity. The histories of the churches of Russia, the Ukraine, Serbia, and Armenia differ from one another enormously in many respects, but with respect to beliefs about church and nationhood and church and state they are much more similar to one another than they are to the history of the American churches. Church, history, peoplehood, and culture are tightly interwoven in these countries, and hence resistant to the corrosive effects of Western formalistic categories of religious freedom, pluralism, civil liberty, and toleration. Like the American churches, these Eastern churches face challenges that test their integrity and faithfulness to the gospel, but these challenges arise out of circumstances largely alien to the Western consciousness. In this chapter, I want to focus on the modern history of the Armenian Church as a case study of this Eastern phenomenon in an attempt to broaden the American perspective on the crisis of faith and ecclesial life that has been introduced by the advent of the post-Christendom era.

I need at the outset to qualify my assertion of Bonhoeffer's helpfulness on this score. His comparison of European religious history and the American context took into account that portion of Europe strongly and permanently affected by the Reformation and Enlightenment, but he did not concern himself much with Eastern Europe or Russia, where Orthodox Christianity, the legacy of Byzantium, and the Russian model of the theocratic state had a lasting influence into this century. Nevertheless, he does have some valuable insights to offer concerning the overall phenomenon of modern national churches, and I will return to his analysis shortly, after a brief survey of the contemporary situation in Armenia.

Old Habits, New Realities

In the late 1970s, during the bleak and repressive twilight of the Brezhnev era, the religious dissident Michael Meerson-Aksenov contributed a powerful piece of samizdat literature analyzing the character of the national churches under Soviet domination. Strikingly reminiscent of Bonhoeffer's writings on the national church, Meerson-Aksenov's essay sounded a note of admonition and hope for the post-Soviet life of the church:

> A local national Church, torn away from other Churches and therefore from any ecumenical position, cannot be free. Depending on how much authority it has and on internal political conditions it can conclude more or less advantageous concordats with the State and can even transform the social order into a theocracy, but all this is a far cry from real freedom. . . .
>
> A national Church must inevitably share the fundamental political views of its government and place the objectives of the State's foreign policy above the interests of love among the churches. . . .
>
> Only the Ecumenical Church can be free [because it is] transnational, is spread everywhere, and no strictly homogeneously organized society has enough power to fully subordinate it.[4]

Meerson-Aksenov insisted that the church needed a new vision of itself to supplant the forms of a bygone sacral order. Though the communist societies had followed a different path than Western societies, they too had permanently altered the future of the Christian faith. He argued that when the system of official atheism was finally lifted, the church would be forced to come to terms with a new secular, pluralistic order filled with people of a variety of religious and nonreligious persuasions. "The Russian Church, . . . [which had] inherited

---

4. Meerson-Aksenov, "The People of God and the Pastors," in *The Political, Social and Religious Thought of Russian "Samizdat" — An Anthology,* ed. Michael Meerson-Aksenov and Boris Shragin (Belmont, Mass.: Nordland, 1977), pp. 524-25.

the caste consciousness of the clergy and the inert psychology of a dependent State establishment," would be tested in its ability to preach the gospel and serve people in new and unfamiliar ways.[5] "The fifteen hundred year era of the Christian empire has come to an end," declared Meerson-Aksenov, "and former Christian societies everywhere are hurrying to remove their priestly vestments. The Christian no longer lives in an environment of co-religionists."[6] Ultimately, even in what had once been Holy Russia, the world of the old national and establishmentarian church would pass. But would the church recognize this, admit it, and respond appropriately?

In the initial phases of the transition from Soviet to free societies, the national churches have followed form in their efforts to reclaim old power and influence. The Armenian Church is illustrative of this behavior. Even as a new, autonomous, secular, and more pluralistic society is emerging, the Church continues to claim that Armenia is a Christian nation (a Christendom) of which it is mother and guardian. Every seven years at the historic center of the Armenian Church, the See of Holy Etchmiadzin, the Holy Chrism is consecrated and distributed to churches everywhere for the sacramental rituals. September 1991 was the occasion for such a blessing. As is customary, His Holiness Vazken I, Catholicos of All Armenians, presided. The event coincided with the extraordinary moment of Armenia's newly gained independence. As one might expect, the patriarch's sermon referred to that event, but it also went much further. Vazken I inaugurated a new civil religion in which the Church's role loomed large and unchanged from the pre-Soviet past. No longer restrained by Soviet dogma and threat, Vazken I asserted that the Church would stand at the very center of the nation's process of rebuilding. He asked the government to grant the Armenian Church de jure status as the established national church. "Today, it is only just to acknowledge the Armenian Church as the proto-witness, the forerunner, of our national independence."[7]

The patriarch carefully made his appeal in the context of a powerful rhetorical rehearsal of the Armenian Church's historic struggle against absorption by the Byzantines and others — the "history of the Armenian Church . . . [in] heroic battle against the expansionist desires of foreign churches." Now this protector of the "souls

---

5. Meerson-Aksenov, "The People of God and the Pastors," p. 525.
6. Meerson-Aksenov, "The People of God and the Pastors," p. 534.
7. Vazken I, "One Free Nation, Free Government, Free National Church," *Window: View on the Armenian Church* 2, no. 3 (1991): 30.

of the Armenian people" was under siege of "proselytizing ('man hunting') . . . churches [which have entered] the bosom of our nation," he exclaimed. That being the case, he argued that "after the proclamation of our independent republic, it is crucial to secure the spiritual independence of the Armenian Church, as the sole authentic church of the Armenian people, free from foreign religious centers. . . . One of the foundations of our new independent government is the freedom and self-determination of the Armenian Church."[8] The patriarch's dramatic remarks betrayed a forgetfulness of what constitutes the true freedom of the church. He defined this freedom as a grant of the state.

On the ideological plane, Vazken I's civil theology leaves few resources to distinguish the freedom of the church from the *raison d'être* of the national state. The patriarch's sermon for the blessing of the Holy Chrism concluded with a peroration in which he drew together all the strong symbols of Armenian Church, nation, and peoplehood:

> One of the foundations of our new independent government is the freedom and self-determination of the Armenian Church.
>
> We profess the Creed: one free nation, one free government, one free national Church.
>
> With this creed, with this understanding, we proclaim this holy chrism, which has been blessed by the power of the Holy Spirit, as the *"Chrism of Independence."*
>
> Armenians, our spiritual children, with this Holy Chrism, unite! Be brothers! Become one will! One happiness! One suffering! One nation! One family! One strong oath! And beneath their eternal sight of biblical Ararat, with the blessings of Holy Etchmiadzin, believe in this one patch of Armenian soil and its future.[9]

The patriarch thus wove strands of the Armenian "sacred history" and the belief in Armenia as a specially chosen people of God into the warp of the Armenian struggle for national independence. This peroration built on remarks made earlier in the sermon reminding the listeners of St. Gregory the Illuminator, who, "with his miraculous works, achieved the conversion and baptism of the Armenian King Dirtad." It was according to the vision of St. Gregory that the Armenian Church and the cathedral of Holy Etchmiadzin were established where "the only

---

8. Vazken I, "One Free Nation, Free Government, Free National Church," p. 31.

9. Vazken I, "One Free Nation, Free Government, Free National Church," p. 31; italics mine.

begotten Son of God descended." The patriarch asserted that this revelation and act of founding forever mixed "the spirit of the Armenian nation . . . with Christ's Gospel. . . . The Armenian people was transfigured and became a creative nation. . . . History is witness to the fact that through Christianity the Armenian nation became a universal phenomenon."[10] This rhetoric gives the illusion of universalism while, in fact, it draws near to national idolatry.[11]

Since Vazken I's sermon, the new government has bestowed on the Armenian Church legal status as the sole church in Armenia; all other denominations are designated religious "communities" and are explicitly prohibited from proselytizing. The Roman Catholics and Baptists have long been present in Soviet Armenia. More recently, Jehovah's Witnesses, Mormons, Seventh Day Adventists, and Pentecostals have been extremely active. In an interview granted during the fall of 1991, the Armenian Minister of Religious Affairs Ludwig Khachadrian echoed the Catholicos's rationale for the Armenian Church's privileged position: "Considering the persecution of the Armenian Church . . . we have created special opportunities for the Armenian Church and have given certain privileges, so that the Church may recover what she lost." Khachadrian did not see a contradiction when he also insisted that "there is no difference between the Armenian Church and other churches or religious groups, because the legal system that we have adopted assumes that everybody is free to choose his religion or faith and is free to practice his religion."[12]

Khachadrian's comments echo the new *Law of Armenia on Freedom of Conscience and Religious Organizations* promulgated in June of 1991. This document contains the same logical contradictions as Khachadrian's statements. The preamble declares "the Armenian Apostolic Church as the national church of the Armenian people and an important

10. Vazken I, "One Free Nation, Free Government, Free National Church," p. 30.

11. For most of this century, Armenians everywhere have listened to incessant preaching of this kind from hierarchs and clergy. They are told, in effect, that the Armenian Church belongs to the Armenian people and *is* in some mystical sense the nation. As John W. de Gruchy has rightly concluded regarding Afrikaner religious nationalism, "There is nothing wrong with the idea of a church for the people, but a major problem arises when 'the people' is confined to a particular race, class, or *volk*, . . . for then the church denies not only its universal or catholic identity, but also the gospel" (*Liberating Reformed Theology: A South African Contribution to an Ecumenical Debate* [Grand Rapids: William B. Eerdmans, 1991], pp. 24-25).

12. "Church and State in Armenia: An Interview with Ludwig Khachadrian," *Window: View on the Armenian Church* 2, no. 3 (1991): 4.

stronghold of its spiritual life and the preservation of the nation." Later under Article 7 of Section 6, "Relations between Religious Organizations and the State," it says, "In the Republic of Armenia the church is separate from the state." The document proceeds to list several senses in which this is the case with respect to powers and limitations that apply to church and state respectively. But the *Law* seems to want it both ways, both separation and establishment. The same article goes on to state that "the Armenian Apostolic Church [is] the national Church of the Armenians, which also operates outside the Republic, [and] shall enjoy the protection of the Republic of Armenia." Part 1, "General Principles," guarantees the "freedom of conscience and religion" of the Armenian citizenry. However, Article 8 of Part 3, "The Rights of Religious Organizations," states that "proselytism [literally, "soul stealing"] is prohibited on the territory of Armenia." The term is not defined any further, although the article goes on to say that "no action within the limits of the rights indicated in Article 7 . . . may be regarded as proselytizing." The most significant of these rights are the freedom to conduct religious services in a variety of places, freedom to provide religious education for members, freedom to train clergy, and freedom to use the media within the bounds of established law. The term *proselytism* has a distinctly negative connotation in Armenia. It is associated with religious antagonists bent on stealing Armenians from the mother church. Section 4 under Article 7 would seem to ensure the freedom to evangelize — as that term is understood in Western democracies. But, without explanation, the *Law* does make a distinction between evangelism and proselytism. Matters are further confused when, under Part 6, the *Law* speaks of "missions which are the privilege of the national church." Among the special rights granted to the Armenian Church is permission "to freely confess and spread its belief throughout the territory of the Republic of Armenia," "to build new churches," and "to contribute in practice to the moral standards of the Armenian people."[13]

Even with all its contradictions and lack of clarity, *The Law on Freedom of Conscience and Religious Organization* leaves one distinct impression: the Armenian Church has a special legal and moral status in Armenia. The reasons why the new Armenian democratic government is willing to oblige the Church's pleas for special favor range from the strong residual existence of an establishmentarian mentality among

13. Foreign Broadcasting Information Service, "Armenia" (USR-91-016), 23 July 1991, pp. 14-16.

even nonreligious people in Armenia to the more pragmatic political calculation that the Church remains for the time being a unifying symbol for the nation.

At this moment in history, the Armenian people need something other than the nationalistic and quasi-established church of the present. The same can be said of other people and national entities in Eastern Europe and the former Soviet Union. As the Soviet empire collapses, nationalism is on the rise, threatening in the Balkans and the Caucasus to break out into general warfare. It is a time of great peril for the people of Armenia in particular, because of the bloody dispute with Azerbaijan over the Armenian enclave of Nagorno-Karabagh. When the Armenian Church identifies itself so closely with the new nation-state, it also jeopardizes other great services it could render for the Armenian people as an agent of national healing and a voice of restraint concerning a nationalism that is threatening to consume goodwill and unleash frenzied horrors against historic enemies.[14]

The Enduring Message of Dietrich Bonhoeffer concerning the National Church

Dietrich Bonhoeffer began to envision a new relation of church and nation already in his doctoral dissertation, *Sanctorum Communio* (1927), in which he struck a keynote for all he had to say through changing

14. Repeatedly in my conversations with average citizens during visits to Armenia in 1990 and 1991, I was told that it is all right for an Armenian to be a Christian up to a point, but it is impossible for an Armenian to take to heart the command to turn the other cheek or forgive one's enemy. There is a deep aversion to the heart of the Christian gospel among Armenians, and the Armenian Church has not had the courage to face that aversion, preach the gospel, and exorcise the demons of national idolatry.

The gospel planted in Armenia by Gregory the Illuminator inevitably pulls humankind toward a peaceable kingdom in which the use of power is morally wrong. Meanwhile, a relentless history of victimization has been persuading Armenians that their survival depends on the appropriation and use of such power. The antinomy between gospel and history knows no earthly resolution. But it is the inescapable duty of the church to strive to live that tension under the discipline of Christian love and humility.

As I write this in the spring of 1994, there is news that an agreement is in the making for a peaceful resolution of the conflict over Nagorno-Karabagh. It remains to be seen whether such a peace will come about sooner than later. After such a peace, the role of the Church would be no less important. Still it will need to choose between the old habits of serving nationalism or presenting Armenians with a lively message of the gospel.

times. "There is a moment," the young theologian declared, "when the church dare not continue to be a national church, and this moment has come when the national church can no longer see how it can win though it be a gathered church . . . , but on the contrary is moving into complete petrification and emptiness in the use of its forms, with evil effects on the living members as well."[15]

Drawing on Ernst Troeltsch's typological analysis of the churchly and sectarian varieties of ecclesial formation, Bonhoeffer distinguished between a "gathered church," which derives its unity from voluntary association, and a *Volkskirche* (national church), which derives its unity almost exclusively from the binding forces of kinship and common national history. Bonhoeffer valued the cohesive organic and historic qualities of the national church. He wrote that the national church "possesses greater firmness and lasting power than the voluntary association. It is a divine grace that we have a church which is deeply rooted in the history of the nation, which makes the divine will for us, given through the power of the church's historicity, relatively independent of the momentary situation."[16]

Yet Bonhoeffer also judged that the German national church was not responding adequately to the new conditions of secular modernity. In characteristic fashion, he set the matter in dialectical terms: "We can affirm that the national church and the gathered [voluntary and evangelical] church belong together." But he found it "all too obvious . . . that a national church which is not continually pressing forward to be a confessing church is in the greatest of peril."[17] He found confirmation of these suspicions and admonitions in the disappointing conservatism of the German national church and the acquiescence of the German Christian (Deutsche Christen) movement to the Nazi program. The national church proved incapable of distinguishing the confession of Jesus Christ from even the most excessive forms of nationalism and chauvinism. In *The Cost of Discipleship* (1937) Bonhoeffer lamented, "We Lutherans have gathered like eagles round the carcase of cheap grace, and there we have drunk of the poison which has killed the life of following Christ." The church had clung to all the right doctrines through the centuries, but nonetheless "a nation became Christian and

---

15. Bonhoeffer, *The Communion of Saints: A Dogmatic Inquiry into the Sociology of the Church* (New York: Harper & Row, 1964), pp. 189-90. This text is a translation of the third edition of the German original.

16. Bonhoeffer, *The Communion of Saints*, pp. 187-88.

17. Bonhoeffer, *The Communion of Saints*, p. 189.

Lutheran . . . at the cost of true discipleship. The price it was called upon to pay was all too cheap. Cheap grace had won the day."[18]

Bonhoeffer's later statements on the confessing church, "religionless Christianity," and a "world-come-of-age" are largely consistent with his early views on the relative weaknesses and strengths of a national church. At the close of his discussion of the national church in *Sanctorum Communio*, Bonhoeffer indicated that the time had in fact come for the church to define a new *modus vivendi* for itself, involving a renewal of prayer and worship and mission in the world.[19] During the 1930s, he watched the rise of threatening nationalisms. He became convinced that the German national church could not remain the kind of church it had been and be faithful to the gospel of Jesus Christ. In 1935 Bonhoeffer warned that "under the onslaught of new nationalism, the fact that the church of Christ does not stop at national and racial boundaries but reaches beyond them, so powerfully attested in the New Testament and in the confessional writings, has far too easily been forgotten and denied."[20]

A decade after his reflections on the national church in *Sanctorum Communio*, Bonhoeffer explored the origins of modern nationalism in his *Ethics*. This analysis bridges the gap between his early work and his loose and incomplete discussion of religionless Christianity and a world-come-of-age in the *Letters and Papers from Prison*. In it, he describes the French Revolution as the "birth of modern nationalism. Whatever national consciousness existed earlier was essentially dynastic in character. . . . The revolutionary concept of the nation arose in opposition to an exaggerated dynastic absolutism."[21]

Bonhoeffer's thinking about nation and church drew increasingly on the conviction that Christendom had indeed been shattered ideologically and geopolitically in the eighteenth and nineteenth centuries. The process began in the Renaissance and Reformation but took on fully modern characteristics only with the Enlightenment and the French Revolution. "The people deemed that they had come of age, that they were now capable of taking in hand the direction of their internal and external history."[22] No longer did they need or want

---

18. Bonhoeffer, *The Cost of Discipleship*, rev. ed. (New York: Macmillan, 1963), pp. 57-58.

19. Bonhoeffer, *The Communion of Saints*, p. 190.

20. Bonhoeffer, "The Confessing Church and the Ecumenical Movement," in *No Rusty Swords*, p. 326.

21. Bonhoeffer, *Ethics* (New York: Macmillan, 1965), p. 100.

22. Bonhoeffer, *Ethics*, p. 100.

peoplehood and government to be defined under the sacred canopy of Christendom. In the nineteenth century, radical voices of anticlericalism and atheism arose in angry protest against Christendom. The vision of a unified Christendom was challenged and hence empirically shattered, although fragments of the original whole survived within national cultures in various political and ecclesial institutions.

In the twentieth century, Nazism and Communism were symptoms of as well as contributing factors to the breakup and final collapse of Christendom. These outbursts of radical politics and totalitarianism had gestated within national environments that fostered both traditional religious forms and virulent anti-Christian forces. "Since the French Revolution," observed Bonhoeffer, "the west has come to be essentially hostile to the Church. . . . Yet the Churches lose remarkably few of their members, and this points to an important fact, namely the ambiguous character of the hostility to the Church."[23] As they entered the twentieth century, most Europeans remained under the sway of various forms of Christian pietism and religious introversion on the one hand and religious, sometimes highly aggressive nationalisms on the other hand. Those who continued to identify with the church often found comfort in corrupted and already anachronistic "religious" conceptions of sacral nationhood. Bonhoeffer called this "godlessness in religious and Christian clothing."[24] Yet for a time this late corruption of Christian existence continued to provide symbols of legitimation for legal establishments of national churches in Europe.

Bonhoeffer believed that the breakup of Christendom everywhere constituted a serious loss and a bad omen. "By the loss of the unity which is possessed through the form of Jesus Christ, the western world is brought to the brink of the void. The forces unleashed exhaust their fury in mutual destruction."[25] Modern nationalism and atheistic ideologies began to take over the unifying role that Christendom had once played, but they did so without satisfactorily acknowledging the transcendent destiny of humanity or the rights and responsibilities that we owe one another as human beings. In the face of this "void made god,"[26] Bonhoeffer tried to envision what new worldly "formations" of faith in Jesus Christ might look like. He began this work in the *Ethics;* he rejoined the task in *Letters and Papers from Prison.*

23. Bonhoeffer, *Ethics,* p. 103. Since Bonhoeffer wrote these words, the European churches have lost huge numbers of communicants.
24. Bonhoeffer, *Ethics,* p. 103.
25. Bonhoeffer, *Ethics,* p. 105.
26. Bonhoeffer, *Ethics,* p. 106.

While the project was never completed, *Letters and Papers* does give us some hints of where Bonhoeffer was heading. He called the new formations of Christian faith a "religionless Christianity," by which he meant faith in Jesus Christ stripped of the religious culture that faith had once inspired. This religious culture had prospered for a millennium as Christendom, fragmented with the birth of modernity, and then persisted for a much shorter time in so-called "Christian" nations. National churches fashioned garments for themselves as best they could out of the remaining fabric of Christendom. Modern nationalisms, meanwhile, often used the loose religious concepts of a fragmented and eviscerated Christendom to promote their own ends. Increasingly, nationalist ideology pushed lingering religious categories of transcendence and spirituality into the recesses of private life or replaced them outright with immanentistic and vitalistic categories of ethnic identity, racial purity, and national destiny.

In this analysis, Bonhoeffer obviously pays more attention to the negative characteristics of national churches, noting their tendencies to make compromises to secular ideology and to abandon the evangelical faith and an ecumenical vision of the church. He still prizes their qualities of organic kinship, common history, and respect for tradition, but he also notes that these features can fuel reactionary forces within church and nation. Because of its very nature and history, the national church finds it difficult to forge a new mode of ecclesial existence. When the socio-political situation changes, the national church naturally resists the conclusion that the community it once sanctified no longer exists. It has much to lose in privilege and influence if the new circumstances are acknowledged. Motivated by a deep desire to ensure its own survival, the threatened national church will be inclined to embrace nationalistic stirrings to preserve the loyalty of its people. It will be tempted to try to retain its privileges through ever more explicit and insistent identification of church with ethnos and nation.

The rise of Nazism in which all these trends seemed to culminate moved Bonhoeffer toward a broader definition of church and an intense examination of the meaning of the freedom of the church, its being and boundaries. As Larry Rasmussen has pointed out, Bonhoeffer experienced the 1930s as years in which "the tensions of being Christian and being German drew taut."[27] When Bonhoeffer decided to leave the United States in 1939 and return to Germany, he was consciously com-

---

27. Rasmussen, *Dietrich Bonhoeffer: His Significance for North Americans* (Minneapolis: Fortress Press, 1990), p. 36.

mitting himself to the particularity of Christian existence as a citizen of the German nation. He elected to enter the church struggle in Germany and try to secure the integrity of the confessing church, which was seeking to resist "both the Aryanizing of the church and the totalitarian claims" of the Nazis.[28] Ultimately, involvement in this struggle for the integrity of the German church took precedence over Bonhoeffer's ecumenical activities, but those activities did provide him with a perspective from which to reevaluate the relationships among faith, nationality, and the people of God. While Bonhoeffer never wholly abandoned the concept of a national church, in the end he did sharply condemn the heresy to which all modern national churches have been prone — namely, the subordination of the ultimate communion of all the faithful in Christ to the penultimate reality of national identity.

The Course of Armenian Christendom and the Origins of the National Church

The sources of the national character of the Armenian Church run as deep and far back as perhaps those of any church. Its history includes a divorce in the sixth century from Greek Christianity over the christological issue. For centuries afterward, the vastly larger and more powerful Byzantine Christendom posed a threat to the Armenian Church. Its isolation and vulnerability were intensified by the Arab-Muslim invasions of the seventh century. Other churches were similarly estranged — the Syrian and Coptic, for example. Five centuries of Ottoman domination completed the transformation of these churches into ethnic and national churches. The Armenian patriarch Karekin II, Catholicos of Cilicia, has summarized this long history:

> A decisive turning-point in the whole history of the Eastern churches, and more specifically in the realm of church-nation relationship, was the Arab-Muslim invasion of the seventh century, which had a strong impact on the development of their national character. . . . The conquerors allowed [the churches] to exist as separate entities within the Muslim world. . . . [They] were given internal independence, an autonomous status, on the basis of . . . religion. . . . The Christian people themselves, after the loss of their political independence or after their emancipation from Byzantine

28. Rasmussen, *Dietrich Bonhoeffer*, p. 36.

rule, regarded the church as the only expression of their national heritage. So they clung to it, and recognized its head as the leader of the nation. Thus, "the national churches found themselves transformed into some kind of ecclesiastical states, where bishops wielded political as well as religious authority, and whose patriarchs blossomed into the political leaders of their flocks, naturally under the supremacy of the Khalifs."[29]

After the fall of Constantinople in 1453, the new Ottoman rulers recognized "two Patriarchates, the Greek and the Armenian, as the centres of the Chalcedonian and non-Chalcedonian Eastern churches, with full authority over their peoples in everything but political action."[30] This did not really constitute a fundamental change for the churches. The Greek Church had previously maintained a partnership with the Byzantine state, and the Armenian, Syrian, and Egyptian churches had formed similar "small" Christendoms. The antinomy of church and world, necessary for both the good of the church and the good of the world, had lost its sharpness some time before. The churches can be said to have ceded additional freedom to the Ottoman rulers, however, in the degree to which the people extended their identification of church with ethnos, turning inward as part of a deepening survival mentality, and thereby diminishing their sense of mission to the larger world.

This basic situation has continued in these churches through the modern period, albeit with some important twists and turns along the way. The European Enlightenment, the French Revolution, and liberal, romantic, and nationalist movements of the nineteenth century caught the imagination of Greeks, Bulgarians, Armenians, and others, and the churches naturally felt the effects. It was especially during the nineteenth century that two contradictory forces developed within these national and church bodies: a traditional folk religion and a very conservative national church shared the same space with virulent anticlerical and antireligious movements. Newly emerging secular intelligentsia and political parties competed with the church for the soul of the nation. At stake was the title to the authentic voice for national aspirations. The story of this struggle is conspicuously absent from the narratives of contemporary church apologists. In an effort to justify a

---

29. Karekin II, *In Search of Spiritual Life* (Antelias, Lebanon: N.p., 1991), pp. 256-58.

30. Karekin II, *In Search of Spiritual Life*, p. 257.

continued intimate association of church and nation, most of the church leadership converts history to myth.

The whole of the history of the Armenian Church cannot be told here, but at least a few elements that influence the Church's self-understanding need to be mentioned. Briefly, then, while the Ottoman millet system that placed civil functions in the hands of religious leaders persisted into the nineteenth century, it was increasingly challenged by rising nationalisms within the various ethnic communities. This led to the final unraveling of the Ottoman Empire itself. Early in the nineteenth century, Greece became independent. Then the Balkan nations broke away, rendering the Empire the "Sick Man of Europe." By mid-century, nationalist fever was running high among the Amenians as well. Because the vast majority of Armenians were situated right in the heart of Asia Minor, however, independence was virtually impossible. Given the geopolitical realities, the Armenians tempered dreams of national renaissance and focused on reforms that would brings greater freedoms short of complete autonomy.

This nationalism had a distinctly secular cast. It was not officially sanctioned by the Armenian Church, and most of those who championed it were inclined to look less than favorably on the Church. They envied its power or openly criticized its conservatism. The new Armenian bourgeois class became discontented with the millet system, which placed virtually all community power in the hands of a feudalistic church. This helps explain why anticlerical and atheist European influences found fertile soil in the Armenian intelligentsia and the first Armenian political parties. These groups viewed the Armenian patriarch's close association with the Ottoman power structure as a source of corruption thwarting the best interests of the Armenian populace.

An opportunity to change the arrangement arose in the 1850s. Weakened by the Crimean War, Sultan Abdul Medjid agreed to reform initiatives including general provisions to create assemblies made up of both clergy and laity among the minority communities. Thus, in 1863 the Ottoman Sublime Porte ratified a new Armenian National Constitution that forever altered the structure of power within the Armenian community, splitting it between the patriarch and the National Assembly. This lent impetus to powerful secular nationalist stirrings among the intelligentsia and the rise of autonomous political parties. However one judges the degree of corruption or conservatism within the Armenian Church at the time, it is beyond dispute that the Church was not solely or even primarily responsible for early Armenian nationalism.

Many important Armenians of the mid-nineteenth century saw

the work of national renewal as a secular and political task for which
the Church was ill suited. These nationalists blamed the Armenian
Church for the woes that had befallen the nation. They charged that
the Church taught the people passivity and pacifism in the face of
threats to national survival. The most influential Armenian novelist of
this period, Raffi (Hakob Melik-Hakobian, 1833-1888), placed in his
novel *Jellaledin* a famous toast typifying the anticlericalism of the time:

> O fathers! O fore-fathers! I drink this glass, but not as toast to your
> remains. Had you built fortresses, instead of monasteries with which
> our country is full; had you guns and ammunition, instead of
> squandering fortunes on Holy urns; had you burned gunpowder
> instead of perfumery incense at the Holy altars, our country would
> have been more fortunate. . . . From these very monasteries the
> doom of our country was sealed.[31]

Echoing Raffi, Grigor Artsouni, an Armenian nationalist and political
writer, proclaimed, "Yesterday we were an ecclesiastical community;
tomorrow we shall be a nation of workers and thinkers."[32]

In her classic study *The Armenian Revolutionary Movement*, Louise
Nalbandian observes that this anticlericalism ran to extremes in the
1860s, on the heels of the formulation of the new Constitution. During
that time, "the Armenian Church was under constant attack."[33] But in
the last two decades of the century, intellectuals and political leaders
began to change their minds about the Church, realizing that inasmuch
as it was a focal point of Armenian life, it could be made to serve as an
instrument for political change. Those holding otherwise radical political views now "looked with disfavor" on the "idea of reform" within
the Church.[34] It already served their purposes by conserving and
cementing ethnic identity, and they felt sufficiently secure with their
position to permit the Church to go on thinking it was at the center of
Armenian life, even if that was no longer the case. For its part, the
Church felt no need to oppose outright the new intellectual and political
leadership. The Church that had been weakened began to employ

---

31. Raffi, quoted by Sarkis Atamian in *The Armenian Community* (New York:
Philosophical Library, 1955), p. 79.

32. Artsouni, quoted by Leonardo P. Alishan in "Crucifixion without 'The
Cross': The Impact of the Genocide on Armenian Literature," *Armenian Review* 38
(Spring 1985): 33.

33. Nalbandian, *The Armenian Revolutionary Movement* (Berkeley and Los
Angeles: University of California Press, 1963), p. 57.

34. Nalbandian, *The Armenian Revolutionary Movement*, p. 57.

nationalism to strengthen its own standing among the people. And so, with a few notable exceptions, church leaders committed themselves wholly to the role of protector of national identity.[35]

As it entered the twentieth century, the Armenian Church generally embraced, often enthusiastically, this role of safeguarding Armenian identity prescribed by secular Armenian nationalism. The history of this coalescence of religion and nationalism and the submission and compromise of the Church to nationalist movements has not been evaluated critically by Armenian church historians and theologians. Instead, in the face of genocide,[36] a worldwide Armenian diaspora, and the Soviet subjugation of the last remnants of the historic homeland, the Armenian Church has expended its energies in rationalizing its behavior.

Archbishop Tiran Nersoyan: An Armenian Theological Critique of the Nationalistic Church

In the eighty years since the genocide, the Armenian Church hierarchy and clergy have constructed a religio-national myth out of the history. This myth traces the origin of the present secularized nationalistic church back to the founding of the Armenian Church in the fourth and fifth centuries. It is preached and argued in all sorts of public forums that the religionized nationalism which the Church now promotes is

35. See John Meyendorff, *The Byzantine Legacy in the Orthodox Church* (Crestwood, N.Y.: St. Vladimir's Seminary Press, 1982), pp. 226-27.

36. Between 1915 and 1922, the Armenian population living within Turkey, especially in the historic Armenian provinces of eastern Turkey, was decimated — reduced from two million to no more than a few hundred thousand. Somewhere between one and one and a half million Armenians lost their lives in forced marches of deportation and bloody massacres. Ancient centers of Armenian culture and learning were wiped clean of Armenians, and historic monuments were deliberately destroyed. Nearly all Armenian communities in a worldwide diaspora carry the memory of the genocide through survivors and their progeny. And the pain of this history is compounded by continuing Turkish denials that it ever took place and the indifference of nations from which Armenians expected sympathy and acknowledgment of the crimes committed against them. For an introduction to the Armenian genocide, see my essay "A Comparision of the Armenian and Jewish Gencides: Some Common Features," *Thought* 58 (June 1983): 207-23. For additional information, see *The Armenian Genocide in Perspective* (New Brunswick, N.J.: Transaction Books, 1986) and *The Armenian Genocide: History, Politics, Ethics* (New York: St. Martin's Press, 1992), both edited by Richard G. Hovannisian. And, for my reflections on the theological and moral meaning of the genocide, see "Armenocide and Christian Existence," *Cross Currents* 41 (Fall 1991): 322-42.

the selfsame faith of the Church's founders and its martyred defenders through the centuries.

To my knowledge, only one modern Armenian churchman has exposed this myth for what it is and explained the danger it presents for the Church and the disservice it does to the nation. Archbishop Tiran Nersoyan (1904-1989) was the most brilliant and influential Armenian clergyman of the twentieth century. Among the several diocesan posts in which he served as bishop was that of Primate of the Diocese of the Armenian Church in America. He was elected to the post in 1944 and served there for eleven years. Nersoyan was a scholar and ecumenist who translated many of the primary Armenian liturgical texts into English. As a young deacon and priest in Jerusalem during the 1920s and 1930s, he launched his career as a theologian with articles written for the publication *Sion.*

In 1928, Nersoyan wrote an article entitled "Nationalism or Gospel" in which he stated boldly that the role of preserving ethnic identity and promoting Armenian nationalism ought not to be the Church's *raison d'être.* He reminded his readers that among those who now were encouraging this role for the Church were the disciples of a generation that had condemned "the Church [as] the graveyard of the people [and] . . . championed the cause of atheism."[37] Nersoyan's message was twofold. On the one hand, he reminded the Church that in its midst there were wolves in sheep's clothing cynically using it to preserve ethnic cohesion and nationalistic fervor. On the other hand, Nersoyan was calling the Church back to its true purpose as witness to Jesus Christ and servant to the Armenian people. He drew the distinction between an enlightened and confessing national church fully engaged in the world and with other churches and a narrowly nationalistic church whose hubris blinded it to the illegitimate uses to which it was being put by enemies of Christ.

> Because of the ignorance of some, the intentional distortion of acts by others, the indifference of still others who should be most watchful, a secondary benefit derived from our Church, i.e. the preservation of our ethnicity, is presented as her only purpose and calling. As this misunderstanding further spreads and gets rooted in people's minds, it obviously harms both the cause of Armenian nationhood and nationalism, and does even more harm to the true

37. Nersoyan, "Nationalism or Gospel," reprinted in the New York *Armenian Reporter,* 5 October 1989, p. 3. Subsequent references to this essay will be made parenthetically in the text.

calling of the Armenian Church, which, alas truthfully, she is still far from understanding and accomplishing. (P. 3)

Nersoyan denounced the view promulgated by the ecclesiastical powers that the Church was identical "with our nation, [and is] . . . the only protector and sponsor of our national identity." The church had improperly assumed the burden of preserving an ethnic identity that was "only a partial quality of . . . its national character" imposed by an accident of history, "a consequence of the circumstances . . . [of an] absence of a viable national institution . . . , i.e. we never had a strong government, a dominant culture, or a nation with a concentrated population" (p. 3). He warned against accepting as normative the Church's current strategy.

Furthermore, Nersoyan argued, the "accented nationalism" of the Armenian Church has to be understood in the context of the larger phenomenon of the breakdown of the "moral and intellectual foundations" of the Western world (p. 3). The "tremors" of this breakdown had been felt already in the old Ottoman Empire. From a distinctively Armenian perspective, Nersoyan was touching on the themes of the European crisis theology of the time that had been forged by such people as Karl Barth, Emil Brunner, and Dietrich Bonhoeffer, a theology that cannot be understood apart from the context of the aftermath of World War I.

We need not dwell at length on the utterly devastating genocidal consequences of World War I for the Armenian people, although Nersoyan certainly had this in mind when he spoke about the sources and meaning of modern nationalism generally and Armenian nationalism in particular. By taking seriously the new context in which theology and ecclesial life had to be conducted, he performed an invaluable service for the Church's self-understanding vis-à-vis Armenian nationhood. Speaking of the breakdown of order, he said, "Every penetrating mind can see [that] the leaders of mankind want to be armed against it and want to take measures for self-defense. The consequence of this presentiment for self defense is the growth of the idea of nationalism." He granted that nationalism had both positive and negative potential. At crucial moments in a nation's history, nationalism can provide the inspiration for either national rehabilitation and health or destructive and suicidal acts. In the best of circumstances, nationalism can foster "continuous and persistent efforts to establish lasting good relations" among nations; in the worst of circumstances it can exercise a ruinous "dominance" in the national life.

Nersoyan worried that the latter was threatening Armenian national life in his day (p. 3).

"Nationalism or Gospel" appeared just a decade after the genocide and only five years after the Soviet takeover of Armenia in 1922. Nersoyan sensed that the tragedy of genocide, the dispersion of hundreds of thousands of remaining Armenians into Europe and North America, and the imposition of Soviet rule had fundamentally and permanently altered the essence of the nation. Especially in the diaspora, where Armenians "motivated by the presentiment of destruction" struggled to preserve their political and religious life apart from their native soil, they were quick to resort to nationalism to sustain their identity. The nation, observed Nersoyan, "wants to cling totally to this idea, and through it open for itself a path of light in this dark labyrinth where everyone is groping." Yet, there was a danger in this passion for the ideology of nationalism. The presentiment of destruction was becoming an obsession. Fear and self-pity were threatening to overcome hope and precluding the creation of institutions that might have helped to realize the highest aspirations of nationhood. "We cannot keep step with modern civilization by creating a culture that is born out of sad recollections and very shallow and often mediocre and worthless works. . . . To overcome all these sad realities we need a new vitality, courage, gentleness, inspiration, a new thinking" (p. 18).[38]

Nersoyan believed that the Armenia Church had a role to play in the redemption of the people, but it was not the role that others had been urging upon it or that circumstance had deflected it toward. The Church should not permit herself to become a "tool to promote nationalism," he argued. "That is not her calling. . . . The virtue of our church's Armenian saints is in their zeal as Christians and not in their nationalism. . . . They strived and they sacrificed their lives to lift up Armenian human beings through the grace of Christ. . . . They were not nurtured by mediocre mentalities like 'preserving the nation.'" Other kinds of political and cultural institutions were far better suited to pursuing the nationalist idea and vision, but "every time [the church] has tried to champion the cause of nationalism, the cause itself has suffered" (p. 18).

Nersoyan understood that modern civilization, especially in its

38. For a similar analysis of nationalism, see Nicholas Wolterstorff, *Until Justice and Peace Embrace* (Grand Rapids: William B. Eerdmans, 1983), pp. 105-11; and Martin Buber, *Israel and the World* (New York: Schocken Books, 1948), especially pp. 197-252.

present condition of "decay," was not Christendom, that Christendom had passed on. But he believed that the virtues of Christendom, its faith and moral character, were worthy of retrieval. The idea of Christendom lingered in Nersoyan's mind not as a romantic reminiscence but as a worthy heritage on the basis of which the Armenian Church might recall and rededicate itself to its only true vocation, that of being a mission of salvation in the world. He did not seek to return the Church to some past golden age. He recognized that Armenian Christendom had been the happy outcome of the evangelical life of the Church — but it had always been this evangelical activity itself that was most important, not the ecclesial-political structures to which it had given birth. At one point in "Nationalism or Gospel" Nersoyan observes, "The accented nationalism of our church is the result of her failure, for various reasons, to embark on foreign missionary activities, which is her top-most Christian duty" (p. 3). The duty of the church before all else is to pursue this mission to the world, not to be a nation builder — not even a Christian nation builder.

In the midst of this ecclesiology, Nersoyan sought to envision a new national life in which autonomous political institutions would carry out the idea of nationhood as a secular goal. "The Armenian nation must look for other sources to assure the perpetuity of its nationhood," he wrote. That does not mean that he felt the Armenian Church should recede into a private sphere of conscience or personal piety. To the contrary, he envisioned for it the truly public role of forming Christ anew in the people. Nationalism is not what the church's purpose is about: peoplehood is. "A healthy character and a pure spirit must be nurtured in our people through Christ and the Gospel. We must express our repugnance of becoming an evil and morally bankrupt nation because such a nation would soon fall. The Armenian Church must be mindful of her calling and devote herself to it alone. That is the only way to revitalize the Armenian people. Our people must have a life, and Our Lord came so we may have life and have it abundantly" (p. 18).

The Fate of the National Church

Like Bonhoeffer, Archbishop Tiran Nersoyan did not reject wholly the idea of a national church. He simply wanted to direct the Armenian Church back to its primary purpose of mission and forming Christ in a people. Nersoyan and Bonhoeffer both understood that if a national church does not make critical adjustments to the new situation of autonomy and secularity after Christendom, it will be in jeopardy of complete ossification and irrelevance. Perhaps worse still, in circumstances when nationalism reaches a fever, a national church of the old establishment mentality will be especially tempted to acquiesce or even lend support to the destructive proclivities of the nation state.

Archbishop Tiran Nersoyan's life ended just before the commencement of the next crucial stage in the history of his Church and the nation. Nersoyan died in 1989, two years before the declaration of Armenia's independence. In conversations I had with him before his death, he spoke frequently of the necessity for completely rethinking the relation of the Church to the nation and of the Armenian diaspora to the people of Armenia. Had he lived longer, he might have helped to envision a new role for the national church.

The jockeying for power by the Russian Church and the Roman Catholic Church in Poland and the terrible tension between competing Ukrainian Orthodox and Catholic churches testifies to the significance of the issue of the national church in the newly emerging international order. National churches are struggling for identity and purpose where the reality of the passing of Christendom is no longer camouflaged by the Soviet system. But the absence of this camouflage also serves to make the external pluralistic world look especially threatening. The behavior of the Armenian Church illustrates the powerful temptation that many of these national churches face to take cover within the nation from outside forces. Just when the future of the new Armenian nation depends so heavily on breaking free from isolation and turning to full participation in the community of nations, the Armenian Church is yearning to return to its former comfortable institutional and ideological inwardness. A genuinely ecumenical church would be of far greater service to the nation. A genuinely ecumenical church would have the perspective from which to be a witness to the nation of the larger universal vision of the Christian faith.

In the samizdat article cited at the start of this chapter, Meerson-Aksenov proposes a *modus vivendi* for the Russian Church that combines total "outward" participation in the world with intense "inward" ecclesial formation.

> The Christian today is called above all to be conscious witness of his faith, and departure from the world is far from the best means to testify to it. . . . Every age finds its own means of seeking God. The Apostles found God in a crowd, and the anchorites followed

Him into the desert. The many voices of the world call out from all sides, showing us where His presence must be sought and where the light of faith which He has lit must be carried.[39]

Meerson-Aksenov insists that today the light of faith must be carried in new descralized, secular places. This would force "the Church out from all of its former comfortable positions," but it would also force it "to strive for the concentration of all its spiritual energies, all its activities, all of its vital powers." A rigorous exercise of a "worldly" Christianity achieves its mission only if there is a commensurate retrieval and renewal of ecclesial community and discipline. To accomplish this, the church "must return to that organic state of unity of the faithful which prevailed in the first centuries . . . when all Christians were 'like living stones built in a spiritual house' (1 Peter 2:5). All participated in the sacraments instead of just being spectators. . . . All were part of the 'royal priesthood.' "[40] Meerson-Aksenov sees the revitalization of these organic, communal, sacramental, and evangelical characteristics of the church as the work of a new lay movement in the line of the apostles and early monastics.

Bonhoeffer had envisioned the same thing, referring to it as the "arcane discipline." And, like Bonhoeffer, Meerson-Aksenov looks to restoring the "inner" ecclesial community of prayer and worship as part of a dialectical movement of the church "outward" in service to the "other." Where might this convergence of ecclesiology in Bonhoeffer, Nersoyan, and Meerson-Aksenov lead in the context of theology and ethics? New possibilities for ecclesial formation challenge the set of options introduced by the birth of modernity. We have moved beyond having to make a narrow choice between either a national church or a "free church." I believe that Bonhoeffer understood this. He realized that the historical free churches were no less developments of the Reformation and the breakup of Christendom than were the national churches. He looked beyond both to a different world historical context.

Even in the early *Sanctorum Communio*, Bonhoeffer argued that the national church and the gathered church are not necessary opposites, though in their modern manifestations of church and sect they may appear to be. Troeltsch himself had left the impression that these two types were mutually exclusive.[41] Ironically, the national church can

39. Meerson-Aksenov, "The People of God and the Pastors," pp. 534-35.
40. Meerson-Aksenov, "The People of God and the Pastors," p. 535.
41. Bonhoeffer, *The Communion of Saints*, p. 186.

conserve its catholic character only if it begins to embody the voluntary principle of the gathered church; if it fails to do so, it becomes little more than an antiquated reserve of national life and ossified theological and ecclesiastical forms. In the wake of Christendom, it is crucial to affirm that "the national church and the gathered church belong together, and" — even more important — "that . . . a national church, which is not continually pressing forward to be a confessing church, is in the greatest inner peril."[42]

Franklin Littell has shown that through this scheme of analysis Bonhoeffer envisioned a confessing church as an alternative to both the national church and gathered church types, both of which he felt were committed to formations of Christian life that were inadequate for addressing the gospel to the new person-come-of-age. The national church presumed an uninterrupted continuum of church and culture; the gathered church clung to the "fortress concept" of a band of disciples huddled together in opposition to the world. "Bonhoeffer's quest was for a new statement of the church, not in terms of static pattern — 'continuum' or 'fortress' — but in terms of mission to the world."[43]

Littell regretted that Bonhoeffer's experience was limited to "the Pietistic, conventicle-type German 'free churches.' "[44] Had he been acquainted with other historic forms of the free church, Littell believed, Bonhoeffer might have concluded that the free church is not necessarily a fortress church. Keith W. Clements has sought to clarify the Bonhoefferian dialectic in a fashion that challenges Littell's reservations. He argues that Bonhoeffer understood all too well that after Christendom the differences between state church, free church, and Roman Catholic Church no longer are what they once were. After Christendom, "all [churches] become confessing churches — and equally all could be inhibited from becoming so, by blindness, fear or inertia."[45] Clements gives the contemporary example of the British free churches, so many of which have become havens from an inhospitable world for middle-class people.

Clements maintains further that Bonhoeffer saw how even a " 'free church' is subject to manipulation by extraneous and sometimes sinister forces, at precisely the point where it feels itself to be free from

---

42. Bonhoeffer, *The Communion of Saints*, p. 189.

43. Littell, "Bonhoeffer's History, Church, and World," in *The Place of Bonhoeffer* (New York: Association Press, 1962), pp. 36-37.

44. Littell, "Bonhoeffer's History, Church, and World," p. 36.

45. Clements, *What Freedom? The Persistent Challenge of Dietrich Bonhoeffer* (Birmingham, U.K.: Church Enterprise, 1990), p. 105.

the godless world, just as the national church can complacently assume that by its very existence it is upholding the divine order in the world. In both cases the question of the gathered people, bound to the Lord and to one another, can become the choice to be a church on one's own terms, in order (consciously or otherwise), to serve one's own particular social, political — and religious — interests." The church ends up accommodating itself "to the society as it is, rather than providing a critique of it."[46] Bonhoeffer had in fact commented on the transformation of the free-church principle of freedom in both Germany and America. American Protestants, he said, had confused the free act of word preached and deed performed with a gift granted by the state under the formal provisions of the "free exercise" clause and the separation of church and state. Even the free churches compromised their historical understanding of freedom as the command and commission of God to take the gospel everywhere in order to take their place within a denominational society under the umbrella of the American Way.[47]

In recent times, South Africa and the Soviet Union have provided further examples of the accommodation identified by Bonhoeffer. With these historical lessons before us, Bonhoeffer's treatment of the national church question is that much more compelling. The specific circumstances of the national churches in post-Soviet societies differ in significant ways, but the general picture, interpreted in a Bonhoefferian light, does advance our understanding of a complex situation. We have seen that the question of the national church raises two distinct issues: church establishment and ecclesial ethnocentrism. Church establishment is powerfully attractive to many of the post-Soviet churches. Many hunger to regain their old status in new forms. They must be denied. The dangers posed to the faith by re-establishment are simply too great. The problem of the ethnocentrism and xenophobia in these churches is even more intractable and grave, for suspicions of those who are racially and religiously different controvert the gospel. Moreover, the problem is not restricted to national churches; free churches, too, can become ethnocentric.

In conclusion, the indigenous character of the national churches will not soon be shed. There is much work to do in addressing the dangers of new and old religious nationalisms alike. If the former Soviet churches fail to take up this task, they will miss golden opportunities

46. Clements, *What Freedom?* p. 103.

47. See, e.g., Bonhoeffer, "Protestantism without Reformation," in *No Rusty Swords*, 108-9; and *Ethics*, pp. 104-5.

for creative renewal. They might manage to hold on to something of the character of a national church, but in most cases the premodern folk-church character will slip away. Nearly half of the population of Armenia lives in the capital city of Yerevan and its environs. The traditional village religion might persist in some places, but not among vast numbers of urban people. The forces of Ottomanization and Sovietization in the past gutted the Armenian Church of much of its doctrinal conviction, and it will not be able to sustain its hold on the imagination and hearts of people with nothing more than old forms of sacrament and liturgy. We have already considered the negative consequences of further and intensified dependence on religious nationalism to sustain churches. If it is to be anything more than a keeper of ancient temples and artifacts, the Armenian Church will have to come to terms with these weaknesses. It will have to take on more of the characteristics of what Bonhoeffer called a confessing church. The voluntary principle of the free churches and the gospel call to witness must more and more define the existence and behavior of the Armenian Church. But this transformation will not come easily.

The Armenian Church is now in a stage of denial — denial of the loss of its old world. Like other similar churches, it will likely have to be shaken out of its present state of mind. There are some recent indications that this is beginning to happen. In an interview given early in 1994, Catholicos Karekin II of the Holy See of Cicilia in Lebanon stated, "The church has to go beyond opposing or condemning the new sects and cults [in Armenia]. It must till the field." He explained that "seventy years of Soviet rule have surely left a mark on attitudes of both clergy and the people, [and] we have to emancipate ourselves from the inherited apathy. We've got to go out and meet the people in their homes, their workshops, in the villages, in the cities."[48]

Meanwhile, there is movement at the grass roots toward ecclesial renewal in Armenia. The *K'tutyune* (literally "Compassion") organization is an example. On the one hand, *K'tutyune* exhibits all the character of a Western-style voluntary charitable group. Its cadres of volunteers visit homes of the sick and needy distributing food, clothing, and medical supplies throughout the country. On the other hand, *K'tutyune* has the character of an evangelical faith movement, which sometimes puts it in tension with the church leadership. But its members regard themselves as faithful to the Armenian Church. Indeed the *K'tutyune* mem-

48. "Rethinking Church and Nation," in *AIM: Armenian International Magazine* 5 (March 1994): 22.

bership overlaps with an even more broadly based church-centered evangelical group, *Yeghpayrutyune* ("Brotherhood"). This organization holds prayer meetings in homes, sponsors large public rallies in which sermons are delivered by lay ministers, and has composed new hymns. *Yeghpayrutyune*, which until 1990 was a parachurch organization alienated from the institutional church, now has the official sanction of the Church. Since independence and the new freedom of religious practice in Armenia, members of *Yeghpayrutyune* have assumed the lion's share of the burden for religious instruction in the parishes. Similar signs of internal renewal, though not on the same scale, have appeared throughout the traditional structures of the Armenian Church. The most significant is a vital lay and youth movement encouraged by the Bishop of Yerevan, Karekin Nersissian, in his diocesan church of St. Sarkis. *K'tutyune* and *Yeghpayrutyune* are important manifestations of a new confessing and evangelical form of Christian community attuned to an Armenia coming of age. They are well ahead of most sectors of the Armenian Church. It remains to be seen, however, whether such movements will become a source of serious ecumenical consciousness with enough power to turn the Armenian Church toward a new and energetic life of witness to Jesus Christ.

It is impossible to say what the future has in store for the national churches of former Soviet societies. Even the most favorable outcomes will not wholly resolve the division of the catholic and apostolic faith into a variety of cultural embodiments. In a world that the Father of Creation has salted with so many different peoples and cultures, it is not always easy to sort out what is sinful in the national church and what is simply an unavoidable product of human finiteness and historicity. Nevertheless, Dietrich Bonhoeffer gave all the churches a theology that fathoms profoundly the complexities of Christian existence and the challenges they face after Christendom. Through his life and death, this Lutheran pastor cast a light forward into our time that illumines for all churches a path of truth and faithful witness to Christ.

III. Applied Ecclesial Ethics:
Family, Medicine, and the Creation

6. Family and Christian Virtue: Reflections on the Ecclesial Vision of John Chrysostom

In these concluding chapters, I want to turn to a discussion of three significant contemporary moral issues: family, ecology, and care for the dying. I chose these topics not only because I know that they weigh heavily on the hearts and minds of contemporary people but also because of the important *ecclesiological* dimensions of these issues.

In his rich and provocative book entitled *God the Economist: The Doctrine of God and Political Economy*, M. Douglas Meeks has argued that the biblical God is "engaged in creating, sustaining, and recreating households." The biblical concept of household, he notes, "can refer to the people of Israel or the church of Jesus Christ, to families, to a royal court or dynasty, to a place of God's abode, or, in the most comprehensive sense, to the whole creation."[1] Meeks explains that *oikonomia* — literally meaning provision for or keeping of a household — is the Greek term employed by the biblical authors to sum up this divine activity. And it early became a vital concept in the church's ecclesiology.

In this chapter I want to consider the household as *family*. Specifically, I want to explore John Chrysostom's *oikic* and ecclesial understanding of marriage and family. I believe that this great Church Father's insights in this area constitute a valuable and often overlooked resource for Christians endeavoring to live faithful lives and build Christian community in a post-Christendom era. The church is God's spirit-filled agency that makes "the world into a household in which all of God's creatures . . . find access to life."[2] The church is also God's agent of healing and reconciliation in a broken and dying world. It is

1. Meeks, *God the Economist* (Minneapolis: Fortress Press, 1989), p. 4.
2. Meeks, *God the Economist*, p. 45.

133

because God is involved in these matters of healing and reconciliation that those who are followers and imitators of Jesus Christ must similarly involve themselves. This is what it means to be the church. In the words of the apostle Paul, "The one who plants and the one who waters have a common purpose. . . . For we are God's servants, working together; you are God's field, God's building" (1 Cor. 3:8).

Culture and Chrysostom's Ecclesial Vision of Family

Of the many quotable passages from the writings of St. John Chrysostom, the one most often cited is located in his twentieth homily on Ephesians: "If we regulate our households [properly] . . . , we will also be fit to oversee the Church, for indeed the household is a little Church. Therefore, it is possible for us to surpass all others in virtue by becoming good husbands and wives."[3] More often than not this passage has been used as a proof text to support high sacramental interpretations of marriage. Only rarely has it been used to initiate a sustained discussion of what might be described as Chrysostom's ecclesial vision of the Christian family and household. That is my interest in this chapter. I also want to show how this vision enables Christians to better understand what is truly at stake for the church in contemporary debates over the family and its values.

Chrysostom lived at a moment of genuine cultural crisis. The pagan culture of antiquity was in decline, and Christianity was beginning to exert a social force, but it was not yet clear what shape a Christian culture might take. Chrysostom was among a minority of Christian writers (St. Basil was another) who voiced serious misgivings about the emerging Christian order. Like Basil, he brought the spirit of monastic reform into his critique of society. He inveighed against the moral laxity of self-professed Christians and their excessive preoccupation with material possessions, power, and social status. Chrysostom's ecclesiology powerfully expressed a spirit of reform as he struggled to steer a course that would lead neither to an imperial church nor a cake-frosting version of Christianity for the masses. His example is relevant all over again for churches today as they enter an era marked by cultural deterioration and are faced with difficult choices about how to relate to the emerging hegemonic secularity.

---

3. *St. John Chrysostom on Marriage and Family Life,* trans. Catherine P. Roth and David Anderson (Crestwood, N.Y.: St. Vladimir's Seminary Press, 1986), p. 57.

Chrysostom might easily have succumbed to the temptation to promote the moral rehabilitation of the family as a means of securing social stability. In our own time, we repeatedly hear even religious sources — Protestants, Roman Catholics, and Orthodox alike — proclaiming the value of the family as a bulwark against social decay. The presidential campaign of 1992 was replete with talk about family values and the importance of healthy and functional families to secure the promises of the American way of life, and these issues are still intensely debated as we move on into the nineties. Less clear in the political rhetoric is what these family values actually amount to or what they are grounded in.

Chrysostom did not ignore the sociological dimension or function of the family. On one occasion he said, "When harmony prevails [in the household], the children are raised well, the household is kept in order, and neighbors, friends and relatives praise the result. Great benefits, both for families and states, are thus produced."[4] But he subordinated this social function of the family to its ecclesial role. The Christian family is called first of all to the kingdom of God, and in order to fulfill this vocation, it must practice a discipline of spiritual and moral *askesis*. Moreover, unlike modern politicians, Chrysostom was clear about the proper source of family morality: Christ in his life and commandments.

Chrysostom's vision of the ecclesial family was radical when he preached it in the fourth century, and it is equally radical in our post-Christendom society. Living after Christendom, we as spouses and parents — and, indeed, the church as a whole — can no longer assume that our children will be nurtured in biblical and Christian values apart from the community of faith, because no substantial body of these values remains in the general culture. It should be obvious to Christian spouses and parents how truly radical their vocation as family is within contemporary society, but we seem regrettably prone to forget what is actually entailed by being married "in the Lord." The printed and electronic media bombard us with powerful and seductive alternatives to the demanding, disciplined life to which the Christian family is called biblically and through the marital rites of the church. It is easy to think of the Christian family as merely a church-going version of any of a number of comfortable and idealized sitcom families.

Chrysostom speaks to our time when he urges the churches to make strenuous and sustained efforts to cultivate and restore the vision of the family as an ecclesial entity and mission of the kingdom of God.

4. *St. John Chrysostom on Marriage and Family Life*, p. 44.

Sociologists tell us that for vast and increasing numbers of Americans, the family has lost its public meaning and outlook. It is being redefined as a haven for private living, consumption, and recreation. Civic mindedness has been replaced with a hunger for privacy. Personal sacrifice for children and community has been replaced by self-centeredness and hedonism. Chrysostom's ecclesial vision of family speaks to this disintegration of community, but it does so in a fashion that can only look strange even to people who otherwise worry about the privatization and moral privation of family. While the sociologists and politicians contend that the family is in trouble because it is not contributing as it should to the formation of viable community and civic virtue, Chrysostom argues that the Christian family is first of all a calling to community in service to God and his kingdom.

Chrysostom's teachings on marriage and family push us into a much larger debate that is at the center of contemporary Christian ethics — a debate over the prospects of the Christian faith and ethics generally within a post-Christendom world. As I have already suggested, there are those who cling to the empty hope that some version of Christendom is still possible and hence that Christian ethics can still be done in the old and familiar way of correlating Christian truth with norms and institutions found within the culture. Others pin their hope on a more modest program of designing a new public theology for a pluralistic order. Efforts in this direction are being made in diverse and even opposing ideological camps, among neoconservatives, mainline Protestants, and both liberal and neo-Thomist Catholics. Still others are persuaded that Christendom has ended and that it never was a good idea in any case. Many of these have turned to alternative models of a confessing church, the "main political task" of which lies "not in the personal transformation of individual hearts or the modification of society" but rather, as Stanley Hauerwas and William H. Willimon have recently put it, "in the congregation's determination to worship Christ in all things . . . and to build up an alternative polis" — that being the church.[5] The contending parties fling accusations back and forth at one another about whether their respective ecclesiological proposals are too accommodating toward the culture or too sectarian.

Chrysostom helps us to see that this perennial question about the appropriate relationship of the church to the culture is reflected in microcosm within the Christian family. With respect to the contemporary

---

5. Hauerwas and Willimon, *Resident Aliens: Life in the Christian Colony* (Nashville: Abingdon Press, 1990), pp. 45-46.

debate, I want to show how Chrysostom's way of stating the relation of family to church and church to culture eludes some of the facile categories in which we have learned to pigeonhole other points of view. Chrysostom was neither sectarian, accommodationist, nor triumphalist. He resisted the Eusebian Christian imperialism of the day. He was not taken with the Constantinian-Theodosian theocratic synthesis of church and state that, as later codified by Justinian, provided the ideological framework for Byzantine theocracy. Nor did he propose that the church retreat into the catacombs or hold to the opinion that the only pure and true Christianity was restricted to the monastery. Rather, Chrysostom's idea of an evangelical and socially responsible Christian faith was bound up with the pastoral and moral theology he addressed to Christian parishioners and Christian rulers alike. In all that he said about the nature of the church/world relationship, Chrysostom returned again and again to the belief of the Church Fathers that salvation is accomplished from within the *ecclesia* through its process of making the kingdom of God present to an unbelieving world. And he viewed the family as an ecclesial entity that figured centrally in this salvific process.

The "Ecclesial" Household

As Gerhardt B. Ladner has observed, by the end of the fourth century, especially in the East, "the ascetic and mystic and the ruler shared between them as it were true kingship. Reformed in the royal image of God, they represented two different but equally high orders of mankind."[6] The Constantinian-Theodosian initiatives to establish a Christian commonwealth, formalized by the Emperor Justinian in the sixth century, tipped the balance away from the ascetic and mystic toward the ruler. The emperors increasingly asserted a "quasi-sacerdotal position [for themselves] in the Church, and generally made it understood that the value of all acts of reform in the Church and empire flowed directly from the fact that they were put into effect by, or on the command of, the emperor."[7]

Early in his career Chrysostom resisted these trends toward imperial domination of the church and society by championing monastic claims of true "kingship" rather than the Eusebian conception of the king-philosopher. This is a clear aim of his short treatise *A Comparison*

6. Ladner, *The Idea of Reform* (New York: Harper & Row, 1967), p. 124.
7. Ladner, *The Idea of Reform*, p. 125.

between a King and a Monk (c. 380). As Ladner puts it, "There was one great exception to the eastern development of [the] Basileia ideology: the thought and life of St. John Chrysostom."[8] The truly significant turn in Chrysostom's thought came, however, as he struggled with his pastoral and homiletic duties in Antioch and later in Constantinople. In these settings, Chrysostom became convinced "that, apart from the privilege of marriage, the Christian who lived in the world had the same obligations as the monk."[9] While expounding an ecclesially centered interpretation of the Christian household as an expression of the mission of the kingdom of God in the world, he also anticipated and answered the later Byzantine alternatives of (1) envisioning the church as the sacramental organism that whispers in the emperor's ear and sacralizes an imperial order and (2) endorsing the view that the monks are the only true representatives of holiness in a compromised and sinful world.

At the close of his Antiochene ministry, Chrysostom wrote the *Address on Vainglory and the Right Way for Parents to Bring Up Their Children* (c. 386-387), in which he speaks "of a child's soul as of a city in which the King of the universe intends to dwell," and he asserts that "God's earthly representative in this city is not the emperor, but the child's father." "Nothing," concludes Ladner, "could be less 'Eusebian' than this conception of the Kingdom of God on earth and it is not surprising that John Chrysostom perished as a martyr for Christian ethical principles in resistance" to the emerging and solidifying ideology of a Christian empire.[10]

From this point on Chrysostom sought to "reform the 'Polis' within the 'Basileia.'"[11] He increasingly identified the proleptic presence of the kingdom of God not primarily with empire or the cloistered monastery but with the near and familiar Christian household. The cardinal "marks" of the kingdom, Chrysostom insisted, are compassion, love of neighbor, and hospitality toward friends and strangers alike. The Christian household, he maintained, is an exact image of the ecclesia when it puts into practice the gospel specifications for our behavior toward one another and God.[12]

---

8. Ladner, *The Idea of Reform*, pp. 125-26.
9. Ladner, *The Idea of Reform*, p. 127.
10. Ladner, *The Idea of Reform*, p. 129.
11. Ladner, *The Idea of Reform*, p. 129.
12. I have learned much about this from Gus George Christo's dissertation "The Church's Identity Established through Images according to St. John Chrysostom" (Ph.D. diss., University of Durham, 1990). Christo's work has alerted me to a number of passages from Chrysostom's work that I will subsequently cite.

Chrysostom thought of the Abrahamic household as the ancient biblical type of the Christian "ecclesial" household. He maintained that the Abrahamic household kept and practiced in an exemplary fashion those virtues of the kingdom of God that should belong to all the people of God in order that they might receive the Messiah when he comes. In his homily on Acts 20:32 Chrysostom says,

> Make for yourself a guest-chamber in your own house: set up a bed there, set up a table there and a candlestick. For is it not absurd, that whereas, if soldiers should come, you have rooms set apart for them, and show much care for them, and furnish them with everything, because they keep off from you the visible war of this world, yet strangers have no place where they might abide? Gain a victory over the Church. . . . Surpass us in liberality: have a room, to which Christ may come; say, "This is Christ's cell; this building is set apart for Him." . . . Abraham received the strangers in the place where he abode himself; his wife stood in the place of a servant, the guests in the place of masters. He knew not that he was receiving Christ; knew not that he was receiving Angels; so that had he known it, he would have lavished his whole substance. But we, who know that we receive Christ, show not even so much zeal as he did who thought that he was receiving men. . . . Let our house be Christ's general receptacle.[13]

Clearly Chrysostom has in mind something even more concrete than the actual network of human family or household relations here. The physical dwelling itself is realized as "Christ's general receptacle." Abraham's tent is the Old Testament type of the Christian dwelling, which has become the house of God. When the members of the household provide for guests and greet them into their home, the dwelling itself serves as the body of the Lord.

Elsewhere in his homilies on the book of Acts, Chrysostom fills this metaphor of the house of God with its members and their relations. "Let the house be a Church, consisting of men and women. . . . 'For where two,' He saith, 'are gathered together in My Name, there am I in the midst of them.'"[14] This household, which welcomes Christ and feeds and clothes him, thereby inherits the kingdom of heaven. Hospitality

13. Chrysostom, "Homily 45," in *The Homilies of St. John Chrysostom, Archbishop of Constantinople, on the Acts of the Apostles*, vol. 11 of the Select Library of Nicene and Post-Nicene Fathers, 1st series, ed. Philip Schaff (New York: Christian Literature, 1889), p. 277.

14. Chrysostom, "Homily 26" (on Acts 12:1-2), in *The Homilies of St. John Chrysostom*, p. 127.

was such an important virtue for Chrysostom that he held it should figure in the selection of one's spouse. Abraham sent his servant to his own country to find a wife for his son Isaac, and the servant determined through prayer that he should choose the woman who offered him water not only for himself but for his camels as well (Gen. 24:11-14). The servant was sent looking for such a bride for Isaac, writes Chrysostom, because "everything good" that happened to the household "came because of hospitality. . . . Let us not see only the fact that he asked for water, but let us consider that it shows a truly generous soul not only to give what is asked but to provide more than is requested."[15] This sort of cultivation of a righteous household, he concludes, is a means of seeking and receiving the kingdom of heaven. " 'Thou receivedst Me,' He saith, 'into thy lodging, I will receive thee into the Kingdom of My Father; thou tookest away My hunger, I take away thy sins; thou sawest Me bound, I see thee loosed; thou sawest Me a stranger, I make thee a citizen of heaven; thou gavest Me bread, I give thee an entire Kingdom, that thou mayest inherit and possess it.' "[16]

Chrysostom cites the home of Aquila and Priscilla as a quintessential New Testament example of an "ecclesial" household. These two workers in the Lord unselfishly opened their home to St. Paul and Christ's disciples. It was "no small excellency, that they had made their very house a Church." In the same context, Chrysostom notes St. Paul's exhortation to the Corinthian Christians to greet one another "with the holy kiss . . . as a means of union: for this unites, and produces one body."[17] As Gus Christo has summarized, Chrysostom held that "a Christian home's transformation into the Church . . . , or a church, happens when its occupants salute each other with the holy kiss . . . , are hospitable to people and remain free of deceit and hypocrisy."[18] Such a home or church becomes a site from which Christ draws the rest of the world into his kingdom through a liturgical and sacramental action. "Charity," Chrysostom once exclaimed, is "a sacrament. . . . For our sacraments are above all God's charity and love."[19]

15. *St. John Chrysostom on Marriage and Family Life,* pp. 103-4.

16. Chrysostom, "Homily 45," p. 276.

17. Chrysostom, "First Epistle of St. Paul the Apostle to the Corinthians," in *The Homilies of S. John Chrysostom,* part 2 (Oxford: John Henry Parker, 1839), p. 620.

18. Christo, "The Church's Identity Established through Images according to St. John Chrysostom," p. 386.

19. Chrysostom, quoted by Emilianos Timiadis in "Restoration and Liberation in and by the Community," *Greek Orthodox Theological Review* 19 (Autumn 1974): 54. The material is taken from Chrysostom's homily on Matthew 22:34-36.

The Christian Family as Mission of the Kingdom of God: Reforming the Polis from within the Basileia

In order to emphasize the larger ordained purposes and calling of the Christian family, Chrysostom repeatedly returned to the stories of the Abrahamic household, even Abraham's willingness to follow God's command and offer his only son in sacrifice. Yet the Old Testament story most often invoked by Chrysostom to illumine the unselfish and heroic qualities required by God of those who assume the office of parenthood is the story of Hannah and her son Samuel. Chrysostom's use of the story shifted over the years from an early defense of monasticism to a later focus on the responsibility of Christian parents to attend consciously to raising their children as true Christians, and not just nominal ones.

In his early work *Against the Opponents of the Monastic Life*, Chrysostom called on parents to raise their children unselfishly to be fit inheritors of the kingdom of Heaven. This entailed especially, though not exclusively, preparing them for the monastic life. Chrysostom described Hannah as an exemplar of such responsible and unselfish parenthood. She "gave birth to one child and did not expect to have another. Indeed, she had scarcely given birth to him, and this after many tears, for she was sterile. . . . When he no longer needed to be nursed, she immediately took him and offered him up to God, and she ordered him to return to his father's house no longer, but to live continually in the temple of God."[20] Thus it was that Hannah fulfilled the community's office of a parent, by dedicating her son to God and to the well-being of his people. For "when God had turned away from the race of the Hebrews because of their profuse wickedness . . . , [Samuel] won back God's favor through his virtue and persuaded him to supply what had been given previously. . . . Such," concluded Chrysostom, "is always the reward for giving our possessions to God . . . , not only money and possessions, but also our very children."[21]

More than a decade after he wrote these words, during his ministry in Antioch, or perhaps even later during his episcopacy at Constantinople, Chrysostom returned to this story in his homily on Ephe-

---

20. Chrysostom, *"A Comparison between a King and a Monk" and "Against the Opponents of the Monastic Life,"* trans. David G. Hunter (Lewiston, N.Y.: Edwin Mellen Press, 1988), p. 171. In subsequent references, this work will be cited as *Against the Opponents of the Monastic Life*.

21. Chrysostom, *Against the Opponents of the Monastic Life*, pp. 171-72.

sians 6:1-3. In the context of instructing parents how to raise their children, he grants that it is not necessary to raise them to be monks; it is enough that they be raised to be good Christians.[22] Still, he cites Hannah as an example that they should imitate. "Look at what she did. She brought Samuel, her only son, to the temple, when he was only an infant!"[23] Chrysostom uses the story to emphasize the importance of raising children on Scripture. "Don't say, 'Bible reading is for monks; am I turning my child into a monk? . . . It is necessary for everyone to know Scriptural teachings, and this is especially true for children."[24]

This instruction that parents should raise their children to be good Christians rather than to prepare them specifically for the monastic life is not at all inconsistent with Chrysostom's earlier use of the Hannah and Samuel story in *Against the Opponents of the Monastic Life*. It is simply a matter of a shift in emphasis. The cardinal obligation and task of Christian parenthood remains the same: to prepare the child for service to God and his people. Hannah "gave Samuel to God, and with God she left him, and thus her marriage was blessed more than ever, because her first concern was for spiritual things."[25]

In an ancient prayer of the Armenian rite of matrimony, the priest beseeches God to plant the couple "as a fruitful olive tree, in the House of God, so that living in righteousness, in purity, and in godliness, according to the pleasure of Thy beneficent will, they may see the children of their children and they may be *a people unto Thee*."[26] This liturgical prayer emphasizes the ecclesial nature of Christian marriage and family. Husband and wife are called to seek the kingdom of God, to raise children in virtue and righteousness in order that they may be "a people unto" God. In *Against the Opponents of the Monastic Life*, Chrysostom quotes 1 Timothy 2:5: "[T]hey will be saved through bearing children, if they remain in faith and love and holiness, with modesty."[27] Hannah's "wisdom" was a matter of comprehending through faith that by dedicating to God "the first-fruits of her womb" she might "obtain many more children in return."[28] Her attention to spiritual

---

22. *St. John Chrysostom on Marriage and Family Life*, p. 67.
23. *St. John Chrysostom on Marriage and Family Life*, p. 68.
24. *St. John Chrysostom on Marriage and Family Life*, p. 67.
25. *St. John Chrysostom on Marriage and Family Life*, p. 68.
26. *The Blessing of Marriage; or, The Canon of the Rite of Holy Matrimony according to the Usage of the Armenian Apostolic Orthodox Church* (New York: Armenian Church Publications, 1953), p. 56; italics mine.
27. Chrysostom, *Against the Opponents of the Monastic Life*, p. 172.
28. *St. John Chrysostom on Marriage and Family Life*, p. 68.

things was not a retreat into the private self or family; it was an affirmation of the existence of a community of faith to which she belonged and in which she held the divinely commissioned office of parent. God in turn bestowed on her the growing company of that community.

A Brief Excursus on the Theology of the Ecclesial Family in Orthodox Liturgy

The theology of the ecclesial family is predictably lodged with the liturgies of the Eastern churches, especially in the rites of initiation and passage. One might expect to find evidences of it in baptismal rites, but it can be found elsewhere as well. Some years back, Alexander Schmemann performed the service of bringing renewed attention to the ancient rite of *churching*, which marks the fortieth day after the birth of a child. This rite recalls the ancient Jewish practices of purification of the mother described in Leviticus 12 and the dedication of the child to God recorded in Luke 2: "When the time came for their purification according to the law of Moses, they brought him [Jesus] up to Jerusalem to present him to the Lord (as it is written in the law of the Lord, 'Every firstborn male shall be designated as holy to the Lord'), and they offered a sacrifice according to what is stated in the law of the Lord" (vv. 22-24).

Churching came into practice as a rite preceding infant baptism, formalizing a very early Christian practice of the mother's "bringing her child, even before it was baptized, into the liturgical assembly of the Church."[29] It joined this occasion with the even more ancient Jewish rite recognizing the recovery to health and purification of the mother following the birth. In fact, the postpartum experience of the mother is as much at the heart of this rite as is the initiation of the child into the ecclesial community. The rite also marks the mother's return to activity in the church community and a change in her status. She returns and is received as a new mother. She is reincorporated into the community not as an autonomous individual or even a spouse but as someone intimately related to and united with the life of her child. (This is especially true in the case of her first child.)

Schmemann argued that the practice of churching says something significant about "the Church's understanding of the *Christian*

29. Schmemann, *Of Water and the Spirit* (Crestwood, N.Y.: St. Vladimir's Seminary Press, 1974), p. 142.

family."[30] Marriage is a union marked and established through public acts of promise and divine blessing. Christianly conceived, family is a natural and sacramental extension of these promises and blessings. Thus understood, marriage expands to include other new lives in the redemptive union of male and female. Chrysostom's vision renders a particularly strong account of this whole ecclesial process; Schmemann, on the other hand, puts the matter quite simply: the Christian family *"belongs* to the Church, finds in the Church the source, the content and the transcendent goal of its existence as family. Therefore the child who belongs to the family, and in a most concrete biological sense to the mother, *thereby* belongs to the Church, is truly *her* child, already offered, already committed to God" in the rite of churching.[31]

In the Armenian rite of churching the celebrant prays,

> Our Lord Jesus Christ who after forty days . . . did come to the Temple to be presented together with Mary Thy Mother and was laid in the arms of Simeon: We pray and beseech from Thee preserve this Thine child (N) and make him/her to grow up by the invisible grace of Thy power and make him/her worthy to receive a portion of the heritage of Thy chosen ones and to be protected by Thy right hand.[32]

Promise, dedication, and blessing draw together under the eschatological hope for the kingdom of God. Through these acts and in this hope, the ecclesial nature of the family is affirmed and established in the Orthodox rites of churching.

Ephesians 5 and the Ecclesial Marriage

The strongest statements by Chrysostom on the ecclesial and christic calling of Christian husbands and wives, fathers and mothers comes not surprisingly in his homily on Ephesians 5:22-23: "Wives, be subject to your husbands as you are to the Lord. For the husband is the head of the wife as Christ is the head of the church, the body of which he is the Savior." Feminist theologians have regarded this passage as a central piece of what they characterize as the theologization of antiquity's

---

30. Schmemann, *Of Water and the Spirit*, pp. 142-43.
31. Schmemann, *Of Water and the Spirit*, p. 145.
32. *Bless, O Lord: Services of Blessing in the Armenian Church*, ed. Garabed Kochakian (New York: Diocese of the Armenian Church of America, 1989), p. 86.

structures of domination.[33] Other theologians have maintained that there is more christianizing of the marital relationship than the critics admit in this and other *Haustafeln* passages. John Howard Yoder, for example, argues that submission here assumes the character of a revolutionary subordination through the Pauline theology of agape and freedom in Christ.[34]

Virtually all who write on this passage, however, agree that it reflects the Pauline author's strong interest in ecclesiology. Elisabeth Schüssler Fiorenza says at one point in her analysis of Ephesians 5, "The reason for . . . [its] theological shortcomings might be the author's interest in clarifying the relationship between Christ and the church, whose unity is his primary concern in the rest of the letter."[35] Chrysostom's interpretation of this passage is strongly ecclesiological. He regards it as establishing a sacramental and even ontological relationship between the institution of marriage and the church. God's economy is channeled first of all through the body of Christ, the church; the peace of the world is guaranteed by the peace of the church; and the peace of the church is a discipline and task of the Christian family. The church is strengthened by the harmony and good order of a godly household. Thus, reasons Chrysostom, the wife does not obey the husband ultimately for "her husband's sake," but "primarily for the Lord's sake."[36]

After discussing the proper attitude of the wife toward her husband, Chrysostom considers the proper attitude of the husband toward his wife. Keeping in mind St. Paul's analogy of the husband as the head of the wife, Chrysostom works together christic and ecclesial metaphors, exhorting each husband to

> be responsible for the same providential care of . . . [your wife], as Christ is for the Church. And even if it become necessary for you to give your life for her, yes, and even to endure and undergo suffering of any kind, do not refuse. Even though you undergo all this, you will never have done anything equal to what Christ has done. You are sacrificing yourself for someone to whom you are already joined, but He offered Himself up for one who turned her back on Him and hated Him.[37]

33. See, e.g., Elisabeth Schüssler Fiorenza, *In Memory of Her* (New York: Crossroad, 1988), pp. 266-70.

34. See Yoder, *The Politics of Jesus* (Grand Rapids: William B. Eerdmans, 1972), pp. 174-75, 180-81, 190-92.

35. Fiorenza, *In Memory of Her*, p. 270.

36. *St. John Chrysostom on Marriage and Family Life*, p. 45.

37. *St. John Chrysostom on Marriage and Family Life*, p. 46.

Both husband and wife must imitate the Lord, but the greater burden is on the husband, precisely because he is in the position of greater power. He who would view himself as master is called to be a servant in the likeness of Christ, who is the head of the church. "What sort of satisfaction could a husband himself have, if he lives with his wife as if she were a slave, and not a woman of her own free will?" asks Chrysostom. "Suffer anything for her sake, but never disgrace her, for Christ never did this with the Church."[38] In his condescending and sacrificial relationship to the church, Christ becomes the example husbands must follow in their relationship to their wives: "imitate the Bridegroom of the Church."[39] Christ condescended to take the church as his bride even though "the Church was not pure. She had blemishes, she was ugly and cheap. Whatever kind of wife you marry, you will never take a bride like Christ did . . . ; you will never marry anyone estranged from you as the Church was from Christ. Despite all this, he did not abhor or hate her for her extraordinary corruption."[40] Rather, Christ loved the church, in order that she might be sanctified (Eph. 5:25-27). The ecclesial metaphor reigns throughout Chrysostom's strong advice about spousal attitudes and conduct within the marital relationship. The nature of the church and the nature of marriage illumine each other.

In this theology, the Christian family figures as the primal and sacramental human community in which kenotic and agapeic love are learned and rehearsed. Husband and wife share this love within the conjugal relationship, and in turn they communicate this love to the children through their parental care. Furthermore, the Christian family, rehearsed in and equipped with the right virtues, is an arena of ascetic combat with the demons of personal and public life. This *askesis* not only perfects individuals but deepens community.

The Ecclesial versus the Sociological Family

As we have seen, Chrysostom viewed the Christian family as a microcosm of the church and hence a sacrament of the kingdom of God. Chrysostom's ecclesial vision of marriage and family has two key elements. First, it positions parenthood as an office within the community

38. *St. John Chrysostom on Marriage and Family Life*, p. 47.
39. *St. John Chrysostom on Marriage and Family Life*, p. 48.
40. *St. John Chrysostom on Marriage and Family Life*, p. 47.

assigned to people by God and the church. This contrasts with interpretations of parenthood popular in our highly individualistic culture, which tend to focus on parenthood as a subjectively defined role assigned by the self to itself. Second, and correlative to the first point, Christian marriage and family, says Chrysostom, is a communal and oftentimes heroic vocation of unselfish contribution to a divine peoplehood. This challenges contemporary notions of marriage and family that tend to focus on its function either to prepare autonomous selves for participation in society or to provide a therapeutic and recreational center in which the individual can find emotional satisfaction and nurturing.

Those of a more Constantinian set of mind join Chrysostom in viewing the family as a microcosm of Christian society, but they tend to take the belief a good deal further, locating the existence and edification of the kingdom of God more in the family than in the church. The classical origins of this Constantinian outlook and the secular transmutations it has undergone since its adoption in Christian forms lie beyond the scope of our discussion here. Suffice it to say that the differences between the ecclesial vision of Chrysostom and various Constantinian and neo-Constantinian points of view continue to exist in our culture today. For evidence, we need look no further than *The War over the Family* by Brigitte and Peter Berger. The thesis of this volume is that the family is the fundamental building block of society. The Bergers claim further that traditional Protestant Christian family values have historically been vital to the proper functioning of American liberal democracy. Not surprisingly, in view of their thoroughly sociological and functionalistic understanding of the family, the Bergers leave wholly unstated the ecclesial context of the Christian family.

The Bergers make no bones about the fact that they are centrally interested in preserving the American democratic order, which they believe to be threatened by powerful cultural trends of privatism and hyper-individualism. They want their readers to "see that *the family, and specifically the bourgeois family, is the necessary social context for the emergence of the autonomous individuals who are the empirical foundation of political democracy.*"[41] The Bergers support their thesis by citing specific virtues that they say are vital to the flourishing of democratic public life and that they believe are characteristically generated within the American family. Among these virtues are "hard work, diligence, dis-

---

41. Berger and Berger, *The War over the Family* (Garden City, N.Y.: Doubleday-Anchor, 1983), p. 172.

cipline, attention to detail, frugality, and the systematic (not sporadic) cultivation of willpower."[42]

While the virtues mentioned by the Bergers might figure significantly in the telling of at least one version of the story of American democracy, it is not clear that they have much to do with the biblical and Christian story of salvation and the kingdom of God. Nevertheless, the strategy is clear: the Bergers claim a Protestant tradition and ethos as the background of such virtues while avoiding the scandal of Christian particularity; they insist that their list of virtues is "in principle accessible to everyone." I'm not much interested in debating the value of their strategy of securing a secular context — a "middle ground" as they call it in the book's subtitle — for cultivating and instantiating public virtues. But I do find troublesome their rather easy correlation of Christian virtue with the virtues of the culture.

Furthermore, I believe the virtues named by the Bergers lack content. They look rather anemic, even in aggregate, when set alongside that scripturally founded pattern of life that Chrysostom discusses. Chrysostom admired the historic virtues of classical culture, but he did not align himself with the company of those who considered the classical and Christian virtues to be identical, always complementary, or easily correlated with each other. When Chrysostom looked out at the culture, he saw Christians captive to its human-centered standards of success and happiness and pleaded with Christian parents to foster another kind of character in their children.

> If a child learns a trade, or is highly educated for a lucrative profession, all this is nothing compared to the art of detachment from riches; if you want to make your child rich, teach him this. He is truly rich who does not desire great possessions, or surrounds himself with wealth, but who requires nothing. . . . Don't worry about giving him an influential reputation for worldly wisdom, but ponder deeply how you can teach him to think lightly of this life's passing glories, thus he will become truly renowned and glorious. . . . Don't strive to make him a clever orator, but teach him to love true wisdom. He will not suffer if he lacks clever words, but if he lacks wisdom, all the rhetoric in the world can't help him. A pattern of life is what is needed, not empty speeches; character, not cleverness; deeds, not words. These things secure the Kingdom and bestow God's blessings.[43]

42. Berger and Berger, *The War over the Family,* p. 110.
43. *St. John Chrysostom on Marriage and Family Life,* pp. 68-69.

Stoic influences alone cannot account for this passage. The beatitudes, which Chrysostom described as the very constitution of the kingdom of God, lie very near to its surface, together with a biblically founded eschatological hope.

The Bible, said Chrysostom, is the basic primer and lesson book for the virtues of the kingdom that God charges parents to teach their children. Scripture provides the narratives of the lives of patriarchs and matriarchs, the parents and siblings who struggled in God's presence to maintain a way of life distinct though not necessarily separate from the world. In his *Address on Vainglory and the Right Way for Parents to Bring Up Their Children,* Chrysostom pioneered what might be regarded as one of the first Christian curriculums for children's Bible study. The responsibility for such education, however, rests first of all with the parents. Chrysostom commended especially the stories of Cain and Abel, Jacob and Esau, Joseph and his brothers, Hannah and Samuel, and the like. His method is worth looking at, as is the subject matter.

Much of Chrysostom's discussion is concerned with identifying biblical models for relations between parents and children and of siblings with each other. For example, he encourages parents to juxtapose the stories of Cain and Abel and of Jacob and Esau, drawing out the distinct lessons of each story as well as the themes common to each concerning sibling rivalry, envy, and fratricide. He urges parents to tell the stories not once but repeatedly. Then they should say to the child,

> "Tell me the story of those two brothers." And if he begins to relate the story of Cain and Abel, stop him and say: "It is not that one that I want, but the one of the other two brothers, in which the father gave his blessing." Give him hints but do not as yet tell him their names. When he has told you all, spin the sequel of the yarn, and say: "Hear what occurred afterwards. Once again the elder brother, like in the former story, was minded to slay his brother. . . ."[44]

In his twenty-first homily on Ephesians, Chrysostom gives his rationale for such instruction and stresses its importance for Christian living:

> Don't think that only monks need to learn the Bible; children about to go into the world stand in greater need of Scriptural knowledge.

---

44. Chrysostom, *An Address on Vainglory and the Right Way for Parents to Bring Up Their Children,* appended to L. W. Laistner's *Christianity and Pagan Culture* (Ithaca, N.Y.: Cornell University Press, 1951), pp. 106-7.

A man who never travels by sea doesn't need to know how to equip a ship, or where to find a pilot or a crew, but a sailor has to know all these things. The same applies to the monk and the man of this world. The monk lives an untroubled life in a calm harbor, removed from every storm, while the worldly man is always sailing the ocean, battling innumerable tempests.[45]

From the perspective of Chrysostom's vision of Christian family and virtue, strategies for the revitalization of the family and preservation of society like the Bergers' are theologically misdirected. Once one defines Christian existence and tradition in merely sociological terms, a certain kind of ecclesiology and definition of Christian family emerges. The family is defined as a training ground for virtues that principally have to do with the proper functioning of the secular polity — a worthy enough goal, but not what lies at the heart of the vocation of Christian parenthood and family. Nor in these post-Christendom times is it helpful to seek to counteract the privatism in the American family with social ministry, as some liberal Protestants and liberal Roman Catholics seem to think.[46] The Christian family, weakened and secularized by powerful cultural forces of privatism, narcissism, and consumerism, is scarcely the fittest agent for social change in any case. There is a crucial interim step missing in such calls to commit the Christian family to social transformation. The Christian family can receive a public vocation only after it has first become engaged in the struggle for the kingdom of God. The jargon of the Christian activists — "intimacy," "shared decision making," "peacemaking," "cooperative projects," and the like — is hardly distinctive; nor is it in any significant way superior to the other kinds of progressivism in our culture that fail to provide a transcendent imperative for ethical behavior. Chrysostom insists on another course: "When we teach our children to be gentle, to be forgiving, to be generous, to love their fellow men . . . we instill virtue in their souls and reveal the image of God within them. This, then, is our task: to educate both ourselves and our children in godliness; otherwise what answer will we have have before Christ's judgment seat? . . . How [else] can we be worthy of the kingdom of heaven?"[47]

45. *St. John Chrysostom on Marriage and Family Life*, p. 69.
46. See, e.g., James and Kathleen McGinnis, "The Social Mission of the Family," in *Faith and Families*, ed. Lindell Sawyers (Philadelphia: Geneva Press, 1986), pp. 89-113.
47. *St. John Chrysostom on Marriage and Family Life*, p. 71.

Back to Ecclesiological Matters

In closing, I would like to field one potential critical response to this exposition and exploration of Chrysostom's ecclesial vision of the Christian family. I realize that those who follow Ernst Troeltsch may be inclined to categorize even the ecclesiology I have described as sectarian. Troeltsch himself once asserted that Chrysostom wanted to turn "Constantinople and Antioch into a communistic fellowship of love like the monastic life."[48] Troeltsch didn't quite want to take Chrysostom on his word either; he charged him with making an "ideal" prescription. In any event, if a theologian's ecclesiology is in any sense associated with the monastic ideal, Troeltsch's reasoning classifies the theologian as drawn to the sectarian paradigm of Christian existence. H. Richard Niebuhr stated the thesis rather baldly in the context of his discussion of the Christ-against-culture type of Christianity in *Christ and Culture*:

> Eventually, . . . many sorts of monasticism arose. . . . Yet the main stream of the movement, as represented for instance by the *Rule of Benedict*, remained in the tradition of exclusive Christianity. Whatever contributions it eventually made to culture . . . were incidental byproducts which it did not intend. Its intention was directed to the achievement of a Christian life, apart from civilization, in obedience to the laws of Christ, and in pursuit of a perfection wholly distinct from the aims that men seek in politics and economics, in science and arts. Protestant sectarianism — to use the term in its narrow, sociological meaning — has given the same sort of answer to the question of Christ and culture.[49]

Chrysostom did not regard monasticism as an escape from culture or civilization. Nor did he think of it as a pursuit of some sort of higher spiritual perfection that obviated responsibility for the reform of society. Troeltsch was right in saying that Chrysostom valued monasticism and wanted to extend its discipline to society, but he was wrong in asserting that this was an otherworldly ideal for the Church Father. To the contrary, Chrysostom viewed it as a theological imperative for life very much in this world, based in his — yes, let us use Troeltsch's other category for the moment — *churchly* type of ecclesiology. And

48. Troeltsch, *The Social Teaching of the Christian Church*, vol. 1, trans. Olive Wyon (New York: Halley Stewart, 1931), p. 127.

49. Niebuhr, *Christ and Culture* (New York: Harper & Row, 1951), p. 56.

where did he get that ecclesiology? In what for Troeltsch would have been the most unlikely of places: the monastery itself. In Chrysostom's understanding, the motive for the "flight" of monasticism *was* reform. Likewise, the motive for Chrysostom's return to the "city" out of the monastery was conversion and reform of a decadent pagan society and the pale cultural representations of Christianity within it. He expected that this conversion and reform would be achieved through God's economy mediated from within the church. "I frequently prayed," he wrote, "that the need for monasteries would pass away, and that I would be able to find in cities such goodness and such order that no one would ever again have to flee to the desert."[50] Under the circumstances it might be just as appropriate to say that monasticism is the preeminently churchly form of Christianity.[51]

But before becoming tangled in the alluring web of Troeltsch's typology, we would do well to look elsewhere for clarification. Some years back, Stanley Harakas published a remarkable article entitled "The Church in the Secular World." While I would want to make a more complete break with Troeltsch's typology than Harakas was willing to do in that essay, Harakas's central thesis is to be commended and is consistent with Chrysostom on such matters. In the midst of a critique of Troeltsch, Harakas reasonably suggests that Troeltsch needs some correction insofar as he leaves the impression that the church type was merely the by-product of the disappointments of an early sectarian church with the unfulfilled eschatological expectation of the Second Coming and rapid establishment of the kingdom of God. Harakas argues that, to the contrary, the world-transforming outlook of the church type was already implicit in this eschatological expectation of the early church.[52] Alexander Schmemann said the same thing in a somewhat different fashion: "The eschatology in whose light the early church indeed judged and evaluated everything in this world was not negative, but a highly 'positive,' experience, not a denial of the world but a certain way of looking at it and experiencing it. For its ultimate content and term of reference was not the world, but the Kingdom of God, and thus rather than being 'anti-world' it was a

---

50. Chrysostom, quoted by Georges Florovsky in *The Collected Works of Georges Florovsky*, vol. 7: *The Eastern Fathers of the Fourth Century* (Belmont, Mass.: Buchervertriebsanstalt, 1987), p. 242.

51. I owe this insight to Fr. Stanley S. Harakas from conversations with him on the subject.

52. Harakas, "The Church and the Secular World," *Greek Orthodox Theological Review* 17 (1972): 181.

'pro-Kingdom' attitude, in which it differed from eschatologies that developed later."[53]

The monastic movement might then be interpreted not as the lingering and uncompromising continuation among a minority of an earlier sectarianism that was once more characteristic of the whole church but rather as a further clarification and affirmation of the original apostolic kerygma and call to conversion of the church in the face of new circumstances. By the fourth and fifth centuries, persecution no longer threatened the church's integrity and evangelism; instead a Christian empire ironically threatened to "absorb Christianity and subject it to itself."[54]

Harakas proposes that under these circumstances the church was faced with two distinct alternatives. He quotes the Russian religious philosopher George P. Fedetov as saying that the church had to choose either "to remain a small community of the pure, expecting Christ to return and judge the world and meanwhile leaving the world to inevitable perdition, or to go into the world in order to teach and save it."[55] Fedetov characterized the latter alternative as a "path of condescension . . . rooted in the very nature and work of Christ 'who, though he was in the form of God, did not count equality with God a thing to be grasped, but emptied himself, taking the form of a servant, being born in the likeness of men' (Philip. 2:6-7)."[56] Harakas concludes that if early Christianity had been "purely sect-type . . . then the most reasonable expectation would have been that the . . . Christian community would have rejected as unnecessary and harmful, Constantine's offer of freedom, the privileges and the subsequent establishment of the Church."[57]

Here I am not sure Harakas has wholly proven his case. This notwithstanding, however, there is much to be said for Fedetov's notion of a "condescending" church. (We have found this theological notion of condescension in Chrysostom's description of spousal relations, which itself has everything to do with his understanding of the church and its relationship to the world.) The temptation of power proved stronger oftentimes than the church's will to follow this path con-

53. Schmemann, *Church, World, Mission* (Crestwood, N.Y.: St. Vladimir's Seminary Press, 1979), pp. 28-29.

54. Schmemann, *The Historical Road of Eastern Orthodoxy* (Crestwood, N.Y.: St. Vladimir's Seminary Press, 1977), p. 109.

55. Fedetov, quoted by Harakas in "The Church and the Secular World," p. 181.

56. Harakas, "The Church and the Secular World," p. 181.

57. Harakas, "The Church and the Secular World," pp. 181-82.

sistently. At various times and places the church capitulated to or made unholy alliance with secular powers. Nevertheless, the notion of condescension enables us to see the potential consistency of monasticism with the best motives of those who chose the parish or episcopal see rather than the cloister. The radicalism of Chrysostom's ethic of the Christian family lies in just this sort of ecclesiology.

Conclusion

There exists a great need in the Christian churches today for ecclesial formation, for they stand to become increasingly dissipated if they continue to depend for strength on cultural supports for the faith that are in fact no longer present. The churches must seek ecclesial formation not for its own sake but to prepare believers to greet the Groom when he returns. If Chrysostom was right about the Christian family as a vocation of the kingdom and about the Christian household as a little church — the household of God *(oikonomia tou theou)* writ small — then we would do well in this time and place to reclaim that vision. We must work to make the Christian family once again a training ground in which by becoming good husbands and wives, fathers and mothers and children, we become "fit to oversee the Church" and good "housekeepers" of God's present and future kingdom.

We also need to join Chrysostom in regarding the church as a body related in various ways to larger society and reject all notions of the church as an elite group concerned solely with so-called spiritual matters and appropriately heedless of all things worldly. Then we will begin to appreciate anew the special value of Chrysostom's ecclesial vision of the family for the re-formation of the church and the introduction of a new discipline into its life for the salvation of the world.

7. *Ecological Ethics: An Ecclesial Event*

> Everything I saw aroused in me love and thankfulness to
> God; people, trees, plants, animals were all my kind, for
> I saw in all of them the reflection of the Name of Jesus
> Christ.
>
> FROM "THE WAY OF THE PILGRIM,"
> A RUSSIAN RELIGIOUS TALE

After Christendom, Christians are challenged to make the theological
and ethical resources of their faith speak to others in new and different
ways. To meet this challenge, Christians need first to assess the loss to
the societies in which they live that has been inflicted by the reduction
and marginalization of biblical faith. Second, they need to correct mis-
conceptions about Christianity's disposition and outlook on fundamental human ethical concerns. The discussion of the family in Chapter 6
moves in these directions. Our discussion of ecology in this chapter
and of death and care for the dying in the final chapter continue the
inquiry.

There is an ecological vision deeply planted within Orthodox
theology and ethics. Nowhere is this vision more pronounced than in
the Orthodox rites of blessing, and so I want to explore the language
and theology of these services in some detail. I will join some constructive arguments to this descriptive account of the tradition in an effort
to engage the long-standing debate over how biblical faith measures
up ecologically.

In the Context of a Debate

Nearly twenty-five years ago, the biblical scholar Claus Westermann wrote an intriguing little book entitled *Blessing: In the Bible and the Life of the Church*. He suggested that the ascendant *Heilsgeschichte* biblical theology of the time had overlooked the primacy of blessing in Scripture. Yes, history is at the heart of the Bible, but "when the Bible speaks of God's contact with mankind," he argued, "his blessing is there alongside his deliverance."[1] He went on to say,

> History comes into being only when both [deliverance and blessing] are together. The element of contingency, essential to historical events, enters the biblical history through the presence together of God's activity in saving and blessing and through their effect upon each other. . . .
>
> It is God's blessing that provides for the sequence of human births generation after generation. . . . It is God's blessing that lets the child grow into a man or woman, that bestows such manifold talents, and that provides physical and spiritual food from so many sources. Without these elements of growth, maturation, and decline, of lesser and greater gifts, of the relations of men and women, there is no real history.[2]

The biblical understanding of blessing (Heb. *berekh*) concerns the divine gift of life and prosperity (see, e.g., Gen. 27:25-30). Those who are touched by God's blessings reciprocate with blessing and praise of God out of gratitude (see, e.g., 1 Cor. 10:16). Westermann insisted that the biblical view of history is not merely about God's mighty acts of deliverance but also about "processes that are usually regarded as 'unhistorical' — the growth and multiplying of the people and the effects of the forces that preserve their physical life. . . . This leads to a modification of the concept of history."[3] With respect to Israel, the Bible portrays God as being concerned not only with those events specifically having to do with human will and volition but also with those elements involving process, nurture, interdependence, and participation. The biblical view of creation (the *ktisis* or *ta panta*) encompasses what we

---

1. Westermann, *Blessing: In the Bible and the Life of the Church*, Overtures to Biblical Theology, no. 3, ed. Walter Brueggemann and John Donahue, trans. Keith Crim (Philadelphia: Fortress Press, 1978), p. 4.

2. Westermann, *Blessing*, pp. 4-5.

3. Westermann, *Blessing*, p. 6.

call nature as well as history, and biblical blessing embraces this fuller vision of God and creation.

Westermann's *Blessing* was published in its original German so soon after the publication of Lynn White Jr.'s now-famous article "The Historical Roots of Our Ecological Crisis" that it hardly seems possible that he could have written it as a response to White's assertions. Nevertheless, Westermann's book does effectively expose some fundamental errors in White's critique. White completely ignores the biblical motif of blessing, as do virtually all of his theological admirers. White embraced the widely accepted thesis that modern science and technology could not have arisen apart from the demystifying and desacralizing of nature effected by the Bible and Christian theology. The basic argument is that the Bible and Christian tradition impose a sharp differentiation between a transcendent God and an immanent nature. This sets up the opposing categories of history as a realm of God's encounters with humanity and nature as a realm of necessity over which humanity is given dominion. This dualism, it is argued, made possible modern science and technological development. Many of those who had adopted this interpretation before White presented it in essentially positive terms: Christianity made a unique contribution to advanced scientific and technological culture. White, however, cast these developments in a negative light, arguing that the biblical myth of creation supplanted "pagan animism" and introduced "a dualism of man and nature" in which humanity, bearing the image of divinity, was radically differentiated from nature and, by virtue of its special status, granted powers similar to those of the Divinity over nature. This gave humanity a warrant to exploit nature solely for its own satisfaction.[4]

White's thesis quickly made its way into much of the secular as well as religious discussion about ecology. In 1972 Gordon Kaufman, for example, asserted that

> the conceptions of God and man, as they have developed in the Western religious traditions, work hand in hand toward the distinguishing of man from (the rest of) nature. Nature is not conceived primarily as man's proper home and the very source and sustenance of his being, but rather as the context of and material for teleological activity by the (nonnatural) wills working upon it and in it. It is not really surprising that this kind of orientation and stance, given certain

4. See White, "The Historical Roots of Our Ecological Crisis," *Science* 155 (1967): 1203-7.

other historical conditions, could eventuate in a tremendous technological explosion in which the earth and her resources would be
increasingly subjected to human purposes; it is also not surprising
that such an attitude would tend to overlook and neglect the question
whether certain "natural boundaries" were being trespassed and
certain "natural balances" upset. If nature were created by (God's)
will for the sake of further volitional activity, how could (human) will
be threatened simply by its strenuous exercise in nature?[5]

Kaufman conceded that his portrait was a bit "overdrawn," that
the tradition also contained resources for tempering human domination
and the use of nature. Nevertheless, he insisted that the preponderance
of evidence demands the conclusion that "the theological problem of
nature [vis-à-vis the tradition] . . . is not simply one of rearranging
emphases or details, lifting up certain motifs in the tradition which may
have been neglected. It goes far deeper than that, into the very logic of
the central concepts of our religious tradition. The very ideas of God
and man . . . are so framed as to" distort or completely hide humanity's
"embeddedness in the natural order as we now are increasingly conceiving it."[6] Kaufman expanded on White's thesis, arguing that the
tradition is unrepentantly anthropocentric, focused on concepts of per-
sonality, will, and volition, of divine and human being and doing (i.e.,
history and eternity), with respect to which the natural world is at best
a backdrop for human history and at worst a threat to that history,
something that must be overcome before human beings can flourish
spiritually and personally.

I will not deny that there have been strong currents within Christianity, especially Western Christianity, of the sort that Kaufman depicts
as typifying the whole (e.g., the legacies of medieval Roman Catholic
distinctions between nature and grace, Cartesian mind/body dualism,
and modern Protestantism's emphasis on the action of God in history
as distinct from nature). But the point remains that White, Kaufman,
and others who follow them have ignored the element of blessing in
biblical and Christian tradition, particularly as it is connected with
sacrament and liturgical practice, and no assessment will be fair or
accurate that makes this crucial omission. How can one hope to construct an adequate theology of nature and ecological ethics without
making use of all the available resources?

5. Kaufman, "A Problem for Theology: The Concept of Nature," *Harvard Theological Review* 65 (1972): 353-54.
6. Kaufman, "A Problem for Theology," p. 354.

Ecology and the Priestly Vocation of Humanity

Christian tradition holds that human beings are created in the image and likeness of God. For this reason alone, humanity is bestowed with an exceptional power over creation. This power entails both a special vocation and a special responsibility. Humanity must mediate God's presence and God's care to the rest of creation. As human beings, we are called out by the very act through which God creates us to be priests and stewards of creation. The first chapter of Genesis tells the story:

> Then God said, 'Let us make man in our image and likeness to rule the fish in the sea, the birds of heaven, the cattle, all wild animals, and all reptiles that crawl upon the earth.' So God created man in his own image; in the image of God he created him; male and female he created them. God blessed them and said to them, 'Be fruitful and increase, fill the earth and subdue it, rule over the fish in the sea, the birds of heaven, and every living thing that moves upon the earth.' God also said, 'I give you all plants that bear seed everywhere on the earth, and every tree bearing fruit which yields seed: they shall be yours for food. All green plants I give for food to the wild animals, to all the birds of heaven, and to all reptiles on the earth, every living creature.' So it was; and God saw all that he had made, and it was very good. Evening came, and morning came, a sixth day. (1:26-31, NEB)

The presiding metaphor for humankind's role in the creation that contemporary theological writers have drawn from this and other biblical texts is stewardship. In broader discussions involving people outside biblical faith, this concept of stewardship has certainly proved useful, but it may turn out that it is not the most important metaphor with respect to an ecclesially centered ecological ethic. The Orthodox tradition out of which I speak interprets this Genesis account of God's blessings at the creation as issuing a call for a response of thanksgiving and blessing from human beings. The presiding biblical metaphor in Orthodox ecological thinking has been the human being as "priest" of creation.

When Orthodox encounter the stewardship metaphor in ecological discussions, they perceive its inadequacy almost intuitively: they see that it fails to incorporate the concept of blessing for ecological reflection. Paulos Gregorios, who has addressed ecological themes in a theological context as much as any Orthodox, says, "I believe it is wrong to set man's domination of nature over and against his stewardship of it. Replacing the concept of domination with the concept of stewardship will not lead us very far, for even in the latter there lies the hidden possibility of the objectification and alienation which are the root causes of the sickness of our civilization. Nature would remain some kind of property, owned not by us, of course, but by God, given into our hands for efficient and productive use."[7]

Gregorios argues that the priest metaphor is a richer biblical concept for ecological theology and ethics than is the stewardship metaphor. Consider the use of the priest metaphor in the story of Noah's crowning response to the redemption of all who were in the ark, for example. "Then Noah built an altar to the LORD, and took of every clean animal and of every clean bird, and offered burnt offerings on the altar. And when the LORD smelled the pleasing odor, the LORD said in his heart, 'I will never again curse the the ground because of humankind, for the inclination of the human heart is evil from youth; nor will I ever again destroy every living creature as I have done. . . . God blessed Noah and his sons" (Gen. 8:20-21; 9:1a). Noah's priestly offering of sacrifice and blessing signifies a reversal of all that has gone wrong with humankind and the whole of creation as a result of the fall. In spite of the fact that "the inclination of the human heart" remains "evil," the reversal is still possible because Noah has assumed anew the priestly vocation abandoned by Adam when he ate of the forbidden fruit. Stewardship is corruptible because of the evil inclination of the human heart, but blessings offered by humanity in gratitude for what God has done to save and renew creation always have worth in God's eyes. While the priestly action of blessing cannot in and of itself overcome the cosmic consequences of human sin and the fall, it does prepare the human heart to perform good stewardship.

James Barr has answered some of the secular and theological critics who place primary responsibility and guilt for the ecological mess on the biblical tradition. After having listed several biblical themes that he thinks need to be amplified, Barr states that "the whole framework of Genesis is intended to suggest that man is man when he is in his place within nature. His dominion over nature is given little definition; but, in general, its content is less exploitation and more leadership, a sort of primal *liturgical place*."[8] While Barr himself does not explain precisely what he means by "primal liturgical place," Orthodox

7. Gregorios, *The Human Presence* (Geneva: World Council of Churches, 1978), p. 84.
8. Barr, "Man and Nature: The Ecological Controversy and the Old Testament," *Bulletin of the John Rylands Library* 55 (Autumn 1972): 31; italics mine.

theology has had much to say about it. The priestly vocation of humanity is a prominent theme in the sacramental theology of the late Alexander Schmemann. Schmemann focused intently on the implications of this theology of priestly vocation for ecological thinking, as in the following passage:

> The fall of man is the rejection by him of his priestly calling, his refusal to be priest. The original sin consists in man's choice of a non-priestly relationship with God and the world. And perhaps no word better expresses the essence of this new, fallen, non-priestly way of life than the one which in our time has had an amazingly successful career, has truly become the symbol of our culture. It is the word *consumer*. After having glorified himself as *homo faber*, and then as *homo sapiens*, man seems to have found his ultimate vocation as "consumer." . . . But the truth is, of course, that the "consumer" was not born in the twentieth century. The first consumer was Adam himself. He chose not to be priest but to approach the world as consumer: to "eat" of it, to use and to dominate it for himself, to benefit from it but not to offer, not to sacrifice, not to have it for God and in God.[9]

Blessing Turned to Curse

The priest metaphor helps illumine both the destructive consequences that sin and fallenness have on the ecology and the remedy that lies within human responsibility and power. Good management alone will not restore health to the ecosystem. At the center of the ecological problem is the fact that the original blessing has turned to curse. Only humanity's willing embrace of its priestly and eucharistic vocation will remedy the deep ontological disharmony of the created order. The Bible describes sin and fallenness as cosmic in scope. St. Paul expresses this in his letter to the Romans when he observes that "the whole creation has been groaning in travail together until now" (8:22, RSV). Before him, the ancient poet of Isaiah had written eloquently of the same thing:

> The earth dries up and withers,
>   the world languishes and withers;
>   the heavens languish together with the earth.

9. Schmemann, *Of Water and the Spirit* (Crestwood, N.Y.: St. Vladimir's Seminary Press, 1974), p. 96.

The earth lies polluted
  under its inhabitants;
for they have transgressed laws,
  violated the statutes,
  broken the everlasting covenant.
Therefore a curse devours the earth,
  and its inhabitants suffer for their guilt;
therefore the inhabitants of the earth dwindled,
  and few people are left. (24:4-6)

At the close of the flood story, God tells Noah that "the fear and dread of you shall rest on every animal of the earth, and on every bird of the air, on everything that creeps on the ground, and on all the fish of the sea; into your hand they are delivered" (Gen. 9:2). God accepts Noah's offering of blessing and promises him that never again will he curse the ground or destroy the whole earth as he did with the flood. Nevertheless, human sinfulness does not cease with the flood, and the creation awaits an even greater redemptive event — the Incarnation.

As a precondition of that ultimate redemption of creation, God bestows a blessing on Noah and his sons, saying, "Be fruitful and multiply, and fill the earth" (Gen. 9:1b). When God gives human beings permission to eat the flesh of the animals after the flood (Gen. 9:3), he is not diminishing the value he places on all life; to the contrary, he is intensifying that value, and he expects human beings to affirm this value through renewed thanksgiving and blessing. It is in this connection that God commands Noah not to consume the blood of the animals along with the flesh (Gen. 9:4). Blood is strongly symbolic of the God-bestowed life of a living being, and the command not to partake of it is a command to return life to the earth as sacrifice and blessing.

Orthodox Christianity's preference for the language of gift and blessing is evident in its eucharistic theology and particularly in its rites of blessing. The ecological ethic that emerges from a study of the rites of blessing is itself founded in a powerful theology of creation and Incarnation. This theology insists on an intimate relationship of humanity with all that is creature and earth. Gregorios has written:

> It was matter that Christ assumed to constitute his "historical" body; it was food that he ate, water or wine that he drank, air that he breathed, the earth and sea on which he walked. It was of the elements of the earth that his body was constituted, the body which was transfigured on Mount Tabor, crucified on the tree, and came

out through the mouth of a tomb, the body in which he appeared to his disciples, in which he ascended to heaven.[10]

I cannot think of a more vivid illustration of this theology of Incarnation than a story told by the Armenian writer Teotig, who gathered accounts of clergy martyred in the Turkish genocide of the Armenians during the First World War. Among the martyrdoms recounted is that of Fr. Ashod Avedidian, a priest of a village in the vicinity of the city of Erzeroum in Eastern Turkey, one of four thousand men who had been separated from their women and children. On the long death march, when no food was left, Fr. Ashod counseled the men to pray in unison, "Lord, have mercy," and in the only sacramental gesture possible, he led them in taking the "cursed" soil and swallowing it as communion. Gregorios emphasizes the Orthodox belief that the whole creation has been redeemed through the incarnate Word. Teotig's story reminds us that there is no human redemption that excludes the earth from which we come and to which we are intimately bound by God's creative and saving acts in Jesus Christ.

Ecology within the Orthodox Rites of Blessing

I hope these observations have clarified the significance of blessing for a Christian ecological ethic. In the Orthodox churches, baptism and Epiphany both celebrate the new creation inaugurated by Christ's baptism. The rites of Epiphany celebrate the renewal — the rebirth — of all creation in the baptism of the incarnate divine Logos. The rites of baptism focus on the re-creation of the human being rather than the cosmos, but they do include a cosmic dimension through prayers of exorcism and blessing of the water as a symbol of life.

The Byzantine service of baptism includes a great prayer of blessing and consecration that reverses the curse of Genesis and the sign of destruction that the waters had become in the flood. The reversal of the curse begins with an exorcism of the water: "We pray thee, O God, that every aerial and obscure phantom withdraw itself from us; and that no demon of darkness may conceal himself in this water; and that no evil spirit which instilleth darkening of intentions and rebelliousness of thought may descend into it with him (her) who is about to be baptized." Only after such an exorcism does it become

10. Gregorios, *The Human Presence*, p. 85.

possible for this same water to be realized and declared as "the water of redemption, the water of sanctification, the purification of flesh and spirit, the loosing of bonds, the remission of sins, the illumination of the soul, the laver of regeneration, the renewal of the Spirit, the gift of adoption to sonship, the garment of incorruption, the fountain of life."[11] The water again assumes the true and good character that God ascribed to it at the creation. It partakes of the essence of the water over which the Spirit hovered at the creation and the water of the Jordan River into which the Spirit descended at Christ's baptism. "Thou didst hallow the streams of Jordan, sending down upon them from heaven thy Holy Spirit, and didst crush the heads of the dragons who lurked there."[12] Through this water, declares the Armenian rite, "the regeneration of all men" is accomplished, Christ having come "and saved *all creatures.*"[13]

In the great Armenian prayer for Epiphany, the cosmic dimensions of this blessing of the waters are amplified:

> To-day the grace of the holy Spirit, hallowing the water, becomes co-worker (with Christ our God)
> To-day the heavens gaily bedew from above with the dew of grace, and to-day shone forth on us the sun inextinguishable, and all the world is radiant with light.
> To-day the moon beams forth with a great light, and withal the world is filled with splendour.
> To-day the light-clad luminaries work hearty good unto all that dwell on earth.
> To-day clouds divine and dews divine bedew men from above.
> To-day the seas and gatherings of waters are spread out for the path and foot-falls of the Lord.
> To-day the Hidden one is manifested, and the Unseen one is seen, that he may make us seers.
> To-day the Incarnate by his own creation, through a mystery, hath laid hands on him.
> To-day the Unhumbled humbly inclines his head to his own servant that he may free us from servitude.
> To-day he humbles the hills unto servitude and makes the rivers

---

11. *Service Book of the Holy Orthodox-Catholic Apostolic Church*, ed. and trans. Isabel Florence Hapgood (Englewood, N.J.: Antiochian Orthodox Christian Archdiocese, 1975), p. 278.

12. *Service Book of the Holy Orthodox-Catholic Apostolic Church*, p. 278.

13. *The Sacraments: Symbols of Our Faith*, ed. Garabed Kochakian (New York: Diocese of the Armenian Church), pp. 25, 30; italics mine.

as the sea. All that nature of the waters is blessed and
hallowed. . . .
To-day come the currents of grace of the holy Spirit, and all
creatures are inundated therewith. . . .
To-day the briny waters of the sea are changed to sweetness, at
the appearing of our God. . . .
To-day all creatures appear clad in splendour at the appearing of
our God.
To-day the waters appear above for the salvation of the world.
To-day the garden appears to mankind, and let us rejoice in
righteousness unto eternal life. . . .
To-day the earth trembling, but joyfully, receives the Creator's
footsteps upon it.
To-day the sins and transgressions of the race of Adam are
blotted out in the water of Jordan, and the earth's face is
renewed at the appearing of our God.
To-day the shut and barred gate of the garden is opened to
mankind.[14]

The hymn is filled with allusions to the first chapters of Genesis.
It celebrates the reversal of the fall, as the curse is replaced with a new
blessing and new covenant. Indeed, the hymn begins with a recollection
of the entire creation account of Genesis 1 and the story of the fall with
its catastrophic consequences. Thus, when later we hear that "the light
clad luminaries" once again "work hearty good unto all that dwell on
earth" and the like, we are being assured that the primal ecological
system in which God intended all things to coexist harmoniously and
in interdependence has been restored. The new "inundation" brings
not death or destruction but a blessing of "the grace of the holy Spirit
. . . for all creatures . . . inundated therewith." This means all of creation
participates in Christ's baptism. Lastly, the original *shalom* is restored.
The waters have been prepared for the "foot-falls of the Lord," and the
earth "receives the Creator's footsteps upon it." This time, however,
unlike those foot-falls heard by Adam and Eve in the garden after they
had eaten of the forbidden fruit, these foot-falls bring news of fresh
blessing. Now "the earth's face is renewed" and "the shut and barred
gate of the garden is opened."
    In *The End of Nature,* Bill McKibben voices a familiar theme of

14. *Rituale Armenorum: The Administration of the Sacraments and the Breviary Rites of the Armenian Church,* ed. F. C. Conybeare (Oxford: Clarendon Press, 1905), pp. 170, 172, 174-75.

the ecology movement. He condemns the biblical creation myth as destructive and anthropocentric. He asserts that the only true nature is nature untouched by the human species. At one point he laments that "we have built a greenhouse, *a human creation,* where once there blossomed a sweet and wild garden."[15] But no garden of this sort is described in the book of Genesis, in either the priestly story of Genesis 1 or the Jahwist account of Genesis 2. These creation accounts present Adam as "cultivator," "steward," and "blesser": there is no uncultivated garden; all who inhabit the garden benefit from it. Human beings have the special vocation of tending the garden and blessing it to proper use and the praise of God. The Eucharist establishes a profound connection both in origin and consummation between humanity and the entire material creation. Eucharistic faith does not look forward to a time when nature will be "liberated" entirely from human presence; rather, it looks forward, as the Armenian hymn of the blessing of the water puts it, to a day when the shut and barred gate of the garden will be opened for mankind. Moreover, the anticipation of this reunion in no way constitutes a warrant for the continued abuse of creation; to the contrary, it calls us to work for a restoration of the original harmony and peace among all God's creatures and a return of Adam to his priestly vocation.

As for the complaint that the Judeo-Christian tradition is anthropocentric, I will concede the point: Scripture and tradition alike do support the claim that God honors humanity uniquely among all his creatures. But inasmuch as these special honors entail concomitant responsibilities associated with our priestly vocation to care for his creation, I do not believe that this anthropocentrism can rightly be characterized as a flaw or a liability. The problem lies not in the anthropocentrism as such but in our failure to live up to our obligations as specially entrusted creatures of God.

Cleansing and Healing of Creation

The theology of the Orthodox rites includes a cosmic notion of evil. Evil is not psychologized, nor is it restricted merely to the human will. The waters that stand for all of creation must be exorcised. The human being is the priestly agent of that exorcism. The church cannot seriously pray that the water be redemptive when it remains polluted. Redemp-

15. McKibben, *The End of Nature* (New York: Random House, 1989), p. 91.

tion is possible only if human beings act as priests to dispel the demonic in all things. "The Bible and the Christian faith reveal and experience matter on the one hand as essentially *good*, yet on the other hand as the very vehicle of man's fall and enslavement to death and sin, as the means by which Satan stole the world from God," wrote Alexander Schmemann.[16] He went on to argue that "the liberation of man begins with the liberation, i.e. the purification and the redemption of matter, its restoration to its original function: to be a means of God's presence and, therefore, to be a protection and defence against the destructive 'demonic' reality."[17] In other words, there is no human salvation apart from the cleansing and restoration to health of the whole creation.

In the Armenian prayer of communion, the celebrant implores the Father "who hast called us by the name of thine Only-begotten and has enlightened us through the baptism of the spiritual font. . . . Impress upon us the graces of thy Holy Spirit, as thou didst upon the holy apostles, who tasted thereof and became the cleansers of the whole world."[18] Planetary waters are scarcely fit symbols of life and renewal when they are filled with deadly chemicals. It would be inappropriate to offer a dirtied and polluted world back to God in thanksgiving for his divine love. The vocation of the apostles includes being healers and "cleansers of the whole world."

In the Old Testament, the Hebrew word for salvation derives from *yasha*, which means "to be at large" or "to save from a danger." Salvation in the Old Testament is intimately connected with metaphors for healing from sickness or illness. In the New Testament, the Greek *sozo* is derived from *saos*, which denotes "health." Faith delivers persons, creatures, and things into the care of a healing God. Orthodox theology retains a strong sense of this meaning of salvation. Just how all-embracing this understanding of salvation has been in Eastern spirituality is reflected in the famous meditation of St. Isaac the Syrian: "What is the charitable heart? It is a heart on fire with charity for all creation, men, demons, every creature. Immense compassion seizes the heart. . . . It can no longer bear even the slightest pain to be inflicted on a creature. . . . It prays even for the reptiles moved by the infinite pity which is awakened in the heart of those who grow like God."[19]

16. Schmemann, *Of Water and the Spirit*, p. 49.
17. Schmemann, *Of Water and the Spirit*, p. 42.
18. *Divine Liturgy of the Armenian Apostolic Orthodox Church*, trans. Tiran Nersoyan (London: Armenian Church of St. Sarkis, 1984), p. 97.
19. Quoted by Paul Evdokimov, "Nature," *Scottish Journal of Theology* 18 (March 1965): 13.

This emphasis on healing within the salvific process is echoed by St. Basil of Caesarea in a prayer for animals:

> And for these also, O Lord, the humblest beasts, who bear with us the heat and burden of the day, we beg thee to extend thy great kindness of heart, for thou hast promised to save both man and beast, and great is thy loving-kindness, O Master.[20]

Within the Armenian tradition there is a variety of rites that locate this theology of healing ecclesially. One of the most impressive is the Washing of the Cross. Virtually all of the ecological motifs of Orthodox theology we have considered thus far are embraced by this rite. It presents the cross as a source not only of salvific healing for human beings but also "for the healing of Plants, and Herds and Flocks and of all disastrous Ailments."[21] The central prayer of the rite recalls the first chapters of the book of Genesis, enumerating the works of creation and thanking God for them. Humanity is especially honored among God's creatures, but, having fallen into "ruin and destruction," humankind needs to be renewed through the "washing of the font," for God did "constitute the waters for purification and hallowing."[22] The well-being and redemption of the rest of creation depends on the restoration of the divine image in humankind.

The prayer calls up the memory of the primal waters that came into being through the activity of the "eternal word," Christ. Through him, God divided the waters into those above and below and gathered what remained "into their several heaps . . . out of which there issued, kind by kind, creeping things at thy command for the profit of man."[23] God is beseeched to cleanse and return this water to a state in which it might once again be fit for the sacrament of salvation and healing.

> And through the prophet Elisha thou didst bless waters that were pestiferous and deadly; and through the great Moses thou didst divide the victorious waters with a rod fashioned in the form of the cross and swallowing up the enemy in the depths. Thou gavest sweetness to the waters of Mera that welled forth a bitter spring, and didst replenish and slake the burning thirst of the people.
>
> And now, Lord beneficent, send the same spirit of grace into

---

20. Cited by John Passmore in "The Treatment of Animals," *Journal of the History of Ideas* 36 (April-June 1975): 198.

21. *Rituale Armenorum*, p. 224.

22. *Rituale Armenorum*, pp. 224-25.

23. *Rituale Armenorum*, p. 224.

these waters and bless the same with thy spotless right hand and with the life-giving power of the cross . . . to the end that everyone who shall drink thereof may derive therefrom a medicine of soul and body; and a health from diseases which afflict.[24]

This prayer is followed by a series of petitions. God is beseeched for his blessings and asked to restore the water to its primal curative and regenerative power. The cross is declared to be the instrument of that renewal as it is immersed in the water in figuration of Christ's baptism.

Bless, O Lord, this water, and hallow it with thy holy cross, in order that the flocks and sheep which may approach and drink of the same, may derive therefrom freedom from disease and fertility; for from them we select sacrifices of fragrant sweetness and offer them as victims to thyself.[25]

As exemplified in this prayer, the rite as a whole lends multivocal meaning to the phrase "for the profit of man" appearing at the opening of the prayer of blessing. On the one hand, we are instructed that animal and vegetable life is "useful" to human beings, a source of nourishment, clothing, shelter, and pleasure. On the other hand, we are informed that the worth of God's creatures consists in more than just their utility to humanity. As part of an ecological system, all life is of inestimable and inherent value to the Life-giver himself. All life comes to us as gift of beauty and harmony, a sign of God's presence and love. This alone qualifies animals and plants as fit sacrifices and gifts to God.

Each petition of the Rite of the Washing of the Cross closes with an explicit reference to sacrifice and sacrament. The second petition invokes a rather powerful eucharistic image. God is asked to grant that the water "impart to the fields, where it is sprinkled, harvests where-from we have fine flour as *an offering of holiness unto thy Lordship.*"[26] The rite closes with eucharistic doxology: "We make offering unto thee of that which is thine own, O all-victorious and all-powerful king, who forever art praised by all creatures, all-holy Trinity, now and ever to eternity."[27]

I concur with Bernard Haring's assertion that "the sacramental people of God will not spurn usefulness but will give it its integrated

---

24. *Rituale Armenorum*, p. 225.
26. *Rituale Armenorum*, p. 225; italics mine.
27. *Rituale Armenorum*, p. 226.

meaning within the knowledge of salvation, in solidarity, service and mutual love. Then the earthly things enter into adoration of God in Spirit and truth. Ecological responsibility is a part of our praise of the Creator and Redeemer."[28] Haring captures succinctly the biblical outlook on and valuation of creation.

Ecology as Oikonomia within the Church

From Genesis onward, we hear that God's providence oversees the whole of his creation. The Orthodox rites of blessing show how closely ecology is related to the theological notion of *oikonomia* in Eastern theology. The object of the divine economy is the *oikumene* — the whole inhabited earth. For, as the Psalmist says, "The earth is the LORD's and the fulness thereof, the world and those who dwell therein" (Ps. 24:1, RSV). Orthodox theology founds this cosmic scope of the divine nurture and restoration and renewal of creation in the Incarnation. In his tract *Against Heresies*, Irenaeus articulates perhaps the most influential expression in all of Christian theology of this cosmic soteriology with his notion of the recapitulation of creation in Christ:

> Thus He took up man into Himself, . . . the Word being made man, thus summing up all things in Himself; so that as in the super-celestial, spiritual, and invisible things, the Word of God is supreme, so also in things visible and corporeal He might possess the supremacy, and, taking to Himself the pre-eminence, as well as constituting Himself head of the Church, He might draw all things to Himself at the proper time.[29]

The Armenian Blessing of the Field *(Antasdan)* lends liturgical expression to this incarnationally centered soteriology and ecological vision. In this rite, priest and worshipers move in procession to a field, which represents the whole world. The congregation circles the field, turning first toward the east, then toward the west, north, and south — the four corners of the world. At these turnings, the "divine care" is

---

28. Haring, *Free and Faithful in Christ*, vol. 3 (New York: Crossroad, 1981), p. 179.

29. Irenaeus, "Against Heresies," in *The Apostolic Fathers with Justin Martyr and Irenaeus*, vol. 1 of *The Ante-Nicene Fathers*, ed. Alexander Roberts and James Donaldson (New York: Christian Literature, 1885), p. 443 (3.16.6). Paul Santmire provides a useful discussion of Irenaeus in *The Travail of Nature* (Philadelphia: Fortress Press, 1985), pp. 35-44.

beseeched for the earth with its fields and crops, monasteries and churches, villages and cities, and ecclesiastic and secular offices. At each turning, a blessing is invoked under the sign of the cross. The rubrics indicate that the ceremony should be performed no fewer than 25 times per year, including such occasions as the Feast of the Presentation at the Temple, all Sundays from Palm Sunday to Pentecost, the Transfiguration, the Assumption of the Blessed Virgin Mary, and the Exaltation of the Cross.[30] All of these occasions center on the Incarnation and salvation by way of the cross.

Orthodox theology insists that the Incarnation does not concern merely the correction of something that has gone wrong. Rather, it completes God's purpose at creation. It is about the flourishing of all life. A traditional Armenian cross sprouts blossoming branches. No biblical story does a better job than the story of Noah and the flood of depicting how not even God's anger and judgment ultimately thwart his intention that all living things should flourish. All of earth's creatures take shelter in the ark with Noah and his family. Early in Christian theology and liturgy, the ark itself was interpreted as a type of the church. Commenting on 1 Peter 3:20-21, St. Cyprian wrote, "Peter also affirmed when he showed that the Church is one and that only those who are within the Church are able to be baptized [that the ark is a type of the baptism in the church]. 'In the ark of Noah,' he said 'a very few (eight souls all told) were saved by water. And it is in just the same manner that baptism will save you also.' By this testimony he established that the ark of Noah (one only) was a type of the Church (also one)."[31]

Cyprian fails to mention that within the household of Noah are included all of earth's creatures. Christian theology, in both East and West, has been much too inclined to spiritualize the flood narrative and to narrow the range of the divine economy to humankind. In the *Catechetical Lectures* of St. Cyril of Jerusalem we have another example of this tendency. Cyril argues that the ark is a type of the universal church, "draw[ing] together into one the wills of all nations," of whom "the various dispositions of the animals in the ark were a figure." He

---

30. *Bless, O Lord*, ed. Garabed Kochakian (New York: Diocese of the Armenian Church of America, 1989), pp. 25-27.

31. Cyprian of Carthage, Letter 69, in *The Letters of St. Cyprian of Carthage*, vol. 4, ed. G. W. Clarke, Ancient Christian Writers, no. 47 (New York: Paulist Press, 1988), p. 34. It is worth recalling that the central portion of the Christian temple is called the *nave* (med. Latin, *navis*). The name for this section of the church in Armenian is *nav*, which literally means "ship."

mixes typology and allegory in a way that seems to discount the narrative's literal description of the animals as members of the household of the ark and as objects of divine blessing. He is not able to escape the narrative entirely, however; immediately following these observations, he comments that with the coming of the true Noah — Christ — "the spiritual wolves feed with the lambs, in whose Church the calf, and the lion, and the ox, feed in the same pasture."[32] While Cyril seems to want to treat the animals allegorically, he nevertheless ends up linking the narrative's placement of the animals within the ark with the status granted them in Isaiah 11 as inhabitants of the messianic kingdom.[33]

Whatever the deficiencies of his exegesis, Cyril juxtaposed three biblically founded ecclesial images that have significant ecological meaning: (1) the gathering into the ark of all the creatures of the earth, (2) the church as antitype of the ark in which the in-gathering of all creation is completed, and (3) the image of the eschatological messianic kingdom in which the original peace and harmony of the garden is restored and all things flourish. The conclusion that Cyril resists but that the Bible invites us to make is that the curse imposed by the flood turns to a blessing that extends to the *entire* family of Noah. This reversal of the curse and renewal of covenant is first mentioned in Genesis 5:29 as Lamech says of his newly born son Noah, "Out of the ground that the LORD has cursed this one shall bring us relief from our work and from the toil of our hands." This is an obvious allusion to Genesis 3:17-19. In Genesis 9:8-10 Lamech's prophecy is fulfilled, and the scope of God's salvation is said to include all living creatures: "God spoke to Noah and his sons: 'I now make my covenant with you and with your descendants after you, and with every living creature that is with you, all birds and cattle, all the wild animals with you on earth, all that have come out of the ark'" (NEB).

In conclusion, I shall venture one final juxtaposition of images

---

32. "The Catechetical Lectures," 17.10, in *Cyril of Jerusalem, Gregory of Nazianzen*, vol. 7 of the Select Library of Nicene and Post-Nicene Fathers of the Christian Church, 2d series, ed. Henry Wace (New York: Christian Literature, 1894), p. 126.

33. The fifth-century *History of the Armenians*, attributed to Agathangelos, explicitly includes the animals within God's redemptive purpose, while nonetheless emphasizing the special status of humanity: "You who saved Noah from the watery flood, save us from the flood of impieties that surrounds us. For if you saved the beasts and animals in the ark, how much the more will you care for your images that glorify you? While if you cared for the reptiles and birds, how much more will you care for us, whom you have called the temple of your will?" (*Agathangelos: History of the Armenians*, trans. Robert W. Thomson [Albany: State University of New York Press, 1976], p. 179).

from the tradition that unites ecclesial and ecological motifs. I want to place the Genesis description of Noah and his family sharing the ark with all of the earth's creatures beside an image of the nativity preserved iconographically in the Orthodox churches. In Eastern icons of the nativity, an ox and an ass stand close by the manger at the center of the picture. The two beasts depict the fulfillment of the prophecy of Isaiah: "The ox knows its owner, and the ass its master's crib" (1:3, RSV). Here the animal creation is portrayed as included in God's old as well as in his new covenant. The beasts take their place permanently within the household of God. The church as God's vehicle for taking humanity into the new creation is a household that, like the ark before it, embraces in hospitality, thanksgiving, and blessing all living creatures. Together with a redeemed humanity, the beasts and all God's creatures welcome joyfully the incarnate Lord who is their Savior. In the words of a Byzantine hymn, "What shall we offer Thee, O Christ, who for our sakes hast appeared on earth as man? Every creature made by Thee offers Thee thanks."[34]

Conclusion

Ecology *is* an ecclesial concern. The strong sense in which that is so, if not made wholly explicit in the passages from Cyril and Cyprian, nevertheless floats just below their surface. The status of the global ecology is an important concern for the church not just because the times bring to our attention the serious jeopardy in which human greed and violence have put God's good creation but because, absent proper care for our environment, the church cannot be church, and redemption is lost. Care for the biosphere lies at the very heart of the redemptive vocation of the church. The divine *oikonomia* involves a risk on God's part. God has entrusted his plan of salvation to humankind, and that plan involves all living beings. God risks his entire work on human freedom. Having witnessed humanity fail to exercise that freedom responsibly the first time around, God has given us one last opportunity to do so from within the church.

I believe that no moral issue of our times more critically tests the inspiration and spirit of Orthodox theology than the ecological problem, because Orthodox theology, especially in liturgy and rites of bless-

---

34. *The Festal Menaion,* trans. Mother Mary and Archimandrite Kallistos Ware (London: Faber & Faber, 1977), p. 254.

ing, affirms that the new household of God reaches completion in and through that church of which the ark of Noah was indeed a type. From an Orthodox perspective, ecclesiology and concern for the global ecology are virtually the same thing. We *must* keep both church and household better. Nothing short of this will do sufficient honor to the name of the One in whom alone there is hope for all God's creatures of liberation "from bondage to decay" and of the freedom "of the children of God" (Rom. 8:21).

A Postscript

In early summer of 1990, I visited Armenia for the first time. The morning after my arrival, I made the pilgrimage to the ancient cathedral of Holy Etchmiadzin. The liturgy for that Sunday commemorated the Feast Day of St. Gregory the Illuminator, the founder of the Armenian Church who laid the foundation of the cathedral in 301. I was given the privilege of being seated with several dozen other people just in front of the high altar under the central dome. The music was exquisite and transporting. Yet there was a joyful surprise still to come. At the hymn of communion, just as the choir sang,

> Christ is sacrificed and shared amongst us. Alleluia. . . .
> Praise the Lord in the heavens. Alleluia.
> Praise ye him in the heights. Alleluia.
> Praise ye him, all his angels. Alleluia.
> Praise ye him, all his hosts, Alleluia,

birds high in the great dome and east bell tower burst forth in chorus. Their song broke the silence of the painted images of the heavenly hosts above. Or perhaps their song was the very voice of those hosts.

8. Death and Dying in the Orthodox Liturgical Tradition: Toward a Pastoral Ethic of Dying Well

> Whether we live or whether we die, we are the Lord's.
>
> ROMANS 14:8

We live in a time that is fixated upon death. The camera eyes of the culture linger on the death masks of the terminally ill, the cancer wards, the AIDS clinics. A morbid curiosity about death is intermixed with a fear that our lives lose meaning when we are faced with prolonged personal suffering, the infirmities of old age, or terminal illness. With the decline of traditional religion, the resources that help us to die well seem to have dried up. There is renewed interest in old answers of suicide and euthanasia. Assisted suicide is now being debated by doctors and medical ethicists, state legislators, media pundits, and people in all walks of life.

Our society is increasingly coming to view euthanasia as an appropriate solution to the problem of pain and suffering. Walker Percy referred to this trend as "the thanatos syndrome." The Greek from which the term *euthanasia* is derived means "good death." In our time, the term has come to cover both the choice of a painless death on the part of people suffering from debilitating or terminal illness and the deliberate putting to death of helpless or infirm persons. The Orthodox Christian tradition offers many important reasons why such deaths cannot be considered good.

This chapter is not an essay on euthanasia, although I do touch on the subject because of the way in which it raises critical ethical questions about how we should treat the suffering in order to help those

175

who are dying to die as well as possible. Christians and non-Christians who are troubled by the thanatos syndrome need to think seriously about what it means to die well — and about what sorts of care to the sick and dying best reflect this value.

"It falsifies the Christian message," wrote Alexander Schmemann in a discussion of the Byzantine Rite of Holy Unction, "to present and to preach Christianity as essentially life-affirming — without referring this affirmation to the death of Christ and therefore to the very fact of death; to pass over in silence the fact that for Christianity death is not only the end, but the very reality of *this world*."[1] He proceeds to point out that the Orthodox tradition embraces neither a morbid religious explanation of and resignation to death nor a therapeutic affirmation of life that avoids the awful reality of death. It was not by accident that Schmemann chose to discuss death and dying in the context of a reflection on liturgy, for within the Orthodox liturgies — especially the rites of holy unction, the prayers for the sick, and the rites of burial — a rich and profound theology of sickness and dying is set forth. My discussion in this chapter draws from this rich Orthodox tradition, from the realistic theology of death to which Schmemann alludes, in hopes of advancing our knowledge of the theological resources available for an ethic of sickness, death, and dying. Some analysis of the current cultural climate is in order before we get down to an exploration of these theological resources, and so it is to this that we will turn first.

The Case of Baby Rena:
Cultural Confusion over the Meaning of Life and Death

In July 1991, the *Washington Post* ran a two-part front-page feature on Baby Rena and her tragic death at the age of eighteen months. The first article of the series opened as follows:

> Murray Pollack, a physician at Children's Hospital, felt the time had come to change the rules. His 18-month old patient, Baby Rena, was dying, a victim of AIDS and heart disease. For six weeks, ever since her arrival at the intensive-care unit in late January, she had been breathing only with the help of a respirator. She was in so much

1. Schmemann, *For the Life of the World* (Crestwood, N.Y.: St. Vladimir's Seminary Press, 1973), p. 96.

pain that Pollack kept her constantly sedated. When nurses performed even the simplest procedure, such as weighing her, her blood pressure shot up and tears streamed down her face. But a tube in her throat made it impossible for her to utter a sound.[2]

Pollack had been called in to take over the case after Baby Rena was brought to the hospital on January 30 for what was her final stay. She died at Children's Hospital on March 25. From the outset, Pollack judged Baby Rena's case as probably "futile." Keeping her on the respirator was not a life-saving measure so much as it was an intrusion into her dying process that only intensified and prolonged her suffering. Pollack argued that he and the medical staff had "a responsibility to do what's best for Rena . . . , and to give her the appropriate care — and that is not always giving her all care."[3] Pollack was not advocating mercy killing. Rather, he wanted those responsible for her care to "let go" — to let Rena die the death she was dying as well as possible — and he judged that that meant removing her from intensive care and the respirator and providing medication to relieve her severe pain. Death would likely come sooner rather than later.

Children's Hospital required the consent of parents or legal guardians before a patient might be removed from a respirator. Rena's mother had abandoned her at birth, making her the ward of the District government. She had been assigned foster parents, and while they had no legal standing in the decision, they did raise strong objections to Pollack's recommendations. They believed that God had told them "to take the child, and rear her in the nurture and admonition of God's word . . . and to battle the spirits of infirmity."[4] They demanded that her treatment "be motivated by a spiritual sense of obedience to God."[5] When the hospital sought the government's permission to take Rena off the respirator, the request was denied.

In the Baby Rena case, the foster parents, the pastor of their church, and their friends were all significant actors. They all professed a Christian belief in the sanctity of life and God's lordship over living and dying. And yet, based on my understanding of the best standards of the Christian tradition, I cannot find good cause to agree with either

2. Benjamin Weiser, "A Question of Letting Go," *Washington Post*, 14 July 1991, p. 1.
3. Benjamin Weiser, "While Child Suffered, Beliefs Clashed," *Washington Post*, 15 July 1991, p. 6.
4. Weiser, "A Question of Letting Go," p. 18.
5. Weiser, "While Child Suffered, Beliefs Clashed," p. 6.

their reasoning or their judgment. I contend that there are within the Christian tradition resources and reasons to draw a distinction between direct killing in health care settings and allowing to die. The former is euthanasia and is morally wrong; the latter is not. In fact, acquiescence in the face of an impending death may sometimes be required by Christian conscience. There are circumstances in which Christians are permitted — even duty bound — to let life ebb away in its natural course. The remaining duty in such circumstances is to provide care that relieves pain and comforts the dying.

Too often today, conscientious religious and nonreligious people lack the moral means to acknowledge and accept such possibilities. The issue, as in so many other moral controversies, gets framed in either/or terms. Either one believes that everything possible must be done to save life or one supports euthanasia. The Baby Rena case illustrates how people get caught up in this sort of moral cul-de-sac. Religious and nonreligious antagonists tend to view one another's arguments as proof positive that they are far apart in worldview when in fact their conflict often disguises a common outlook: both their positions are grounded in secularity.

In defending a distinction between direct killing (euthanasia) and allowing to die, Paul Ramsey once observed that people in our society who hold opposite positions on euthanasia often end up defining euthanasia in the same way. Religious convictions or the lack thereof are not the important determining factors.

> The case for either of these points of view [favoring euthanasia or favoring relentless efforts to save life] can be made only by discounting and rejecting the arguments for saving life qualifiedly but not always. In both cases, an ethics of only caring for the dying is reduced to the moral equivalent of euthanasia — in the one case, to oppose this ever, in the other case, to endorse it. Thus, the extremes meet, both medical scrupulosity and euthanasia, in rejecting the discriminating concepts of traditional medicine.[6]

In spite of — or perhaps because of — their simple definition of God's sovereignty over life, and certainly because of an almost Manichaean identification of sickness and death with the demonic spirits, Baby Rena's foster parents were unable to distinguish euthanasia from caring for the dying to the point of letting them die. Ramsey insisted

6. Ramsey, *The Patient as Person* (New Haven: Yale University Press, 1970), p. 146.

that the traditional ethic (grounded in the belief that God is Creator, Lord of Life, and Redeemer) clearly holds that " 'letting life ebb' away is *not* the same as 'actively encompassing' a patient's life."[7] How is it that Baby Rena's foster parents, who were religious people, failed to see and act on this important difference? Why is it that they were held captive to the current popular meaning of euthanasia, to thinking in terms of the restrictive alternatives of either a utilitarian devaluation of life or an ethical vitalism that mystifies and absolutizes human life?

I think Alexander Schmemann had it basically right when he argued that the mark of secularism is the absence of God experienced in society and in people's lives. Vast numbers of religious and nonreligious people in our culture carry this mark of secularism in their understandings of God and/or the world, and it is nowhere more evident than in their attitudes toward death and dying.

The nonreligious respond to the perceived absence of God by attributing all meaning and purpose in life solely to human agency and human projects to eliminate suffering, injustice, and the like. God may or may not exist, they say, and there may or may not be an afterlife; since we cannot know either way, we must proceed as if there were no God. The only life of which we are certain is the life we live now, and that life inevitably ends in death. Nonreligious secularists refuse to explain "the world in terms of an 'other world' of which no one knows anything, and life . . . in terms of a 'survival' about which no one has the slightest idea." Rejecting religious orthodoxies that ground the value of life in terms of death and an afterlife, they explain "death in terms of life."[8]

These nonreligious secularists still differ among themselves about the scale of value on which human life ought to be measured, however. Some hold personal existence as the only concrete value and adhere to an ethical vitalism that insists on using every means possible in all circumstances to ward off personal death. Others argue out of a utilitarian framework that the value of a life is qualified by the degree of good or happiness, pleasure or fulfillment that might reasonably be expected in it. They would argue that some lives might not be worth living, and, that being the case, we might properly choose to end some lives through suicide or euthanasia.

On the face of it, religious people like Baby Rena's foster parents seem to be the opposite of nonreligous secularists. They measure all value

7. Ramsey, *The Patient as Person*, p. 156.
8. Schmemann, *For the Life of the World*, p. 98.

in terms of a spiritual world. But the views of both camps are grounded in a presumption that the world is essentially meaningless. Both world-views are profoundly secular. From the standpoint of the classical Christian understanding of life and death and how God is related to them, both outlooks devalue the world and empty it of God's presence. The difference between the religious and the nonreligious outlooks arises at the practical level, with respect to how each invests an essentially meaningless and valueless world with meaning and value. As I have suggested, those at the nonreligious pole of secularism believe life obtains meaning through human endeavor. Contrarily, those at the religious pole insist that God is the only source of meaning, inasmuch as God is spiritual and the only true meaning in life is gained on the spiritual level of our existence, which is radically distinct from this world.

I believe the religion of Baby Rena's foster parents approximates this religious secular worldview. At the root of the foster parents' kind of religion is a metaphysical and moral dualism that radically separates physical existence (this world) from spiritual existence (the other world). This body-and-spirit dualism moved otherwise loving adults to insist that a small child's extreme physical pain be prolonged. What does it mean to care for the spiritual well-being of a loved one if it does not involve concerns about physical pain and the imminence of death? During one conversation between the hospital staff and the parents, the foster father sketched three pictures, representing Rena's body, soul, and spirit. "We see that she has AIDS," he said. "It's real, because you can see it under the microscope." He went on to thank the hospital staff for working hard to meet her medical needs — the needs of her body. But he went on to say that they were ignoring her spiritual side. Pointing to the third sketch, he said, "It seems to me that until the hospital really addresses the spiritual area we won't be able to defeat these various spirits of infirmity, including AIDS, that we're fighting against here." He explained his belief that the decisions for Rena needed "to be motivated by a spiritual sense of obedience to God. It's most important to find out what God desires or what God wills for Rena." At one point, a hospital social worker said, "What you're saying is that you don't want to give up on the spiritual part even though we're giving up on the physical part." The father nodded his head. He recalled an earlier occasion on which Rena had rallied after the hospital staff had given up hope. "If we give up now, we won't fully understand. . . . We won't fully know that God's word is true."[9]

9. Weiser, "While Child Suffered, Beliefs Clashed," p. 6.

The foster father spoke of the necessity of discovering what God wants as if that was not already to be discerned at the level of Baby Rena's fleshly suffering and dying. What more could the parents possibly have been waiting for to reveal God's will in the situation? Again, as Ramsey once so aptly put it, "No Biblical theologian should take umbrage at the suggestion that a pronouncement of death is a medical question." Indeed, I would broaden that to say that no Christian should take umbrage at the suggestion that judgments about when death is imminent or further medical treatment is futile are properly medical determinations. "What personal life do we know except within the ambience of a bodily existence?"[10] God does not need respirators to work miracles, but God entrusts determinations of whether we are biologically dying to our physicians whether they themselves trust in him or not. One writer of a letter to the editors of the *Washington Post* who commented on the foster parents' reasoning from their "faith in God" questioned their identification of the will of God with doing everything possible to keep Rena alive.

> I hope that people reading the article on Baby Rena do not get the impression that keeping her on the respirator was the only decision that people with faith in God could have made. . . . Having faith [sometimes] requires people to voluntarily give control over a situation to God. Although giving up control is the key to doing God's will, you still need to figure out what it is that God wants you to do — that's the hard part.[11]

In his remarkable little book *The Patient as Person*, Paul Ramsey ruminated,

> It may be that only in an age of faith when men know that the dying cannot pass beyond God's love and care will men have the courage to apply limits [to life-saving interventions in] medical practice. It may be that only upon the basis of faith in God can there be a conscionable category of "ceasing to oppose death," making room for caring for the dying. It may also be that only an age of faith is productive of absolute limits upon the taking of the lives of terminal patients, because of the alignment of many a human will with God's care for them here and now, and not only in the there and then of his providence.[12]

10. Ramsey, *The Patient as Person*, p. 61.
11. "The Agonizing Decisions Surrounding Baby Rena" (letter from Monica Michelizzi), *Washington Post*, 22 July 1991, p. 10.
12. Ramsey, *The Patient as Person*, p. 156.

Baby Rena's parents were far more fixed upon the there and then of God's providence than on the alignment of many human wills with God's care for her. This fixation on the there and then to the exclusion of the here and now belongs to a spiritualism and other-worldliness that is a symptom and product of secularism itself, not its opposite, as those who hold such religious views typically assume. Ironically, secularistic Christianity and modern fundamentalism of the kind evidenced by Baby Rena's foster parents can be one and the same thing. If the nonreligious expression of secularism involves the descralization of human life and the experienced world, then Christian or Jewish religious secularism involves the breakdown of the symbolic and sacramental structures in and by which individuals and communities relate God and world so as to experience God as both transcendent over the world and wholly manifest within it. In spite of the foster parents' repeated appeals to God and his law, they simply could not see that in the here and now God's encompassing love might permit a practical distinction between direct killing and letting die.

The articles in the *Washington Post* did not say whether Dr. Murray Pollack was a religious man. Nevertheless, compared with the desires of Baby Rena's foster parents' concerning her medical treatment, Dr. Pollack's practical proposals were more in keeping with the classical Christian conviction that in the here and now God's care should be aligned with human reason and judgment in decisions about when life is ebbing and need not be heroically extended. I say this with one very important qualification: there is nothing in the criteria on which Pollack based his ethical judgment — namely, the futility of additional treatment and the quality of the patient's remaining life — that speaks to the issue of a distinction between allowing the patient to die and putting the patient to death. We are not told whether Pollack considered euthanasia as a possible solution to Baby Rena's plight, but there is nothing in the newspaper's description of Pollack's reasoning to suggest that it would have violated his ethical standards to have advocated such a course of action.

It has been argued that, contrary to Ramsey's opinion, one need not believe in the biblical God in order to believe that there are good reasons for prohibiting or at least severely limiting euthanasia or putting limits on efforts to prolong life.[13] The matter is not settled. Like the arguments of those who challenge his position, Ramsey's argument

---

13. See, e.g., chap. 2 of James F. Childress's *Priorities in Medical Ethics* (Philadelphia: Westminster Press, 1981).

is not logically conclusive. Still, all things considered, I side with Ramsey. In the relatively rarified atmosphere of medical ethical discourse we may well be able to establish principles and rules that secure a distinction between killing and letting die. But Ramsey's argument is more realistic regarding the fact that biblical theism no longer plays a powerful moral role in this particular culture. Biblically rooted theism provides people with the conviction that God, the absolute source and sustainer of our being and our redeemer, is with us in death as much as in life. As St. Paul says in Romans 8, "Neither death, nor life, . . . nor anything else in all creation can separate us from the love of God" (vv. 38-39). Biblical theism gives a vision of the *summum bonum,* but this vision is not predominant in our culture. Indeed, the momentum in the culture is demonstrably toward a utilitarianism and secularism that lack this conviction and provide no strong vision of human ends. In such a context there is no sure ground for sustaining a distinction between killing and letting die — not even appeals to such things as a principle of trust between patient and physician or the doctor's Hippocratic oath.

I have already granted that any discussion of the resources within the Orthodox liturgical tradition for a medical ethic of death and dying would be abstract and irrelevant if we were to ignore the present cultural situation and the moral confusion even among self-professed religious people. But, having made an effort to engage some of the elements of that cultural context, I believe that an exploration of this religious vision of living and dying can give guidance not only to those who profess and practice a biblical faith but also to nonreligious people who are interested in exploring every available resource for doing what is right for the terminally ill and dying. And so I turn now to a discussion of the Orthodox rites of burial and anointing of the sick, confident that they will provide us with means to overcome the moral dilemmas, false reasoning, and confusion that threaten to hamper our ability to think clearly about terminal illness and dying well. There are valuable ethical insights in these rites and prayers that can strengthen our impoverished moral vision with regard to care for the dying.

The Byzantine Rite of Holy Unction: On Sin and Death

The Orthodox rites of burial and anointing of the sick incorporate a belief at the crux of a Christian understanding of death and what constitutes a good death — the belief that sickness and death cannot be understood apart from sin, that "the wages of sin is death" (Rom. 6:23) and "the sting of death is sin" itself (1 Cor. 15:56).

St. Paul's writing is not the only place in Christian scripture where this connection between sin and death is made. It belongs to the Gospels also. We need look no further than the second chapter of the Gospel of Mark for a powerful narrative presentation of the reality of sin in death. At the beginning of chapter 2, the story is told of Jesus' healing of the paralytic in Capernaum. Word had gotten out about Jesus' return to that region, and "some people came, bringing to him a paralyzed man" (v. 3). The man was lowered through the roof of the house in which Jesus had been staying. The Gospel writer reports that when Jesus saw the faith of the man and his friends, "he said to the paralytic, 'Son, your sins are forgiven.'" This response is bound to strike the ears of modern folk as just a bit strange. Jesus does not immediately heal the man. Instead, he forgives him his sins. Only after his authority to forgive sins is questioned by certain "scribes" who "were sitting there" does Jesus go ahead and heal the paralytic of his physical ailment. "'But so that you may know that the Son of Man has authority on earth to forgive sins' — he said to the paralytic — 'I say to you, stand up, take your mat and go to your home.' And he stood up, and immediately took the mat and went out before all of them" (vv. 5, 6, 10-12).

This Markan lesson about the connection between sin and sickness is sealed later in the chapter when the story is told of Jesus' visit at the house of Levi the tax collector and his meal with certain "sinners." Pharisees saw this and "said to his disciples, 'Why does he eat with tax collectors and sinners?' When Jesus heard this, he said to them, 'Those who are well have no need of a physician, but those who are sick; I have come to call not the righteous but sinners'" (vv. 15, 16-17). The Matthean version of this story (Matt. 9:9-14) is read in the Byzantine Rite of Holy Unction.

Set these portions of the biblical narrative beside the commonly held misunderstanding that the practice of anointing the sick is just about curing physical or psychological illness and one begins to see to what extent the biblical belief about the relation of sin, sickness, and death has broken down in our culture. The fact is that the anointing of the sick and dying is first of all about penance and forgiveness of sins. The deep meaning given to healing in the rite of holy unction eludes us if these central themes of penance and forgiveness of sins are forgotten. Witness the Byzantine rite, which opens with Psalms 143 and 51. The whole of each of these psalms is said in the rite, but I need cite just a few stanzas from each to make the point:

Hear my prayer, O LORD;
　　give ear to my supplications in your faithfulness;
answer me, in your righteousness!
Do not enter into judgment with your servant,
　　for no one living is righteous before you. . . .

Answer me quickly, O LORD;
　　my spirit fails.
Do not hide your face from me,
　　or I shall be like those who go down to the Pit.
Let me hear of your steadfast love in the morning,
　　for in you I put my trust. (143:1-2, 7-8)

Have mercy on me, O God,
　　according to your steadfast love;
according to your abundant mercy
　　blot out my transgressions.
Wash me thoroughly from my iniquity,
　　and cleanse me from my sin.
For I know my transgressions,
　　and my sin is ever before me.
Against you, you alone, have I sinned
　　and done what is evil in your sight,
so that you are justified in your sentence. . . .
Indeed, I was born guilty,
　　a sinner when my mother conceived me.

You desire truth in the inward being;
　　therefore teach me wisdom in my secret heart.
Purge me with hyssop, and I shall be clean; . . .
Let me hear joy and gladness;
　　let the bones that you have crushed rejoice.
Hide your face from my sins,
　　and blot out all my iniquities.

Create in me a clean heart, O God,
　　and put a new and right spirit within me. . . .
Restore to me the joy of your salvation,
　　and sustain in me a willing spirit. (51:1-10, 12)

In the Old Testament, the Hebrew for "salvation" derives from
yasha, which means "to be at large, to save from a danger." Salvation,
in these psalms, is intimately connected with themes and metaphors

for healing of body and soul. God delivers us — literally *snatches* us — not only from our enemies and from persecution and the like but also from sickness and from the power of death. In the New Testament, the Greek *sozo* is derived from *saos,* which means "healthy." Prayer and penance for the sin that attaches to all "flesh" and makes that flesh subject to a corruptible death (the destruction of the unity of body and soul) issue from the belief that God wants to heal all of our infirmities. Penitential prayer issues also from the conviction that this healing is a part of the whole process of salvation. A reading from the Epistle of James in the Byzantine rite makes it abundantly clear that the church holds to such a belief.

> Be patient, therefore, beloved, until the coming of the Lord. . . . As an example of suffering and patience, beloved, take the prophets who spoke in the name of the Lord. Indeed we call blessed those who showed endurance. You have heard of the endurance of Job, and you have seen the purpose of the Lord, how the Lord is compassionate and merciful. . . .
>
> Are any among you suffering? They should pray. Are any cheerful? They should sing songs of praise. Are any among you sick? They should call the elders of the church and have them pray over them, anointing them with oil in the name of the Lord. The prayer of faith will save the sick, and the Lord will raise them up; and anyone who has committed sins will be forgiven. Therefore confess your sins to one another, and pray for one another, so that you may be healed. The prayer of the righteous is powerful and effective. (5:7, 10-11, 13-16)

Motifs of prayer, penance, forgiveness of sin, healing, and salvation are joined together in this passage. Anointing with oil is the sign and sacrament of these divine and human healing actions. According to the rite, the actual anointing of the sick or dying person follows soon after this reading — but not before the story of the good Samaritan is recited also. God's love and mercy are like that of the Samaritan. We can have hope in the face of sickness and death because love like that of the Samaritan is the very being and character of God. From this we also gain assurance that God forgives us our sins, heals us, and raises us to life eternal. Immediately following the reading of the story of the Good Samaritan is this prayer: "For thou art a great and marvellous God, who keepest thy covenant and thy mercy towards them that love thee; who givest remission of sins through thy Holy Child, Jesus; who regeneratest us from sin by holy Baptism, and sanctifiest us with thy Holy Spirit; who givest light to the blind, who raisest up them that are cast down, who lovest the righteous, and showest mercy unto sinners; who leadest us forth again out of darkness and the shadow of death."[14]

The Messiah, wrote Paul Ramsey, did not "bear epilepsy or psychosomatic disorders to gain victory over them in the flesh before the interventions of psychoneurosurgery. Rather is he said to have been born *mortal* flesh to gain for us a foretaste of victory over sin and death where those twin enemies had taken up apparently secure citadel."[15] The healing done by Jesus is not merely a metaphor or external sign for salvation; it is a deep symbol and sacrament of salvation binding together heaven and earth, leading to eternal life. All Jesus' miraculous healings were signs and foreshadowings of his victorious death on the cross, through which we gain entrance into the kingdom of his Father.

Further, the God whose love is "steadfast" and whose "mercy is abundant" could never euthanize. It is in the character of God to act finally to *save* all fleshly, personal life, not end it. From a Christian standpoint, the euthanizers' motives, however humanitarian or well-meaning, can never justify what they do. Their *aim* (i.e., their specific intent to bring about the death of an individual) is more important than their *motivation* (e.g., their desire to bring about an end to grievous suffering) when it comes to evaluating the rightness or wrongness of the act. Or, to put it another way, the fact that they mean well is less important than the fact that the result of their "good intentions" is a person's death.[16] The aim of euthanasia is contrary to everything God intends for us and does for us in a fallen and sinful world that, apart from his presence and saving activity, is a cosmic cemetery. There is a difference between a God-centered humanism and naturalistic humanitarianism, and Christians must observe and promote that difference. While they might grant the good intentions of those who in the name of humanitarianism practice euthanasia, they are called to condemn the act as sinful.

14. *Service Book of the Holy Orthodox-Catholic Apostolic Church*, ed. Isabel Florence Hapgood (Englewood, N.J.: Antiochian Orthodox Christian Archdiocese, 1975), p. 344.

15. Ramsey, "The Indignity of 'Death with Dignity,'" in *On Moral Medicine*, ed. Stephen E. Lammers and Allen Verhey (Grand Rapids: William B. Eerdmans, 1987), p. 192. Originally published in *Hastings Center Studies* 2 (May 1974): 47-62.

16. For more on the ethical significance of the distinction between aim and motive, see Gilbert C. Meilaender, "Euthanasia and Christian Vision," in *On Moral Medicine*, pp. 455-57. Originally published in *Thought* 5 (December 1982): 465-75.

The Images of Life and Death in the Armenian Rite of Burial for the Layman

Anointing of the sick and dying is no substitute for medical care and treatment. Anointing is not a kind of Christian magic. But penance and requests for God's forgiveness of the sick person's sins are healing practices that convey an understanding of health broader and deeper than the narrow naturalistic and mechanistic understandings prevalent in modern medical practice. Health, rooted in incarnational faith, has sacramental, soteriological, and eschatological dimensions that are evident in the Byzantine Rite of Holy Unction.

At this point, however, I want to turn to the Armenian Orthodox Rite for the Burial of a Layman. This rite continues the themes of penance and atonement we have encountered in the Byzantine rite of holy unction but it goes on to set forth a far more exhaustive theology of the Incarnation, the church's answer to death. This service gives voice to the Christian conviction that care for the dying is care for that flesh among us that is near to the end of the perishing in which we all participate from birth. Christian care for the dying values this flesh not only because God created it but also because the Son assumed it as his own form in life and death. The despair over the perishing of flesh that is expressed in suicide and euthanasia is not only unreasonable but irreverent from the standpoint of the Christian story of creation and salvation.

The great prayer attributed to St. Basil in the Armenian rite of burial conveys a story with profound implications for those who believe that Jesus Christ is Lord and Savior. Christians must dispose themselves toward living and dying as Christ did. The following passages from that prayer are representative of its principal theological statements:

> We thank thee, Father of our Lord Jesus Christ who because of thy love of mankind has visited us, and saved [us] from the machinations of the traducer [of] the race of men that were driven out and banished afar. For Satan was jealous of us, and drove us out of eternal life by his deceits and wiles, proscribing and banishing us unto our destruction and ruin. But thou, O God, who art benevolent and lovest man, didst not permit the bitterness of his poisoned fangs to remain in us. Wherefore thou didst summon death, and poured it out upon creatures, in order that the wickedness that had befallen might not remain immortal: but by removing us from this life, and cutting us from our sins, the punishment of the beneficent One became salvation.

But in the last of days thou didst send thy only-begotten Son beloved in the image of the death of sin; and he condemned sin in his own body, and by his voluntary crucifixion shattered the hosts of the enemy. He became the firstfruits of them that slept, and by his divinely marvellous resurrection he invited us to share in his own immortality.

Now this thy servant believing in him has been baptized into the death of thy Christ. . . . Remit to this man his debts incurred either willingly or unwillingly, and heal all the wounds which the disincarnate enemy hath inflicted. . . .

And now do thou heal his wounds, and convey him peacefully past the principalities of darkness, . . . and efface the handwriting of their influences and inworkings, which they have sown in him and vouchsafe to him a goodly journey. . . . Let him through [the path of the Tree of Life so that he may] arrive at the place of safety where all thy saints are massed and wait for the great wedding, when the great God and Savior shall appear, Jesus Christ, at the sound of the great trumpet. . . . Then . . . at the glance of the judge the earth shall be shaken, and the sealed sepulchres be opened. The bodies that were turned to dust are built up afresh, and the spirits swooping down like eagles reach them and array themselves in the incorruptible body.[17]

One has to marvel at this prayer. For in it virtually all of the church's theology of death is powerfully and poetically expressed. One should also recognize that in a culture in which belief in the soul and in the immortality of flesh and spirit is all but lost, those who would pray this prayer and take it to heart as physicians, nurses, or family members in their care for the dying are bound to look odd to even the most well-meaning of observers.

What is perhaps most incomprehensible to modern people is the belief that death is more than just a biological or physical reality. This prayer and the whole of the Orthodox tradition inform us that death is also spiritual. The full ramifications of our dying extend beyond the otherwise medically useful fiction of a precise moment of death measured in terms of the cessation in function of the brain or the shutting down of the body's system of vital organs. "For in . . . [the] Christian vision, death is above all a *spiritual reality*, of which one can partake while being alive, from which one can be free while lying in

---

17. *Rituale Armenorum: The Administration of the Sacraments and Breviary Rites of the Armenian Church*, ed. F. C. Conybeare (Oxford: Clarendon Press, 1905), pp. 130-31.

the grave."[18] This spiritual definition of death does not entail a Platonist dualism of body and soul. And it is a very different thing from familiar, modern notions of the mortality of the body and the immortality of the soul. Spiritual death, in the classical Christian understanding, happens and is defined in strict relation to the body. It encompasses our whole being, whereas medical definitions of death do not take the whole person into account (and need not do so).

Perhaps moderns would begin to grasp what I'm talking about here if I were to say that death spiritually understood includes that which we call the human psyche. I could point to clinical depression and behavioral disorders as examples of phenomena that involve the whole person, body and spirit alike. But psychological aspects of being don't take in the whole of what classical Christian belief has in view either. Spiritual death is here and now — and forever after. It involves the soul together with the body. It is eschatological. The Armenian rite describes the nature of this death as expulsion from the garden with the Tree of Life. This means separation from God, the sole Giver of life. Death Christianly understood is not the same thing as personal extinction. It is not the opposite of immortality. Only God has the power to annihilate our existence (and he will not do so), but we have the power to reject the true Life, "the light of all people" (John 1:2). Sin is the character of the creature alienated from the Creator — alienated from true Life. The death referred to in the prayer of St. Basil brings an immortal death — an unceasing separation from God, a separation that begins in the here and now. A sign of this separation from God is our separation from our fellow human beings. A longed-for but not grasped (and, paradoxically, habitually rejected) true communion with others is missing from our lives. We all sin, and we all experience desolation.

Death understood in its spiritual reality threatens personal existence with another form of separation or alienation: the separation of the soul from the body. The Church Fathers called this "corruptible death," the decomposition of the body-soul unity that constitutes the living person. It is a kind of fading away of the image of God in the human being. The anthem of St. John of Damascus in the Byzantine rite of burial exclaims, "I weep and I wail when I think upon death, and behold our beauty, fashioned after the image of God, lying in the tomb disfigured, dishonored, bereft of form."[19] The Armenian prayer

18. Alexander Schmemann, *Of Water and the Spirit* (Crestwood, N.Y.: St. Vladimir's Seminary Press, 1974), p. 62.

19. *Service Book of the Holy Orthodox-Catholic Apostolic Church*, p. 386.

states that such a death "was summon[ed] by God and poured . . . out upon creatures in order that the wickedness that had befallen might not remain immortal."[20] Note that the prayer does not say that God created death: it says that God allowed the natural inclination of the creature toward dissolution to be realized.

This complete dissolution of the person is death in all its horror. It surpasses the horror of mere physical death, which itself holds a terror for most human beings. Even those uninformed by a Christian understanding of personal existence dread the process of dying, the sense that sickness or approaching death is robbing them of control over their body and with it their identity and their whole world, both personal and impersonal.[21] For it is only in and through this body, this "flesh" in its wholeness and integral connection with soul and psyche, that we are able to participate in the world. The experience of the dissolution of our being and loss of our world is more profoundly real than any secular psychological or social science is able to comprehend, because it extends beyond the scope of such science, beyond space and temporality, into eschatological time.

The Byzantine tradition includes an office of the parting of the soul from the body that is to be said when physical death is near. It beseeches God to bring this process to a conclusion by allowing "the destructible bond" of body and soul to "be dissolved, . . . the body . . . [to] be dissolved from the elements of which it was fashioned," and the soul to be "translated to that place where it shall take its abode until the final Resurrection."[22] The Armenian prayer completes this picture of death when it envisions the reconstitution of resurrected humanity: "The bodies that were turned to dust are built up afresh, and the spirits swooping down like eagles reach them and array themselves in the incorruptible body." The image of God within us is thus restored. The Byzantine and Armenian prayers together present the picture of a spiral of life and death.[23] The Byzantine prayer identifies the nadir of death;

20. Gregory of Nyssa makes the same point: "Divine providence introduced death into human nature with a specific design so that by the dissolution of body and soul, vice may be drawn off and man may be refashioned again through the resurrection" (cited by Georges Florovsky in *The Collected Works of Georges Florovsky*, vol. 3: *Creation and Redemption* [Belmont, Mass.: Nordland, 1976], p. 108).

21. For this point, I owe a debt of gratitude to William F. May, "The Sacral Power of Death in Contemporary Experience," in *On Moral Medicine*, pp. 175-85 (especially pp. 181-82).

22. *Service Book of the Holy Orthodox-Catholic Apostolic Church*, p. 366.

23. I have drawn this analysis from Jaroslav Pelikan's extraordinary little book *The Shape of Death* (Nashville: Abingdon Press, 1961), especially chap. 5.

the Armenian prayer captures the beginning of the spiral upward again, beyond earthly life into eternal life.

We are assured that this path is a spiral, not a circle, by the Incarnation. Christ has not only repeated or recapitulated in his living and dying our living and dying, but he has added something new. Whereas Adam was, like all his sons and daughters, disobedient unto sin and death, Christ, the new Adam, was obedient unto new and eternal life. Christ opened up the possibility of eternal life in the presence of God that had been closed to Adam and Eve when they were expelled from the garden. The circle of sin and death opens into a spiral leading to new life with God. The Armenian prayer of St. Basil presents this theological linchpin of the Orthodox understanding of death tersely and forcefully:

> But in the last days thou didst send thy only-begotten Son, beloved in the image of the death of sin; and condemned sin in his own body, and by his voluntary crucifixion shattered the hosts of the enemy. He became the firstfruits of them that slept, and by his divinely marvellous resurrection he invited us to share in his own immortality.[24]

From this vantage point and this vantage point only can we make sense of the Easter proclamation that death has been overcome once and for all in Christ Jesus. It is this mystical death of which physical death is only a part and visible sign that Christ came to destroy and abolish. Christ has taken the sting, the spiritual poison of sin, out of death by denying it a final eschatological triumph over life. Through his own voluntary death on the cross, Christ transformed dying and death into a passage and entrance into a fuller life of communion and love with God and his saints.[25] The physical death that medicine knows, studies, and endeavors to delay is not the first issue here; certainly it is not the whole of what Christ came to abolish. But neither is physical death inconsequential. We are not permitted to inflict such death on the sick and innocent, for "whether we live or whether we die, we are the Lord's" (Rom. 14:8). The life we have is a gift.

In George MacDonald's wonderful tale *The Princess and the Goblin*, the mysterious great, great grandmother presents the child princess Irene with a magic ball of thread and then returns it to a drawer while fastening the end of it to Irene's ring. Irene asks if she has done some-

24. *Rituale Armenorum*, p. 130.
25. Schmemann, *Of Water and the Spirit*, p. 64.

thing wrong which accounts for the grandmother taking back the ball of thread. "No, my darling," says the grandmother. "But you must understand that no one ever gives anything to another properly and really without [also] keeping it. That ball is yours."[26] The divine gift of life is given yet kept in this way by God. Life is ultimately God's gift to give or take back as he chooses; it is not ours to take from another or ourselves.

The Church and Care for the Dying

The truth about life and death, about living and dying, that the church embraces and proclaims in its liturgies and rites is not easily understood or accepted by people outside the church today. In his last novel, *The Thanatos Syndrome*, Walker Percy identified and explored the disagreement between modern secularism and Christianity over the meaning and end of life. The novel introduces the eccentric character of Fr. Simon Smith. We meet him at the very beginning of the story after he has fled from his responsibilities in a hospice to the top of a fire tower, where he is praying and meditating. Some in the community view Fr. Smith as a failed priest, but there is more in his "failure" than meets the eye. He is viewed as a failure because he has declined to assume the role of divine therapist for the modern narcissists who populate Feliciana parish — a respectable, successful population that Fr. Smith addresses in a sermon at the close of the novel. "I don't see any sinners here," he says. "Everyone looks justified. No guilt here."[27] These wry words belie the reason Fr. Smith climbed the tower in the first place. At least one of his parishioners sees through the irony, though: "For God's sake. Like Jonah, I mean, really. Has it ever occurred to anybody that he might be up there for a much simpler, more obvious reason. . . . He could be doing vicarious penance for the awful state of the world."[28]

Fr. Smith will not turn his face from the evils being committed around him, especially the false care for the dying being provided in the government Qualitarian centers where abortion and euthanasia are routine therapies for the physically and mentally impaired, the "unwanted," and the socially "useless." Nor will he withdraw judgment

26. George MacDonald, *The Princess and the Goblin* (New York: Dell, 1986), p. 101.

27. Percy, *The Thanatos Syndrome* (New York: Farrar, Straus, Giroux, 1987), p. 360.

28. Percy, *The Thanatos Syndrome*, pp. 112-13.

from the lives of people who want to believe that there is no such thing as final accountability for one's life, that all we need expect of ourselves is to be well adjusted, tolerant of others, and "decent" toward our fellow human beings — even, and in fact especially, when putting them to death. In a society such as ours, the capacity to rationalize killing, from fetuses to the geriatric ward, knows no limit. We have invented for ourselves the right to inflict death on others as we would have them inflict death on us.

"If you have a patient, young or old, suffering, dying, afflicted, useless, born or unborn, whom you for the best of reasons wish to put out of his misery — I beg only one thing of you, dear doctors! Please send them to us," Fr. Smith pleads in his sermon. "Don't kill them. Please send them to us! I swear to you you won't be sorry. . . . We will even call on you to help us take care of them! . . . God will bless you for it." Would that our church was better prepared to make this sort of witness to our society. Would that the church was better prepared to express its deepest convictions about life and death and provide more institutions and services to meet the needs of the sick and dying.

I have identified two tenets of Christian faith that demand greater attention from the church as it responds with compassion to the sick and dying: the mystical relationship between sin and death and the work of healing and hope through the Incarnation and resurrection. The first calls for penance, not merely as a punitive measure but as a healing sacrament. The second calls for devotion in eschatological hope. Neither calling has been easy in any time, but they are especially difficult in the utilitarian, narcissistic, therapeutic ethos of our time. I want briefly to take a closer look at each of them.

There are those who are bound to object to the extraordinary attention given to sin and penance in the Orthodox rites. Many consider sin and penance to be unhelpful concepts in any context, and they will be especially prone to consider them inappropriate in the context of care for the sick and dying. What a cruel thing to impose on people who are weakened with sickness or facing imminent death. I am quite willing to concede that these themes can be twisted and misused by those who are commissioned to practice the theology of the church in pastoral and medical care settings. Condescension and a punitive impulse often turn what is supposed to be healing into another form of torment for the afflicted.[29] There exist among the clergy and laity of

---

29. For a powerful discussion of this, see May, "The Sacral Power of Death in Contemporary Experience," p. 181.

every church contemporary counterparts of Job's so-called friends who are motivated by an inflexible orthodoxy or other reasons to add to the suffering of those who are afflicted by assuming the divine prerogative of judgment or by reminding them incessantly of their failures.

But these misuses of penitential theology do not discredit the profound and practical wisdom of the church in placing repentance and forgiveness at the center of its prayers for the sick and dying. This emphasis makes perfect sense in light of the Gospels and indeed the whole of Scripture. We have already seen that the Bible and the Orthodox tradition both teach us that sickness is often enmeshed, "consciously or not, in the complexities of sin, personal and/or social."[30] This is not to say that we can always account for sickness as a punishment for individual sins. Jesus repudiates such a view in Luke 13:3-4. It is simply to acknowledge the very real connection between sickness and death and sin. Sometimes this connection is easy to see, as in "the statistical correlation between overeating and heart disease, or sexual license with venereal disease."[31] In such cases it may even be appropriate for pastors to remind their parishioners of the link between their behavior and their sickness. But whether it is easy to see or not, we must pay appropriate attention to the reality of the relationship.

The Orthodox rites wisely take account of the burden of guilt and remorse that often weighs even more onerously on those who are sick or dying. In such circumstances, the wrongs and injustices we have committed over a lifetime can suddenly return to haunt us in devastating ways. They may deeply and existentially confound what meaning we have found in our lives. We may well begin to think in terms of accounting for our failures and transgressions. In Iris Murdoch's *Nuns and Soldiers,* an atheist dying of cancer speaks to an estranged nun. "I wish I believed in the hereafter," he says. "Not for any vulgar reason of course. Not just to be let off this thing that's happening in the next few weeks. But — it's something I've always felt. . . . I would like to be judged."[32] The gist of his desire is that he would like the assurance of having "a clear account" of his life. He feels that his life project should have some consequences, even if they were to include punishment. But why an afterlife, he is asked. "Oh but one can't *see.* I would want to understand it all. I would want to have it exhibited, explained. That's

---

30. Thomas C. Oden, *Pastoral Theology* (New York: Harper & Row, 1983), p. 251.

31. Oden, *Pastoral Theology,* p. 251.

32. Murdoch, *Nuns and Soldiers* (New York: Viking, 1981), pp. 71-72.

why the idea of purgatory is so moving."[33] The church's serious concern about sin and penance answers such needs and helps us to see how our living and dying are important matters.

The theme of forgiveness is of course closely related to the issues of sin and penance, as is the notion that dying persons have a responsibility to the living to die in a manner that contributes to the good of the community that has nurtured them. The need to forgive and be forgiven and the responsibility of expressing goodwill and trust toward those with whom one's own life has been bound up are reflected in the Armenian Rite for Communion of the Sick. The rubrics indicate that the priest shall take "the saving mystery and the cross and censor . . . , and go to the sick man. . . . But it is *fitting* that the sick man should first hold converse with his intimate friends or with any one else with all vigilance and circumspection. And if he has any grudge against any one, he shall forgive him."[34]

These rubrics nicely anticipate yet another characteristic of the prayers in the Orthodox rites: the prayers set personal sin firmly within a social matrix of evil and suffering. This is especially the case concerning death, which is understood theologically as a consequence of sin. We all abide and participate in Adam's sin as one mystical body of fallen humanity condemned to death. Thomas Oden has correctly observed that Scripture places a greater emphasis on corporate sin than on personal sin in accounting for the suffering and death in the world.[35] This is not to diminish the significance or effects of personal sins, however. We have already noted how sinful behaviors can lead to illness, but personal sins can wreak havoc in many other ways as well. Stress in the workplace, for example, is inevitably bound up with the lying and deception, the vengefulness and manipulation in which we all engage. And our institutions, subverted by this collective personal sin, produce yet more individual suffering. Personal sin thus begets corporate sin, and corporate sin begets personal sin. We are only beginning to understand just how much, for example, the stress created by the social and institutional matrix of injustice contributes to physical and psychological illness and mortality. It is a truly vicious circle.

A prayer in the Byzantine Rite of Holy Unction expresses this idea of the social matrix of sin and injustice:

Yea, O Lord who art easy to be entreated; who alone art merciful

---

33. Murdoch, *Nuns and Soldiers*, pp. 67-68.
34. *Rituale Armenorum*, pp. 114-15; italics mine.
35. Oden, *Pastoral Theology*, p. 251.

and lovest mankind, who repentest thee of our evil deeds; who knowest how that the mind of man is applied unto wickedness, even from his youth up; . . . and didst thyself become a created being for the sake of thy creatures; thou hast said: I am not come to call the righteous but sinners to repentance. . . . Do thou O tenderhearted Master, look down from the height of thy sanctuary, overshadowing us sinners, who are also thine unworthy servants, with the grace of the Holy Spirit, at this hour, and take up thine abode in thy servant, N., who acknowledgeth his (her) iniquities and draweth near unto thee in faith.[36]

The prayer wisely focuses not on the sins of the individual alone but also on the sins of the family and friends gathered at the bedside or in the church during the performance of the rite. This principle should extend to all pastoral care, to prevent further intensification of a sense of failure on the part of the sick and further alienation from the healthy. The prayer contributes to a reconstitution of the church as a community of sinners and penitents aware of their common frailty and mortality who, in the words of the Armenian service for communion of the sick, look together to God "for wholeness of souls and bodies . . . and for the perfection of good works and of all virtues."[37] The healthy are reminded that they are not so very different from the afflicted in their midst.

The church's theology of resurrection and eternal life is, of course, the obvious place to locate a resource of hope in the care of the sick and dying. Unfortunately, this theology, like that of sin and penance, has traditionally been subject to much abuse. A condescending cheerfulness and insistence on Christian hope can be just as alienating and tormenting to a sick or dying person as an insensitive or morbid preoccupation with sin and penance. But here I think the strong emphasis on sin and penance in the Orthodox rites precludes such a cheapening of the hope in the resurrection. Christ died for the *sins* of all to remove the curse of guilt and abolish death, with its sting of emptiness and desolation. Through his dying and our participation in it, death is transformed into a passage to eternal life. Death, which was the wages of sin, becomes the end of sins. God does not remove all the pain and anguish of dying — Christ himself experienced that pain and anguish — but the hope of the resurrection includes faith that God can reach "even into the hollowness of nonexistence . . . to confer life."[38]

36. *Service Book of the Holy Orthodox-Catholic Apostolic Church*, p. 347.
37. *Rituale Armenorum*, p. 116.
38. Pelikan, *The Shape of Death*, p. 27.

Conclusion

It has been my intent in this chapter to illumine the theological convictions within the Orthodox tradition that define its understanding of death, euthanasia, and care for the dying. I cautioned at the outset that our culture is not disposed to give these convictions a full hearing. Walker Percy rightly showed that Fr. Smith's position will be perceived as extreme by devotees of the utilitarian ethos.

It is no small task to put into practice an Orthodox and Christian ethic of death and care for the sick and dying in an increasingly "pagan" environment. A culture once deeply informed by biblical faith is fast losing its memory of the reasons why it once objected to the casual taking of life. In this environment, I believe that Christians must concentrate more of their energies on the life and instruction of the church. The ethic I have been describing is first of all ecclesially centered: it makes whole and complete sense only within a church setting. It cannot be disconnected from the community of faith in which it is received and practiced. It cannot be reduced to a set of universal principles and taught as such in courses on professional or medical ethics. It is intimately joined with the cardinal convictions and narratives of the Christian faith regarding creation and redemption. It is meant for a people who have been formed by these convictions and stories and who have received the care of the church, starting with baptism. It is naturally located within a larger tradition of pastoral theology and practice. Care for the sick and dying begins with care for the healthy and living. The sacraments, Christian catechetical instruction, and preaching are the precedents and in some real sense the prerequisites of the ethic I have been describing. The resources that the Christian faith offers to help the living face death in freedom and with hope and courage are not like some miracle drug that can be effectively administered to a sick person awaiting imminent death, whose flesh is already ravaged and mind tormented by disease. The meaning for living and dying that faith provides must be owned by the person over a lifetime.

Yet at the risk of sounding self-contradictory, let me state by way of conclusion that even though I believe that the primary location of the ethic explored in this chapter is ecclesial, the church's own special ministry of healing need not — indeed, *must not* — be limited to believers. There are secular outlooks on medical ethics that converge with the diagnoses, prescriptions, and prognoses of the church. Those who hold these outlooks will see in limited but crucial ways the truth in the Christian ethic. And others can be persuaded. Christian medical professionals who bring their faith into their practice can make a difference for sick people who do not believe in the God of the Jewish and Christian scriptures. I agree with William F. May's assertion that "it is angelism to assume that the sole witness of the church to the dying and the bereaved is the testimony of theology alone. A ministry to the flesh is a true and valid ministry."[39] Christian faith has the power to comfort and heal individuals outside the church. This must be true because the Word assumed flesh, a flesh that all human beings have in common. We live and die as one humanity. The Son of God demonstrated this when he endured death for the salvation of all on the life-giving cross.

39. May, "The Sacral Power of Death in Contemporary Experience," p. 181.

Index of Subjects and Names

Abortion, 17-21, 22, 85, 87, 95, 193
Abraham, 69-74, 139-41
Adam, 159, 192; and humankind's
  priestly vocation, 161, 165-66
Agathangelos, 172n.33
AIDS, 175-76, 180
Allegory, 66, 67n.29, 68, 172
Anabaptists, 56-57
Anamnesis, 46, 47, 71n.41
Armenia, 4, 104-6, 108-10, 122, 124,
  128-29, 174
Armenian Blessing of the Field, 8,
  99, 170-71
Armenian Church, 4, 99, 104-10,
  115-24, 128-29
Armenian Rite of Churching, 144
Armenian Rite of Communion of
  the Sick, 196
Armenian Rite of Epiphany, 8, 164
Armenian Rite of Holy Baptism, 34,
  164
Armenian Rite of Holy Matrimony,
  142
Armenian Rite of the Blessing of
  the Water, 165
Armenian Rite of the Burial for a
  Layman, 188-92
Armenian Rite of the Washing of
  the Cross, 168-69
Artsouni, Grigor, 118

Askesis, 135, 146
Augustine, 26-27, 40-41, 100

Baby M, 73
Baby Rena, 176-82
Baptism, 8, 69, 80, 99, 103, 107, 143,
  163-65, 186, 198; and ethics, 43;
  and tradition, 34, 36, 41-43; and
  typology, 76, 77, 171. *See also*
  Armenian Rite of Holy Baptism;
  Byzantine Rite of Holy Baptism
Barr, James, 68, 160
Basil of Caesarea, 25, 34, 40, 51,
  134, 168, 188, 190
Basileia, 27, 138, 141
Beatitudes, 27, 60-66, 149
Bellah, Robert, 44
Benedict, Saint, 26, 33
Berger, Brigitte and Peter, 147-48, 150
Blessing, 156-57, 159-62, 165-66,
  170, 172
Bonhoeffer, Dietrich, 5-6, 102-4, 105,
  109-15, 121, 123, 125-29
Bush, George, 19
Byzantine Divine Liturgy, 57, 63,
  66, 71n.4, 74
Byzantine Office of the Parting of
  the Soul from the Body, 191
Byzantine Rite of Burial for a Lay-
  man, 183, 190-91

Byzantine Rite of Churching, 143-44
Byzantine Rite of Holy Baptism, 8, 34, 163
Byzantine Rite of Holy Matrimony, 74-75
Byzantine Rite of Holy Unction, 176, 183-84, 186-87, 188, 196

Cartwright, Michael G., 70
Chalcedon, Council of, 8n.8
Christo, Gus, 138n.12, 140
Christology, 23-25, 43, 46, 64-65, 68, 170. *See also* Incarnation
Chrysostom, John, 7, 11, 27-28, 51, 63, 65, 66n.27, 68-72, 79, 100, 133-42, 144-54
Church and state. *See* Separation of church and state
Civil religion, 51, 84, 88-89, 93, 106
Clements, Keith W., 126-27
Communism, 113
Constantine, 1, 21
Constantinianism, 21-22, 27, 87-88, 137, 147, 153
Council of Chalcedon, 8n.8
Curran, Charles E., 61-62
Cyprian, Saint, 171, 173
Cyril of Jerusalem, 171-73

Death, 155, 175-81; and care for the dying, 193-99; and sin, 26, 167, 183-84, 186-87, 189-92
De Gruchy, John W., 108n.11
De Kruijf, Gerrit G., 90
Denominationalism, 32, 83-84, 88-89, 104
Diakonia, 27, 55
Divine Liturgy of the Armenian Church, 78
Doxology, 40-41, 46, 59, 63, 65, 78, 169

Ecclesia, 56, 76, 137-38
Ecclesial and ecological symbolism, 171-73, 174
Ecclesiology, 3, 49, 123, 125, 150-52,

174; and eschatology, 47; and ethics, 54-55; and family, 133-40, 143-47, 154. *See also* Eucharist; Family; Marriage
Ecology, 8, 133, 155-74. *See also* Ecclesial and ecological symbolism
Eisenstadt v. Baird, 20
Eliot, T. S., 12-15, 16, 17, 29-33, 37, 48, 51-52
Employment Division v. Smith, 14
Enlightenment, 6, 14, 16, 24, 51, 86, 91-92, 94, 96, 104, 112, 116
Epiphanius, 41-42
Epiphany, 163
Eucharist, 33, 36, 46, 69-71, 161-62, 166, 169; and Bible, 57, 59, 63; and ethics, 54, 55; and hermeneutics, 76, 77, 78
Euthanasia, 175, 178-79, 182, 187, 188, 193, 198

Falwell, Jerry, 16, 17
Family, 7, 85, 189; and ecclesiology, 133, 135-39, 141-44, 146-47, 154; and virtues, 150-51. *See also* Marriage
Faulkner, William, 35-38, 44
Fedetov, George P., 153
Figural interpretation. *See* Typology
Fiorenza, Elisabeth Schüssler, 145
Florovsky, Georges, 27, 40-41, 67
Forgiveness, 184, 186, 195-96
Free-church tradition, 1, 22, 125-28
Freedom, 30, 37, 39, 97, 101, 102-5, 107, 109, 114, 116, 127, 153, 173
Frei, Hans, 66, 68, 71-72
French Revolution, 90, 112-13, 116

Genocide, 100, 119, 121-22, 163
German National Church, 102-3, 111-12, 115
Gregorios, Paulos, 159-60, 162-63
Gregory of Nyssa, 63n.28, 191n.20
Gregory the Illuminator, 107, 110n.4, 174

Griswold v. Connecticut, 20
Guilt, 160, 195, 197
Gustafson, James, 55

Handy, Robert T., 2
Hannah, 72, 141-42
Harakas, Stanley, 152-53
Haring, Bernard, 169
Hauerwas, Stanley, 1, 7, 12-13, 17-18, 22, 29, 53, 55, 56, 98, 136
Heilsgeschichte School, 68, 156
Herberg, Will, 83-86, 88-89, 91, 95-96, 98
Hermeneutics/hermeneutical problem, 53-61, 67, 72, 76
Holy Etchmiadzin, 106-7, 174
Hospitality, 69-70, 140, 173
Human rights language, 18-19, 21, 22
Hunter, James Davidson, 85-87, 89, 95-96

Icon, 41-42, 49-50, 64
Iconoclasts/Iconodules, 41
Incarnation, 31, 74, 77, 162-63, 170-71, 188, 192, 194. *See also* Christology
Individualism, 15, 21, 23, 32, 44, 59-60, 86, 147
Irenaeus, 170
Isaac the Syrian, 167

Jefferson, Thomas, 14
John of Damascus, 41-42, 190
Justinian, 1, 137

Karekin II, Catholicos of Cilicia, 4, 5, 115, 128
Kaufman, Gordon, 157, 158
Kavanagh, Aidan, 53
Kennedy, James, 17
Khachadrian, Ludwig, 108
Koinonia, 78
K'tutyune, 128-29

Ladner, Gerhardt B., 27, 137-38
Lash, Nicholas, 60, 76

Lazarus, 69-71
Lee v. Weisman, 90
Lehmann, Paul, 54-57, 58, 78
Lesser Entrance, 63-64
Lex credendi, 33
Lex orandi, 39-40
Liberalism, 2, 16-18, 24, 29-30, 32, 39, 44, 52, 92
Lindbeck, George A., 12-13, 17, 66-67
Littell, Franklin H., 2n.3, 88, 126
Locke, John, 14
Lockmann, Thomas, 87
Lossky, Vladimir, 32-33, 43, 44, 45n.24

MacDonald, George, 192-93
MacIntyre, Alasdair, 7, 12-13, 17, 26, 29, 33, 39, 50-51
Marriage, 7, 20, 21, 49, 80, 98, 133-34, 136; and Christian vocation, 72-75, 142; and ecclesiology, 138, 144-47. *See also* Family
Marsden, George M., 100n.37
Marty, Martin E., 93-96
May, William F., 191n.21, 199
McCann, Dennis P., 94-96
McClendon, James William Jr., 55, 56
McKibben, Bill, 165-66
Meeks, M. Douglas, 133
Meeks, Wayne A., 42, 48-49, 57-58, 60, 76, 78
Meerson-Aksenov, Michael, 105-6, 124-25
Meilaender, Gilbert, 13, 22, 24-26, 97, 187n.16
Melik-Hakobian, Harob (Raffi), 118
Monasticism, 27, 100, 137-38, 141-42, 149-50, 151-54
Murdoch, Iris, 195
Murray, John Courtney, 2, 89, 91, 93-94

Nalbandian, Louise, 118
National church(es), 4-6, 104-6, 111-16, 125-29

Nationalism, 5, 22, 110, 112-14, 116-24, 128
Natural law, 18, 22-25, 51
Nazism, 102-3, 111, 113-15
Neoconservatives, 3, 18, 92, 136
Neo-orthodoxy, 2, 17
Neo-Thomism, 2
Nersissian, Karekin (Bishop of Yerevan), 129
Nersoyan, Archbishop Tiran, 120-25
Neuhaus, Richard John, 17-18, 90, 91n.19
New (Christian) Right, 16
Newman, John Henry, 40
Niebuhr, H. Richard, 2, 98, 151
Niebuhr, Reinhold, 55, 91
Noah: ecclesial and ecological symbolism of, 171-73, 174; and humankind's priestly vocation, 160, 161, 162

Oakeshott, Michael, 92
Oakley, Francis, 13
Oden, Thomas C., 196
Ogletree, Thomas W., 55
Oikonomia, 133, 170, 173
Ontology, 24-25
Oriental Orthodox, 8n.8
Orthodox Church, 56-58, 65, 66-67, 74-75, 79-80. *See also* Armenian Church; Oriental Orthodox
Ottoman Empire, 115-17, 121

Palmer, Parker, 99
Paradosis, 34
Parenthood, 141-42, 146-50
Paul VI (pope), 21
Paul, Saint, 25, 37, 44, 48-49, 76-78, 79, 134, 140, 145, 161, 183, 184
Pelikan, Jaroslav, 33, 38, 39, 47
Penance, 186, 188, 194-97
Percy, Walker, 175, 193, 198
Pius XII (pope), 97
Planned Parenthood v. Casey, 20-21
Pluralism, 14-15, 50-51, 83-95, 99, 104-6, 136

Pollack, Murray, 176-77, 182
Privatism, 14, 32, 38, 87, 93, 136, 147, 150
Proselytism, 109
Protestants, 7, 12, 16, 46, 56, 83, 85, 87-89, 92, 94-97, 102, 127, 135-36, 147-48, 150, 158
Public church, 94-96, 100
Public theology/philosophy, 3, 18, 25, 87-97, 100, 136

Raffi (Harob Melik-Hakobian), 118
Ramsey, Paul, 178, 181-83, 187
Rasmussen, Larry, 114
Rauschenbusch, Walter, 15
Reformation, 2, 5, 6, 86, 104, 112, 125
Renaissance, 112
Robertson, Pat, 16, 17
Roe v. Wade, 20
Roman Catholics, 7, 12, 22, 46, 62, 83, 85, 92, 94-96, 102, 108, 124, 126, 135, 150, 158
Russian (Soviet) Church, 5, 103, 105-6, 124, 127

Samuel, 72, 141-42
Schlinder, David L., 18-19, 22-25
Schmemann, Alexander, 38, 47, 57-59, 63, 76, 143-44, 152, 161, 167, 176, 179
Sectarianism, 14, 26, 93, 98, 136-37, 151
Secularism, 3, 4, 5, 7, 11, 14, 32, 105, 157, 193; and American religion, 84-93; and education, 100; and Christian family, 150; and liberalism, 16-17; religious and nonreligious, 179-80, 182-83
Separation of church and state, 84, 87-89, 92-93, 104, 109, 127
Sin, 26, 41, 160-62, 167, 183-84, 186-87, 188, 190, 192, 193-97
Social Gospel movement, 15-16
Soviet Union, 103-4, 106, 110, 122, 124, 127

Stackhouse, Max L., 91n.19
Suicide, 175, 179, 188
Surrogacy, 72-76

Theodosius, 1, 21, 137
Tiel, John E., 59
Tocqueville, Alexis de, 5, 88-89, 92, 93, 95
Toetig, 163
Tradition, 15-17, 22-24, 29-52, 56-57, 59-60, 114, 150, 157-60, 166, 173
Trinity, 8, 23-24, 31, 169
Troeltsch, Ernst, 54, 88, 95, 111, 125, 151-52
Typology, 64, 66-69, 71-72, 74, 76-77, 88, 111, 152, 172

Ugolnik, Anthony, 50, 67

Vazken I, 4, 5, 106-8
Virtue(s), 17, 30, 32, 35-38, 43, 66, 97, 136, 140-41, 146-50

Wainwright, Geoffrey, 79
Webster v. Reproductive Health Services, 19-20
Weigel, George, 90, 91n.19
Westermann, Claus, 156-57
White, Lynn, Jr., 157-58
Will, George, 14-15
Willimon, William H., 136
Wuthnow, Robert, 85-86, 89, 95, 101

Yeghpayrutyune, 128-29
Yoder, John Howard, 1, 7, 22, 44-47, 49, 50-51, 55, 56, 57, 98, 145

Zizioulas, John D., 46-47

Index of Scripture References

OLD TESTAMENT

Genesis
1:26-31	159
3:17-19	172
5:29	172
8:20-21	160
9:1a	160
9:1b	162
9:2	162
9:3	162
9:4	162
9:8-10	172
12:10-20	74
20:1-18	74
24:11-14	140
27:25-30	156

Leviticus
12	143

Psalms
24:1	170
34	78
51:1-10	185
51:12	185
103	63
143:1-2	185
143:7-8	185
146	63

Isaiah
1:3	173
11	172
24:4-6	162

NEW TESTAMENT

Matthew
5:1-12	60, 62, 63, 65
5:45	70
5:48	65
9:9-14	184
13:52	48
25:40	71

Mark
2:3	184
2:5	184
2:6	184
2:10-12	184
2:15	184
2:16-17	184

Luke
2:22-24	143
6:17	60
6:20-23	60
13:3-4	195
16:19-31	69

John
1:1-5, 14 78
1:2 190
1:14 54
2:15 47
3:16-17 47

Acts
17:28 25
20:32 139

Romans
6 44
6:23 184
8:21 174
8:22 161
8:38-39 183
13 49
14:8 .... 175, 192

1 Corinthians
3:8 134
6:1-7 49
6:9-20 49
7 49
8:1-13 77
8:4-13 78
10-11 76
10:14-17 77
10:16 156
10:18-21 78
10:23-33 78
11 44
11:1 77
11:3-17 77
11:17-33 77
11:23-26 77
14 49
15:56 184

2 Corinthians
3:17 37

Ephesians
5:21-33 49
5:22-23 144
5:25-27 146
6:1-3 141

Philippians
2:6-7 153

Colossians
1:16-17 25
2:6 43
2:8 42
2:11-12 43
2:18 42
2:20-21, 23 43
3:1-4 43
3:9b-10 43
3:12b-14 43
3:15 43

1 Timothy
2:5 142

James
5:7 186
5:10-11 186
5:13-16 186

1 Peter
2:5 125
3:20-21 171

1 John
3:1-3 62

Revelation
7:2-4 62
7:9-14 62